AMERICAN VOICES OF THE **CHICAGO RENAISSANCE**

. . .

AMERICAN VOICES OF THE
CHICAGO RENAISSANCE

Lisa Woolley

NORTHERN ILLINOIS UNIVERSITY PRESS

DEKALB 2000

Library of Congress Cataloging-in-Publication Data

American voices of the Chicago renaissance / Lisa

Woolley.

    p.   cm.

Includes bibliographical references and index.

ISBN 0-87580-258-3 (acid-free paper)

1. American literature—Illinois—Chicago—History

and criticism. 2. Dialect literature, American—

Illinois—Chicago—History and criticism. 3. English

language—Spoken English—Illinois—Chicago.

4. Chicago (Ill.)—Intellectual life—20th century.

5. Chicago (Ill.)—In literature. 6. Speech in

literature. I. Title.

PS285.C47W66 2000

810.9'977311—dc21   99-20974

                    CIP

To Mother, Larry, Robin, and Oscar

CONTENTS

PREFACE

• *American Voices of the Chicago Renaissance* places writing considered to represent midwestern speech in a historical perspective and delineates the ways that women and African Americans established and worked against this paradigm. As other critics have done, I assert that writers associated with Chicago transformed American literary standards by representing the diverse and changing accents of modern urban life. I expand on this premise by examining specific contexts in which authors merged literary and spoken language or created the illusion of doing so, such as journalists' experiments with dialect, the speaking tours of Carl Sandburg and Vachel Lindsay, the oratory of reformers Jane Addams and Ida B. Wells, the conversational manner in which Harriet Monroe and Margaret Anderson ran their magazines, and the emerging vernacular aesthetic in African-American literature. The authors discussed here confirm the degree to which Chicagoans strived to imitate spoken language in writing; however, by asking whose speech was valorized and why and to what effect, I call into question the meaning of traits commonly associated with Chicago literature: plainness, simplicity, Americanness, and democracy.

By privileging the speech of their region, these authors both challenged and confirmed linguistic prejudices toward immigrants, the working classes, African Americans, and women. To try to capture the speech of a particular group of people was to deem their language worthy of representation. Such efforts, however, competed with a history of using dialect for the purposes of comedy and ridicule. Moreover, debates about the future of spoken English in the United States made calling attention to variations in speech a complicated gesture. While some writers celebrated the singularity of Americans' vocabulary and phrasing, other educators and critics, fearing that Americans were corrupting English, organized to prevent further deterioration of the language. Chapter 1 focuses on the relationship between linguistic purity movements and writers' use of dialect, colloquialisms, and slang. Chapter 2 treats Carl Sandburg's and Vachel Lindsay's interests in African-American culture and their efforts to make popular wisdom multicultural. Chapters 3 and 4 examine women's language, and chapter 5 addresses stereotypes of African-American speakers and two writers' uses of literary trends in order to confront them.

ACKNOWLEDGMENTS

• I wish to thank Wilson College and the Department of English and the Graduate School of the University of Minnesota for their support of this research. Thanks also go to the staff at the O. Meredith Wilson and Walter libraries at the University of Minnesota; at the Harry Ransom Humanities Research Center, The University of Texas at Austin; and at the John Stewart Memorial Library at Wilson College. Appreciation is extended to Marjorie S. Williams, Allyn Rose Ransom, Robert L. Seiffert, and John C. Pryor for permission to quote from the letters of Marjorie Allen Seiffert, to Ann Monroe for permission to quote from the letters of Harriet Monroe, to Hilary Masters for permission to quote from the letters of Edgar Lee Masters, and to Thomas B. Catron III for permission to quote from the letters of Alice Corbin Henderson. I am grateful as well to all who have read parts of this study as it progressed, including my doctoral committee, Shirley Nelson Garner, Philip Furia, John S. Wright, Toni A. McNaron, Rey Chow, and Helen Hoy; my dissertation study group, Kathleen R. Wallace, Maureen Heacock, Michele Moylan, and Mary Alice Brenk; and participants in the Feminist Studies in Literature research group at the University of Minnesota. John Ward and John Edgar Tidwell offered the encouragement I needed to persist. Wilson College work-study students Heather Thomas, Lori Snyder, and especially Melanie Faith helped with innumerable details. Phyllis Woolley, Dee and Tom Shillock, and Jaimie and Mark Granger provided countless hours of babysitting. Lee and Elizabeth Woolley, Cyndi and Scott Westermann, Katie and Andy Shillock, and the Grangers kept our family in clothes and toys. My husband, Larry Shillock, who says he now knows why writers use the tone they do when acknowledging spouses, has read and reread this study, argued with me about it, and done a great deal of cooking, cleaning, and shopping so that I could finish. I also would like to thank Martin P. Johnson, Susan Bean, Wendy Warnken, and the staff at Northern Illinois University Press. Many people have improved this study; deficiencies that remain are attributable to my own stubbornness.

An earlier version of the Vachel Lindsay segment in chapter 2 appeared as "Vachel Lindsay's Crusade for Cultural Literacy" in *MidAmerica* 22 (1995). An earlier version of the Fenton Johnson segment in chapter 5 appeared as "From Chicago Renaissance to Chicago Renaissance: The Poetry of Fenton Johnson" in *The Langston Hughes Review* 14.1–2 (1996). I am grateful to both publications for permission to reprint.

I would like to thank the following: the Jane Addams Memorial Collection (JAMC neg. 1003), Special Collections, University Library, University of Illinois at Chicago, for permission to reprint the portrait of Jane Addams; the Man Ray Trust © 2000 Man Ray Trust / Artists Rights Society, NY / ADAGP, Paris, for permission to reprint Man Ray's portrait of Margaret Anderson; and AMS Press for permission to reprint the portrait of Harriet Monroe from their edition of *A Poet's Life*. I also wish to thank The Crisis Publishing Co., Inc., the publisher of the magazine of the National Association for the Advancement of Colored People, for the use of the photograph of Marita Bonner.

AMERICAN VOICES OF THE CHICAGO RENAISSANCE

. . .

Jane Addams

Marita Bonner (c. 1928)

INTRODUCTION

There is a city of English and American words and it has been a neglected city. Strong

broad shouldered words, that should be marching across open fields under the blue sky,

are clerking in little dusty dry goods stores, young virgin words are being allowed to con-

sort with whores, learned words have been put to the ditch digger's trade. Only yesterday

I saw a word that once called a whole nation to arms serving in the mean capacity of ad-

vertising laundry soap.

—Sherwood Anderson, Introduction to *Geography and Plays*, 7

• To praise the American expatriate Gertrude Stein, Sherwood Anderson tellingly uses the city as a metaphor for her vocabulary. The comparison calls attention to Anderson's own association with Chicago, for, in the early decades of the twentieth century, that city supported a network of writers who expressed the increasingly urban character of American life. Scholars acknowledge that this group (including Anderson himself, Theodore Dreiser, Vachel Lindsay, Edgar Lee Masters, Frank Norris, Carl Sandburg, and Upton Sinclair) made a lasting contribution to American literature because, by attempting to represent the speech of ordinary Americans, they translated nineteenth-century literary diction into a modern, urban idiom.

This book contextualizes the representation of speech during the Chicago Renaissance, in part by including the litera- ture of women and African Americans. It argues that portray- ing spoken language produced multiple, often contradictory, effects and that Chicago writers both confronted and af- firmed linguistic stereotypes. Moreover, descriptions of Chicago literature, including such terms as *plain, simple, American,* and *democratic,* depended on and disguised

Chicago's multiethnic character and the new status of women in the city. In light of these issues, the literature of the Chicago Renaissance remains vital for understanding the continuing struggle over cultural representation, linguistic differences, and the dissemination of knowledge.

The Chicago Renaissance drew from the city's history of conflicts and disasters. The 1795 treaty of Grenville with the "Delawares, Wyandottes, Shawnees, Ottawas, Chippewas, Pottawatomies, Weas, and Kaskaskias" (Masters *Tale* 28) made the region part of U.S. territory. As one consequence, Fort Dearborn was built to protect vital water routes, but during the War of 1812 settlers leaving the fort were killed by Potowatomi in a struggle that became known as the Fort Dearborn Massacre.[1] The Blackhawk War of 1832 was the last armed conflict in the region. Extraordinarily rapid population growth in the century following Chicago's incorporation in 1833 fueled the social upheavals for which it became famous. Fires destroyed large parts of Chicago in both 1839 and 1871. In contrast to the destruction that often would characterize the city's history, the World's Columbian Exposition of 1893 prompted new construction and brought visitors from far and near. At that time Chicago was known particularly for its labor disputes, such as the Haymarket Affair of 1886, when a bomb exploded as demonstrators protested the deaths of some McCormick Harvester Company workers at the hands of police. Although circumstances surrounding the bombing remained a mystery, a group of anarchists was held responsible and executed. Similarly, in 1894 a violent strike pitted Eugene Debs's American Railway Union against the Pullman Company.

Large-scale immigration to Chicago in the late nineteenth century brought attention to the city's inadequate sanitation system, poor child protection laws, and lack of social services. In response, Jane Addams founded Hull-House in 1889 to serve inner-city immigrants and to provide middle-class women with an outlet for their education. With the new century, and particularly World War I, African Americans from the South migrated to Chicago, where segregation and substandard housing sparked racial tensions and the deadly race riots of 1919.

By the turn of the century, Chicago was considered peculiarly modern. As Henry Claridge points out, "Chicago possessed no relics, physical or otherwise, of a republican or colonial past; indeed, its rapid development made it, virtually, a city without a history" (88). Its western location, rapid growth, business- and industrial-based economy, transportation networks, and ethnic diversity made it thrilling to some, revolting to others, but noteworthy to all. Henry Adams declared that Chicago's 1893 Columbian Exposition profoundly shocked those who were unacquainted with new technologies, forcing them "to sit down on the steps and brood as they had never brooded on the benches of Harvard College" (342). Theodore Dreiser emphasized a different facet of the city's modernity in *The Titan*: "A city with but a handful of the native-born; a city packed to the doors with all the riffraff of a thousand towns . . . all the dreams and the brutality of the day seem gathered to rejoice . . . in this new-found wonder of a metropolitan life in the West" (7).

Contemporary writers and critics believed the literature of Chicago to be distinctly American. Like the city of underemployed words Sherwood Anderson imagined, early-twentieth-century Chicago was populated by a variety of workers clamoring for the opportunity to improve their lives. Injustice and neglect frequently led to the tragedies that have made the city's past dramatic for its historians, writers, and inhabitants. Civic unrest also precipitated linguistic change, as Anderson's portrayal of role reversals would seem to indicate. Trade unions, social work, and suffrage campaigns made women outspoken. Immigrants struggled to learn English and added new expressions to the language in the process. Obscene labor conditions demanded a new vocalness on the part of workers, and African Americans of the post-Reconstruction era began to make themselves heard in the upper Midwest.

Chicago's turmoil became fodder for realists and naturalists wishing to portray an American economic, industrial, spiritual, or cultural crisis. Although neither literary movement was invented in Chicago, both realism and naturalism seemed well suited to capturing this extraordinary city and its rural environs. Indeed, muckraking journalism and American socialism's zenith encouraged a didacticism not always embraced by modern writers elsewhere.

Until now, a relative handful of authors have shaped our understanding of both the literature and the city of Chicago. Dreiser's accounts of consuming ambition perhaps best match popular images of Chicago and its writers. The son of struggling German immigrants, Dreiser became a journalist despite the many disruptions in his education. The prose style that his journalism helped create has incited debate for nearly a century; some critics saw innovation, others ineptitude. F. R. Leavis even suggested that Dreiser did not seem to possess a first language (Markels 186). Thomas P. Riggio proposes that the initial outcry against *Sister Carrie* was occasioned not by Carrie benefiting from her illicit sexual affairs but by the victory of a woman "two generations removed from the emigrant" and the failure of a mainstream American man (59, 62). Dreiser's overturning of nineteenth-century literary conventions depended upon his portrayal of America's most modern city; it remained for critics to foreground gender and ethnicity in his work.

Upton Sinclair raised further controversy by portraying the injustice of capitalism. While best known for prompting legislation to ensure the safe processing and distribution of food, *The Jungle* (1906) also examined the plight of workers, especially immigrants whose lives were consumed by Chicago's packinghouses. Sinclair's socialist agenda prevented him from depicting the efforts of immigrants to found life-sustaining institutions (Wade 80), but his novel covers a surprising gamut of social issues, including prostitution, child labor, sexual harassment, discrimination against those who do not speak English, and the exploitation of seasonal workers in the rural Midwest. Chicago literature would ever after be associated with investigative journalism.

Although Frank Norris spent most of his adult life in California, his early residence in Chicago, his portrayal of urban life, and his account of the Chicago Board of Trade in *The Pit* (1902) have contributed to his being associated with America's second city. Norris sought adventure as a journalist, and he shocked American readers with vivid fictional depictions of violence and sexual desire. His eclectic literary style also puzzled readers. *The Pit* merges naturalism and domestic fiction, telling the story of the high-strung, art-loving Laura Dearborn and her suitor, the lowbrow, maniacally competitive Curtis Jadwin. Clare Virginia Eby has noted that *The Pit* is often seen as Norris's weakest novel, but she argues that it skillfully challenges masculine codes of naturalism: "In *The Pit* Norris constructs a dialogue between femininity and masculinity, between sentimental fiction and the business novel, without giving the last word to either" (164–65). In this sense, *The Pit* perhaps best captures the range of Chicago literature, which included sentimental fiction as well as the more celebrated naturalism and its offshoot, the business novel.

Sherwood Anderson and Edgar Lee Masters are best known for their portrayals of American small towns. Yet Anderson's volume of poetry, *Mid-American Chants* (1918), has an urban sensibility; the title suggests the oral aesthetic favored by other members of the Chicago Renaissance. Masters's *Spoon River Anthology* (1915) makes little attempt to represent midwestern speech, though the volume consists of a series of dramatic monologues that the reader imagines to be delivered by the inhabitants of the local cemetery. An Illinois lawyer, Masters was more interested than many of the other Chicago Renaissance writers in traditional signs of literariness. Yet his inclusion of representatives from all parts of the social spectrum links *Spoon River* to other writing from this period. Anderson's *Winesburg, Ohio* (1919) and Masters's *Spoon River*, albeit in different genres, both tell a collective story; they portray a place by sketching the lives of assorted citizens. This format proved popular among Chicagoans attempting to represent a many-voiced city and nation. Sandburg used a similar technique in *Chicago Poems*, as had Hamlin Garland in *Main-Travelled Roads,* and Marita Bonner later brought to life a multiethnic neighborhood through a series of short stories in *Frye Street and Environs.* Critic Sidney H. Bremer credits Edith Wyatt with creating a format that could accommodate an ensemble of equally important characters in her 1903 novel of Chicago life, *True Love* ("Lost Chicago Sisters" 214–15).

Several scholars have already drawn the broader outlines of Chicago's literary history. Bernard Duffey's *The Chicago Renaissance in American Letters* (1954) puts the city's literature in the broader American context of the end of romanticism (6). Duffey discusses three kinds of Chicago writers: early journalists, "genteel" writers who were part of the city's attempts to prove that it could support culture as well as commerce, and realists who portrayed the city's harsher sides (6–7). Dale Kramer's *Chicago Renaissance: The Literary Life in the Midwest, 1900–1930* makes accessible the lives and work of key writers. Hugh Dalziel Duncan's *The Rise of Chicago as a Literary Center from 1885 to 1920* examines the institutions that supported Chicago writers—the newspaper room and the artist's studio. Kenny J. Williams analyzes the role of the artist in Chicago in light of its predominant culture of business. Her *In the City of Men* traces the influence of commerce on literature and architecture by concentrating on the careers of Henry Fuller and Louis Sullivan. *Chicago and the American Literary Imagination, 1880–1920,* by Carl S. Smith, addresses literary artists' responses to modern, urban life. Bremer's important article "Willa Cather's Lost Chicago Sisters" focuses on the city's women writers. Unlike the men, who were mainly newcomers to Chicago, many of these women grew up in the city and emphasized its sense of community, ties to the past, and connection to the natural world. Their representations contrast with the alienating experience of the city portrayed by most of the men (211–12, 215). With *Chicago in Story,* Clarence A. Andrews moves beyond the period of the Chicago Renaissance to detail the history of Chicago as a literary subject.

Both Duffey and Duncan have discussed the Chicago Renaissance in terms of a departure from genteel American literary standards. Duncan credits Chicago's authors with codifying spoken American English in a literary style that would henceforth differ from British English (177). I take this achievement as my starting point and consider what it might mean in the wake of feminist and multicultural approaches to American literature.

British writers were changing their own literary diction, and such Americans as Mark Twain and the local colorists already had brought features of the New World's speech into print. Yet, as Duncan discusses, a decidedly urban point of view made what the Chicago writers were doing

Ida B. Wells (1920)

new (178)—as did the desire to be accessible and authoritative—rather than just modern or realistic. Alfred Kazin refers to Chicago's "tough-talking 'literary' reporters" (238), and, indeed, a series of journalists, including Eugene Field, George Ade, Finley Peter Dunne, Ring Lardner, Ida B. Wells, Carl Sandburg, Floyd Dell, Ben Hecht, and Frank Marshall Davis, would make Chicago writing synonymous with the pithy speech attractive to a large reading audience.

Not every twentieth-century writer in Chicago wrote realistic dialogue for characters, integrated vernacular language into literary prose, or relaxed poetry's formal diction, but several self-consciously advanced these techniques. "For a long time I have believed that crudity is an inevitable quality in the production of a really significant present-day American literature," Anderson wrote. "How indeed is one to escape the obvious fact that there is as yet no native subtlety of thought or living among us? And if we are a crude and childlike people how can our literature hope to escape the influence of that fact?" He invited those skeptical of his claims for crudity to travel across America to eavesdrop on conversations and read local newspapers (*Sherwood Anderson's Notebook* 195). Crudity was not Harriet Monroe's cause, but she saw the poets she published in *Poetry* magazine making an "effort at modern speech, simplicity of form, and authentic vitality of theme" (*New Poetry* xxxvi). Midwesterners involved in this new poetry movement included Sandburg, Masters, Lindsay, Eunice Tietjens, Florence Kiper Frank, Marjorie Allen Seiffert, Mary Aldis, and Fenton Johnson.

Although crudity, simplicity, and vitality were vague concepts applicable to a great deal of literature, several stylistic devices popular among Chicago writers specifically inspired these labels. Overall, the subject matter appealed to the concerns of a broad population, and writers went out of their way to avoid beautiful settings, preferring to astonish readers with descriptions of strikes, slaughterhouses, railroads, the board of trade, poverty, adultery, and the desperation of small towns. Sinclair's *The Jungle* would come to epitomize the use of disgusting detail to shock an audience into recognizing America's social problems. Vocabulary in Chicago writing, moreover, usually coincided with general usage. Diction was not elevated or archaic. For the most part, poetry did not rely on elision or inverted word order, and nontraditional poetic lines, especially free verse, attracted the most attention. The new poetry movement left behind Chicago poet William Vaughn Moody, for example, who was considered a precursor by those in the next generation. He anticipated the topics of interest to the younger writers, but his style perhaps best illustrates the changing tenor of his city's poetry. "The Brute" describes the spirit of the new century:

> Through his might men work their wills.
> They have boweled out the hills
> For food to keep him toiling in the cages they have wrought;
> And they fling him, hour by hour,
> Limbs of men to give him power. . . . (49)

The description of the brute's raw energy is consistent with the urban poetry to come, but the end rhymes and such words as "might," "boweled," and "wrought" distinguish the poem from Sandburg's personification of a twentieth-century city: "Laughing the stormy, husky, brawling laughter of Youth, half-naked, / sweating, proud to be Hog Butcher, Tool Maker, Stacker of Wheat, / Player with Railroads and Freight Handler to the Nation" (Sandburg *Complete Poems* 4). The ordinary vocabulary, irregular line length and meter, and shift from fear of the young man's muscles and perspiration to pride in them mark the new Chicago paradigm.

Many believed that they found in the Midwest and the West the natural, artless expression of democracy. The literature of Chicago, especially, came to be seen as representative, in style and content, not just of a region but also of the true character of America. In her essay "Modern Poetry," Chicagoan Edith Wyatt refers to "the great prairie plainnesses of Carl Sandburg" (123). An expatriate artist from *Spoon River Anthology* suggests that Midwesterners could not escape their simple, democratic roots, no matter how much they tried. Many a face the Midwesterner paints "has a trace of Lincoln's" (Masters 170). An opinion from outside the Chicago school linked midwestern writers to the true spirit of America in yet another way. In her 1923 study of poetry, *The American Rhythm,* Mary Austin offered a theory about the relationship between American poetry and landscape and set out to demonstrate that Native American and European-American poets shared a common response to their unique American environment (Ford 4). Austin believed that, with the exceptions of Lincoln and Whitman, however, American writers had largely ignored American rhythms for the cadences of Europe. Sandburg, Lindsay, and Anderson, though, were close to realizing the American beat (Ford 5–6).

The political effects of representing speech varied with style, genre, and date of publication, and individual works are often at odds with themselves. As "agents of cultural formation" (Tompkins *Sensational* xvii), then, the texts discussed here encouraged varied and sometimes contradictory responses on the part of their readers. Many Chicago authors relied on dialect, slang, colloquialisms, vernacular language, and oratory in order to make their writing accessible, modern, or democratic. Others avoided these kinds of language for the same reasons. Sinclair, for example, would in all likelihood have lost his audience's sympathy and patience had he tried to represent "realistically" the speech of his Lithuanian immigrant characters. Dreiser cashed in on the popularity of realistic dialogue while also including within his novels warnings about the dangers of uneducated speech, apparently (dis)satisfying rebels and purists alike. Similarly, many authors both confronted and confirmed ethnic and racial stereotypes about language.

Lesser-known works help to illustrate these contradictions within better-known texts. The literature of Chicago's women, for instance, especially serves this purpose as it reveals a competition over the authority to represent the urban poor. More to the point, Chicagoans' valorization of crude language brought attention to the working classes but effectively marginalized women, who nevertheless struggled to present themselves as American authors. The historical specificity of techniques for representing speech is illustrated by Fenton Johnson's career, which swung widely from poetry conforming to stereotypes of African-American music to free verse bearing few traces of African-American oral tradition.

By calling attention to the privileging of sound and speech, I allude to both the work of Jacques Derrida and a set of questions only tangentially related to it. Derrida maintains that the Western philosophical tradition has conceptualized speech as a "representation of the self-present voice, of the immediate, natural, and direct signification of the meaning" (*Of Grammatology* 30), whereas writing has been considered a mere imitation of spoken language, "the exterior representation of language and of this 'thought-sound'" (31). His reading of philosophical texts overturns this hierarchy and presents all language as a form of writing.

Rethinking the relationship between speech and writing is particularly important in considering the problem of reproducing spoken language. In most cases, writing that attempts to copy speech by altering the spelling of standard English only underlines the degree to which the maintenance of "proper" or educated speech relies on a concept of writing. In other words, deviating from standard spelling in order to call attention to phonetic difference begs the question of the pronunciation from which written dialect differs. Attempts at phonetic spelling suggest that standard spelling represents somebody else's spoken language—that is to say, white, middle-class Americans' proper or normal speech. Yet spelling is a matter of convention and does not accurately reflect anyone's pronunciation. Dialect in pulp fiction and vaudeville often influenced perceptions of spoken language and the means of putatively reproducing it in writing; in Derridean terms, popular entertainers ensured that their audiences heard dialect as commonly written whenever African Americans spoke.

Newspapers frequently did the same, reproducing expected rather than actual speech. In his autobiography, James D. Corrothers, a journalist and minister who attended Northwestern University, recalled a *Chicago Tribune* story he wrote about his fellow African Americans. It was edited to the extent that, according to him, "nearly every sentence of my work had been recast into what was then the customary newspaper way of speaking of coloured folk" (84). This incident illustrates the complex social relations that determined how readers perceived the authority established by writing. The matter is further complicated by Corrothers's own examples of writing in dialect (see *The Black Cat Club* 1902).

Despite such abuses as Corrothers experienced, Chicago writers often called attention to those whose speech literate people had ignored, ridiculed, or considered ineffectual and even dangerous. Literature from Chicago shocked audiences in part by valorizing the new masses of city dwellers who could not write for themselves. "[L]iteracy," as Henry

Louis Gates, Jr., reminds us, "is the emblem that links racial alienation with economic alienation" ("Writing" 6). While not exactly disagreeing with Derrida, Gates shifts the focus from the set of relations that Derrida reads in Western philosophy to the words of African Americans, who often have been unheard within it. In the process, Gates stresses the privileged place of writing in Western culture, a place so privileged that it historically has been used as a test of the humanity, or lack thereof, of non-European peoples.[2] The equation of writing with humanness, and illiteracy with nonhuman status, did not make speech seem particularly privileged to early African-American writers (Gates *Figures* xxiii–xxiv).[3] Sandburg's and Lindsay's celebrations of Americans' speech also questioned the elevated position of writing as they endeavored to base a multicultural, national literacy on American oral traditions.

My methods of analysis vary somewhat with the texts under scrutiny. Scholars of African-American literature have influenced my understanding of history and race, in the work of both black and white authors. Feminist scholarship on the conditions under which literature is produced has shaped my conception of region, and I thus concentrate on the influence of literary peers rather than on landscape in discussing a Chicago school. Although some see feminism and the new historicism in conflict (Erickson 329; Newton), a study such as this one certainly is indebted to recent developments in literary criticism that have reinvigorated the relationship between literature and history (see During). One effect has been that I concentrate more on the discourse of a particular era when interpreting texts than on the authors' statements in autobiographies, letters, and essays. Jane Tompkins's emphasis in *Sensational Designs* on "what a text had *in common* with other texts" (xvi) also affected my decision to look carefully at now obscure works, not necessarily to resurrect them but to illustrate patterns of thought that remain with us today.

Jane Heap, coeditor of the *Little Review,* once remarked, "Chicago has a thrall" (Anderson *Little Review* 273). It certainly does, but, by and large, this study will resist the allure of Chicago as a symbol or physical place and will focus instead on the discussions, debates, friendships, and foment that gave men and women with literary ambitions the opportunity to be heard in Chicago. Although this study examines the conditions in and perceptions of the Chicago area that led to the privileging of certain kinds of speech, I do not limit myself to literature set in Chicago or to authors who lived there. Instead, I include texts that partake of a Chicago aesthetic of one kind or another. Much of the so-called Chicago writing, for instance, deals with small towns and farms. *Main-Travelled Roads, Spoon River Anthology, Winesburg, Ohio, Cornhuskers,* and other works with rural settings contribute to the sense of a Chicago voice. Some works discussed here were written after their authors had left

Chicago or, as in the case of Marita Bonner, before they moved to the city. Such literature nevertheless offers insight into the particular styles that, though not limited to Chicago, became part of the city's literary identity; Chicago's claims on its authors did not always depend on their physical presence. Although Dreiser and Sandburg, for example, eventually took up residence in the East, their reputations did not change as a result, for they never became identified with another movement or school. Susan Glaspell, in contrast, whose plays and novels have an affinity with the Chicago circle in which she spent her early days as a writer, is better known in connection with the Provincetown Players.

Challenges to literary canons have emphasized the arbitrariness of a period's parameters. Nonetheless, the appearance of two works in 1900 and the onset of the depression by 1930 frame this study. The changes Chicago would see in the early twentieth century were signaled in 1900 with two accounts of female aspiration, one well known and the other little known: Dreiser's *Sister Carrie* and Fannie Barrier Williams's essay "The Club Movement Among Colored Women." Dreiser's book raised eyebrows because of its amoral depiction of sexual desire and financial acquisitiveness. Williams's essay, published in *A New Negro for a New Century,* called attention to the accomplishments of African-American women. Both captured the changing consciousness of urban America. Although some believe that any renaissance of Chicago writing generally was over by the 1920s, I see a longer period of continuity. After 1930, however, WPA money created new dynamics, and the authors of the Depression era, including Nelson Algren, Saul Bellow, Marita Bonner, Gwendolyn Brooks, Jack Conroy, Frank Marshall Davis, Katherine Dunham, James T. Farrell, Fenton Johnson, Studs Terkel, Margaret Walker, Richard Wright, and Frank Yerby, deserve a study of their own.

Thus many different Chicagos existed simultaneously, some defined by generational lines, others encircled by streets and railways, and still others set off by profession, gender, race, or ethnicity. As Edgar Lee Masters wrote on 14 February 1927 to Alice Corbin Henderson, *Poetry*'s associate editor in the early years, "I still keep Chicago as my residence; though I don't know what Chicago it is. The Chicago of those to whom Chicago is now Chicago is not, however, the Chicago that I adored."[4] This study draws from some of the various Chicagos in order to look at an assembly at once coherent and in conflict with itself, part of both national and international movements, yet locally specific. These Chicagos and writers were connected by exchanges about what kind of language most effectively would reach an American audience, would produce a regional, national, or racial aesthetic, or would influence popular thinking about America's new linguistic realities. Authors contended over, rather than agreed on, how best to represent the new urban areas and the problems their rise revealed in other parts of the country. Although shaped by national and international trends (including realism, naturalism, feminism, modernism, and the Harlem Renaissance), these conflicts also resulted from such local pressures as the authority granted to journalism and social work.

The inherent classism of attempts to represent speech calls for attention to our own involvement in century-old linguistic debates. Literary texts frequently make social distinctions obvious by foregrounding written slang, vernacular language, colloquialisms, and dialect and thus open the question of writers' complicity in maintaining hierarchies. Much of the literature discussed here aimed to include as many kinds of voices as possible, raising the issue of the relationship between literary and political representation, but mere inclusion has not led to a transformation in social status. As Robyn Wiegman discusses, images from popular culture today suggest that racial minorities have become more visible than ever before and belie a stagnation in economic advances (116–17, 132–33). The issue of positive stereotypes, in which so many turn-of-the-century writers unwittingly invested, remains very much with us today.

Richard Terdiman has observed that "In classes we learn to class" (227). Belonging to a social class, whose relative authority is naturalized by schools, certainly extends beyond the domain of language. Yet students' futures may depend on how well they learn to class their speech. Milroy and Milroy write that language forms the basis for legal discrimination in England, which ostensibly does not allow employers to disqualify people due to their race, religion, or class (3). Although linguistic markers of class are less distinct in the United States than they are in England, the situation is otherwise much the same. Teachers and professors can help empower others by teaching them standard language, but they most likely will meet with resistance unless they acknowledge the counterdiscursive potential and ample pleasures of students' mother tongues. "If there is a language crisis in the United States, it is not because there is no official language," Dennis Baron writes, "nor is it because too many Americans use 'foreign' languages or nonstandard varieties of English. Rather, it is because large numbers of Americans do not learn to read or write well enough in any language or language variety to make that language work for them" (*English-Only* 199). The literature of Chicago provides an excellent illustration of the enfranchisement of linguistic variety because it demonstrates how individual works have helped to change what gets accepted as standard. The early-twentieth-century "classics" used today to teach receptiveness to the power of the English language often propagated the colloquialisms, slang, and underprivileged speech of their time.

Dreiser is a case in point. When the University of Pennsylvania Press issued a new edition of *Sister Carrie,* they tried to eliminate revisions made by printers, editors, typists, Dreiser's wife, and his friend Arthur Henry. The new edition contains a note on "Editorial Principles" that explains, "Dreiser's Germanic rhythms and cumulative sentence structures dominate most of the narrative, but Henry's 'improvements' crop up throughout, altering and often emasculating the original writing. The Pennsylvania edition has as one of its goals the preservation, wherever possible, of Dreiser's original prose, with its awkward power and forcefulness intact" (West 581). This passage suggests that, despite intermittent bans on teaching German in the United States, its influence upon American literature now is accepted (and even romanticized).

My own education exemplifies the process by which the unorthodox literature of another era seems normal today. Growing up in the town where Carl Sandburg was born and raised, I regularly heard his poetry and stories read in schools, churches, and other public places. My generation was too young to have heard him read in person, but his literary voice was internalized for some of us as the sound of our ministers, teachers, and fellow citizens. Away at college, I discovered how well he had captured the idioms of my mother's relatives, Swedish-Americans, who, like his family, mainly worked for the railroad. I, therefore, was surprised recently when I listened to recordings of him reciting. He sounded liltingly ethnic and self-consciously poetic, not at all like the current residents of Galesburg, Illinois.

Such is the course of literature as it defies conventions and then eventually redefines expectations. The teaching of American literature should include the fact that certain works have become "correct" when their authors chose to use a particular variation of language insightfully and precisely. In contrast, literary celebrations of linguistic difference do not necessarily expand opportunities for the speakers they represent and may, in fact, cloak social inequalities. Similarly, the study of literature will not lead directly to positive social change for most students. Attention to language cannot be neglected, however, for students' own language use can advance or inexplicably thwart their progress. This book argues not so much for attention to the words of Anderson's neglected city as to the way literature can privilege or delegitimize its speakers. The scorned urban terms now dwell among us, and although Chicago writers did not abolish stereotypes by employing these words, the city's literature still can alert us to prejudice's habitation in sound as well as in images.

1

DIALECT IS A VIRUS
Chicago's Literary Vernacular amid
Linguistic Purity Movements

[T]h' best way to masther th' language iv anny furrin' counthry is to inthrajooce ye'er

own. . . . Faith, whin us free born Americans get through with th' English language we'll

make it look as though it had been run over be a musical comedy.

—Mr. Dooley, in "Mr. Dooley on Slang," by Finley Peter Dunne, 39

• In addition to reporting the struggles of reformers, workers, farmers, women, African Americans, and immigrants,
turn-of-the-century Chicago writers responded to linguistic
conflicts, both legislative and literary. The craze for representing the speech of immigrants, African Americans, and the
working classes became part of a program to represent changing social realities. Most of these efforts appear racist or clas-
sist today, in part because writing in dialect often affirmed the
era's linguistic stereotypes. Yet seeing nonstandard English in
print pushed readers to confront their prejudices as well. Indeed, the context in which dialect literature was produced
and commented upon explains the nature of its popularity
among Chicago writers, many of whom professed that they
abhorred racial and class prejudice. As two long-standing attitudes toward the English language in the United States contended in Chicago's literary production, artists, editors, journalists, and critics insisted—with varying levels of
intensity—on either the consistency of English across time and
geography or the distinctness of the American version. These
conflicting attitudes pitted proponents of linguistic purity
against writers who challenged their taste.[1] Because the ethical, political, and aesthetic implications of these philosophies

of language ultimately overlapped, however, experiments with dialect produced contradictory effects.

Chicago served as a laboratory for testing literary and legislative approaches to polylingualism and variations within English at a time when the nation as a whole was arguing about the purity of the English language. Although Henry James's complaints about American speech being "an absolutely inexpert daub of unapplied tone" (*Question* 25) take the debate to esoteric levels, his making the 1905 Bryn Mawr commencement ceremony a forum addressing orthoepic decline indicates the currency of such topics. "[T]he early 1890s, the period during and after World War I, and the present" have seen debate about the official status of the English language, according to Dennis Baron, who finds that Illinois has historically taken a stand "firmly in the middle of the road" ("Legal Status" 14). Both British traditions of standardizing English and American patterns of proclaiming linguistic uniqueness created a climate for attempts to declare an official language in the United States. In the United States and Great Britain, maintaining standard language traditionally has involved moralism; discrimination in education, employment, and social standing; an assumption that spoken usage should be modeled on the written form; and outraged letters over issues of correctness to editors of newspapers and magazines (Milroy and Milroy 2–3, 21–22, 37–38, 40–41). James Milroy and Lesley Milroy, who define standardization as an "intolerance of optional variability in language," trace what they call "the complaint tradition" in English as far back as Jonathan Swift's "Proposal for Correcting, Improving, and Ascertaining the English Tongue" (26, 33).

Advocates of a unique American English have praised the language's no-frills, no-nonsense, down-to-earth serviceability. Its lack of pretension has been credited to its use by a wide range of people. Baron discusses the American notion that the character of language is shaped by democracy, including in his discussion examples from Noah Webster, John Adams, Walt Whitman, and James Fenimore Cooper.[2] While in England, Cooper "idealized his compatriots as living more simply, and communicating more naturally and directly, with less deviousness and artificiality, than their English counterparts" (*English-Only* 50). Such attitudes had a strong influence on the course of Chicago's literature as midwestern speech came to be linked with a mythical, forthright, truly American form of communication. The popular association of the Midwest with democracy also occurred outside literary circles. The connection arises, for example, in the arguments Illinois legislators made for and against prohibiting instruction in languages other than English and requiring English literacy of voters. Chicago's Charles J. Michal "argued that prescribing education was despotic and inimical, something more appropriate to New England (where nativism had been strong in the mid-nineteenth century) than to an all-American midwestern state: 'I think it is blue-bellied Yankeeism. I think it is not Americanism'" (Baron *English-Only* 125).

Protectionist and laissez-faire linguistic philosophies overlapped because associating a New World language with patriotism encouraged linguistic chauvinism that resulted in attempts to keep American English consistent throughout the country (43). The Chicago writers illustrate the shortcomings of both standard English and "all-American" views, and they vary in their awareness of these complicated issues. As Baron writes, "the very definition of what constitutes a language or a dialect is influenced by political factors as well as by linguistic ones" (5). For my purposes, writing in dialect refers to any attempt to call attention to the speech of a particular region, social class, or ethnic group, especially when the effort involves a departure from conventional spelling, syntax, or word choice. By continuing to use the categories of dialect and standard English, I reluctantly reaffirm the hierarchy that the terms connote but also confirm the failure of dialect literature to silence the call for standardization. The distinction between dialect and standard English still exists, but standards have become less rigid.[3]

American and British authors long have attempted to render "language really used by men" (Wordsworth 434) into written form, and the portrayal of local color has a lengthy history in the United States. By the 1890s, however, a large influx of non-English-speaking immigrants to America, the African-American migration from South to North, labor movements that captured the imaginations of writers, especially those in Chicago, and the new prominence of certain regions of the country made literary experiments with dialect a charged subject in the United States. Not all writers from Chicago communities took an interest in making the colloquial literary, but writers there did become more involved with questions of empowering the public, uniting citizens through language, and applying folk wisdom to the industrial world than with the questions of perception, vision, and defamiliarization that concerned other modern writers. A fascination with American accents extended Chicago writers' interests beyond their own city, and passages from midwestern literature suggest that performing in dialect also became an American pastime. As early as 1893, one of the characters in Henry Fuller's novel of Chicago, *The Cliff-Dwellers*, asks a young man about the kind of writing he does: "Well, what is it—dialect or psychological?" (27). In *Babbitt* (1922), Sinclair Lewis satirized the popularity of imitating varieties of the American vernacular when he described correspondence courses in public speaking that offered, among other lessons, instruction in "how to tell dialect stories" (66). Lewis also parodied the trend by making the idiom of Babbitt and his friends a source of humor. Hence Lewis gave middle-class, Anglo-Saxon citizens the same treatment that other writers were giving the lower classes.

Some Chicagoans made dialect literature notorious rather than popular, as was apparent in the literary magazine the *Dial*. Unlike Hobart Chatfield-Taylor's and Slason Thompson's Chicago-based periodical *America* (1888–1891), which stood explicitly for anti-immigration in its hyperpatriotism (Duffey 57–62, K. Williams "Pretzel to Grobnik" 174, Szuberla "Reborn" 39), the *Dial* stood for the New England philosophy of its editors and expressed what Fredric John Mosher has called an "intelligent conservatism" (107, 430). Its founder, Francis Fisher Browne, opposed imperialism and protested publicly against the execution of the anarchists involved in the Haymarket affair (Mosher 158, 153). Fluent in French, Norwegian, German, and Italian, and a self-taught expert on European literature (187, 389), *Dial* associate editor William Morton Payne did not base his judgments opposing dialect literature on the common prejudice against anything that sounded foreign.[4] Yet, despite the editors' interest in questions of justice and their endorsement of such issues as non-English library books for immigrants, the *Dial*'s appeals for the maintenance of standard English often relied on the rhetoric of xenophobia.

For many of its thirty-eight years in Chicago, the *Dial* "was widely regarded as the leading literary review in the United States" (Mosher 42). Founded in 1880, the journal was meant to stimulate cultural activity in Chicago, involve area writers as contributors (81), and participate in national debates about publishing, libraries, education, the arts, literary criticism, and other forms of scholarship ("Dial" 28:328).[5] The *Dial* had a national circulation but also reported on news at the University of Chicago and cultural events in the city. Its editors struggled to avoid appearing provincial while simultaneously publicizing their city's cosmopolitan accomplishments. In order to maintain this balance yet ensure that Chicago writers of merit received critical attention, Browne adopted a policy of either encouraging local writers or overlooking them altogether. "[I]f a book was not worthy of some commendation," writes Mosher, "it was simply ignored and not mentioned in Browne's columns" (81). Despite this attempt to accommodate local and national interests, some felt that the *Dial* did not do enough to promote Chicago writers, and readers sought to even the score by writing letters in praise of what was happening in the area or to complain about the general lack of publicity local authors received. One reader lamented, "Whenever there shall be, among our millions, a few thousands, who on seeing any Chicago book announced, cry, 'Hello! What's this? I must buy it and see,' there will be a Western literature. Then it will be the second book of a worthless writer which is neglected; now it is the first book of a worthy writer—if he happens to be 'a Westerner'" ("Who Reads" 13:131).

The *Dial*'s attitude toward the use of dialect in literature stemmed in part from associate editor Payne's dislike of realism (Mosher 331) and from the desire to raise the quality of books written and published in the midwestern and western United States. Arguments for and against the notion of a uniquely "western" literature raged in the *Dial* for months. The magazine took an unequivocal position in an 1893 editorial by Payne[6] entitled "The Literary West":

> Some composer of dialect doggerel, cheaply pathetic or sentimental, gains the ear of the public; his work has nothing more than novelty to recommend it, but the advent of a new poet is heralded, and we are told by Eastern critics that the literary West has at last found a voice. Some strong-lunged but untrained product of the prairies recounts the monotonous routine of life on the farm or in the country town, and is straightway hailed as the apostle of the newest and consequently the best realism. Some professional buffoon strikes a new note of bad taste in the columns of the local newspaper, and the admiring East holds him up as the exemplar of the coming humor. (15:174)

Here the burlesque of eastern critics' attitudes toward western literature illustrates the intersection of regional issues and linguistic purity movements.

For Payne and some readers, the debate over a western literature—and its characterization as a new breed of written American English—was tied to the question of America's literary relationship to England. Payne drew parallels between Easterners condescending to Westerners and the way British critics earlier had treated American writers, concluding that literature in English could be grouped by era of publication but not by geography (15:173). Critics of American literature still argue that the notion of a national literature is flawed and that American literature cannot be divorced either from the European traditions out of which it grew or from European concepts of a land called America. Unlike the *Dial*'s position, these challenges emphasize that American literature has not all been written in English and cannot be separated from the history and culture of the other countries of the Americas (Spengemann 26–27, Wiget 209). For its part, the *Dial* rested its case against a distinct American or regional literature on notions of literary excellence and the unifying power of the English language: "Except in their relation to choice of subject-matter, the terms Eastern and Western, Northern and Southern, have absolutely no literary meaning in a country all of whose parts have a common speech. The same standards apply to all the literature written in the English language" (15:175).

Editors and contributors to the *Dial* saw literature ensuring that Americans shared this "common speech" with England. In another 1893 editorial, "The Future of American Speech," Payne at once exalted in and was repulsed by the linguistic imperialism of Great Britain: "However desirable may be the increased use of our language by the nations of the earth, we cannot regard with equanimity the tendency of the language, in its territorial extensions, to assume corrupt dialectic forms." Payne expresses his concern about the United States in his reminder that "the English language, in its native environment, is still substantially the language created by Chaucer and Shakespeare, but observers are not wanting who declare that the English language, transplanted to the American continent, is undergoing radical changes, and becoming a dialect of the parent form of speech" (14:233).

Issues of literature and speech raised the question of national identity, and Payne's answer—basing that identity on English culture—denied differences between speech and literature, the sixteenth and nineteenth centuries, the United States and Great Britain. It also indirectly denied differences among American citizens of various ethnic origins. A similar welding of English and American history had taken place in the 1880s with the publication of textbooks on literary history. "In view of the Americanizing aims of the American literary history textbooks," Nina Baym writes, "the histories rather emphasized than played down the English origins of the American nation, thereby instructing classrooms of children of non-English ancestry to defer to the Anglo-Saxonism of their new country's heritage. This most important point was often left implicit, but it appears to have been well understood" (463). In "The Future of American Speech" Payne likewise emphasized the importance of schools in preserving Anglo-American culture, concluding with the thought that only proper education could bring us "once more into secure possession of the rich heritage, so nearly lost, of the speech of Shakespeare and of Tennyson" (14:235).

Two decades later, a *Dial* editorial would sound a desperate note that made explicit the cultural and political issues raised by an American literature:

> All the white races represented in America are beginning to intermarry. But biology does not promise that the result will be a composite type in which the characters we call Anglo-Saxon will predominate. . . . Indeed, we know that there is no assimilation of races without modification. We

cannot be certain that so much as the language will remain to us. Our vernacular may be so modified that there will be more difference between the speech of an American and an Englishman than there is now between the speech of an Italian and a Spaniard.

But long before that happens we shall have begun to produce an American literature distinct from English literature. ("American Literature" 58:38)

The call to clean up speech—and to keep written English standard—was an attempt to hold together a national myth that had little basis in the nation's history or in the heritage of its citizens. At times, the *Dial's* rhetoric suggested that everyone must exercise vigilance in an effort to maintain what William Cranston Lawton called the "ties which still bind us to the happiest of our many fatherlands" in his praise for the *Dial's* "effective warfare, of argument and ridicule, against the notion that American literature in general, and sectional Western literature in particular, should cut loose from the English traditions that make up the past" (25:39). "The Future of American Speech" stressed that "Americanisms"—or the coining of new words or idioms—were not the problem. "But we do refer to the mushroom growths of speech that spring up everywhere among us, the modes of expression that result from mere slovenliness of mind, and find no warrant either in the genius of the language or in the necessities of the situation," Payne explained (14:234). Everybody's slouchy speech habits and their proliferation in dialect literature, then, threatened the national identity. Beginning around 1918, the National Council of Teachers of English cosponsored "Better Speech Week" in American schools, where children pledged to "not dishonor my country's speech by leaving off the last syllable of words"; to "say a good American 'yes' and 'no' in place of an Indian grunt 'um-hum' and 'nup-um' or a foreign 'ya' or 'yeh' and 'nope'"; to "improve American speech by avoiding loud rough tones"; and to "learn to articulate correctly as many words as possible during the year" (Daniels 9).

The shape the debate took in the *Dial* intimated that crusaders against solecisms were trying to help the lower classes come into their American heritage on an equal basis with other citizens. For instance, in his article "Conversational English," Percy F. Bicknell chides the upper classes, the clergy, and members of the bar for letting their speaking habits slip and concludes, "Let us beware of reaching the condition of Greece and Rome of old, and of Turkey and parts of Germany and France and other European countries of to-day, where the literary and the spoken languages are entirely distinct, and the uneducated man is obliged to study a book in his own tongue as he would a foreign language" (21:107). Evidently, as Bicknell suggests, careless speech on anyone's part could lead to the development of a two-tier language that would alienate the working classes in their pursuit of education. Rampant variability in spoken language was feared because it might eventually make the written form unrecognizable to all but an elite group.

Despite the *Dial*'s concern for the working classes, some of its commentary suggests that insisting on proper speech was a way of maintaining class distinctions and keeping inferiors in their places. Moreover, there was the implied concern that representation in literature might also correspond to admittance into other exclusive, but vaguely defined, institutions. For instance, a letter from Marion E. Sparks of Urbana, Illinois, implies that allowing the speech of the lower classes into literature may be only a first step toward letting them into other spheres:

> The growth and popularity of the dialect story has caused words unknown to polite literature to appear in conservative periodicals. That seems to be accepted as necessary. But how far can we permit this to go? Can we afford to admit these tramps in the world of words into the society of their betters on terms of equality? Can dialect and colloquial terms take the place of words which are acknowledged as standards in literature apart from the dialect story? (24:39)[7]

In an 1899 editorial entitled "Idiom and Ideal," the *Dial* used a similar metaphor, expressing a fear of educated citizens and undesirable people competing for space:

> There are few features of the recent literary situation as noteworthy as the large production and wide vogue of writings which exploit some special form of idiom and rely for their main interest upon the appeal to curiosity thus made. The idiom of the sailor and the soldier, the rustic and the mechanic, have elbowed their way into literature, and demand their share of the attention hitherto accorded chiefly to educated speech. The normal type of English expression has to jostle for recognition with the local and abnormal types of the Scotchman and the Irishman, the negro and the baboo, and, in our own country particularly, with such uncouth mixtures as those of the German-American and Scandinavian-American. (27:305)

Dialect literature created controversy because it introduced variability, did not sustain the myth of an Anglo-Saxon–based American culture, and gave "Others" legitimacy through writing. Elizabeth Frick has observed that throughout American history "the immigration of non-English speakers is almost always described as a problem, but with remarkable consistency it is seen more specifically as a *disaster by water*" (27). In addition to making an occasional reference of this type (see, for example, Duffield 15:86), the *Dial* often associated nonstandard language with disease. Payne's 1895 editorial on "The Use and Abuse of Dialect" identifies incorrect English as the agent causing a national literary illness:

> There are indications—not very marked as yet, but still indications—that the day of the dialect versifier and story-teller is waning. The literary epidemic for which he is responsible has raged with unabated virulence in this country for the past ten years or more. It has had almost complete possession of the *bric-a-brac* popular magazine. Its contagion has even extended to those periodicals which we too fondly fancied to stand for the dignities, as opposed to the freaks, of literature. At the other extreme, it has been disseminated and vulgarized by the newspaper and the popular reciter. A few of the men and women whom we count as real forces in American letters have been numbered among its victims. But all epidemics exhaust themselves in time, and we are encouraged to believe that this one is nearly spent. (18:67)

As Sander L. Gilman argues, "The most powerful stereotypes in nineteenth-century Western Europe and the United States were those that associated images of race, sexuality, and the all-pervasive idea of pathology" (11–12). These stereotypes attached themselves to languages because, according to Gilman, "language implies the correct and meaningful use of language. Any other use is 'crazy.' Thus one of the inherent definitions of any linguistic group is that it is the norm of sanity. The Other is always 'mad'" (129). In the nineteenth century, literature, popular dialect fiction, and vaudeville had depicted African Americans, among others, as incapable of using language correctly. As a result, there existed many good reasons for objecting to the use of dialect; yet in protesting the worthlessness of dialect literature, the *Dial* associated ideas about race, class, and country of origin with metaphors of disease, thereby reaffirming the stereotypes perpetuated by the conventions of writing in dialect. Payne's conceit emphasized physical health, rather than sanity, but conformity to standard written English nevertheless became a test of cultural well-being.

The editorial "Idiom and Ideal" asked, "Does the speech of Tommy Atkins and Marse Chan, the dialect of Drumtochty and Donegal, the locution of the Hoosier farmer and the Bowery tough, have anything of the antiseptic quality that preserves a story or a poem and enables it to delight successive generations of readers"? (27:305–306). If great literature had an "antiseptic quality," then were nonstandard versions of English toxic? According to one of the *Dial*'s contributors, even college students, who presumably had many positive models, were not immune to the dangers of poor speech. In a *Dial* opinion piece from 1897, W. H. Johnson complains about college students not reading enough good literature, getting credit for working on the school newspaper, and making a "habit of taking the most grotesque liberties in its [English's] morphology, phonetics, syntax, and meaning, for no more adequate reason than the supposition that such linguistic butchery is humorous." Johnson warns, "Now it is utterly impossible that such loose habits of speech indulged in constantly during student life should have no permanently deleterious effect upon the speech of after days" (22:271). Venereal disease appears to provide the analogy here, and an earlier *Dial* editorial entitled "The Use and Abuse of Dialect" had similarly connected speech and sexuality by alerting readers about textbooks containing "examples of perverted diction that cannot fail to exert an evil influence upon the impressionable years of childhood" (18:68). Metaphors of pathology represented written dialect as unhealthy or deviant despite the legitimacy that writing granted nonstandard speech.

Some of the *Dial*'s readers and contributors felt strongly enough about the threat to literature that they added their voices in support of legislation to restrict immigration to the United States. In a letter that appeared in the *Dial* under the title "A Literary Phase of the Immigration Question" in January 1893, Henry W. Thurston of La Grange, Illinois, refers to a writer from *The Forum* who "believes that the literary decay of New England has been largely due to the great influx of foreigners in recent years." The writer continues, "Furthermore, . . . no considerable literary product of the highest excellence can possibly be obtained from a polyglot people." Thurston wonders, "[S]hould all immigration to this country, except from Teutonic or possibly from English-speaking peoples, be entirely prohibited for a period of years, would there be an unmistakable literary gain to the United States?" (14:41). William Trent also advocates homogeneity in an article entitled "American Literature" for the *Dial*'s twentieth-anniversary issue in 1900: "The great centres of artistic and literary production in the past, from Athens to the Boston of the Transcendentalists, have been also centres of a homogeneous population. Can a really great literature grow up in the midst of a heterogeneous population, and how far are we Americans a heterogeneous people?" (28:337).

Midwestern fiction writers, even though they were often the target of invectives against the use of colloquial language, expressed some of the same attitudes as the *Dial* had about the unhealthy effects of immigrant slang. Although Theodore Dreiser did not make overt moral judgments in *Sister Carrie*, he, too, characterized vernacular speech in terms of pathology by his juxtaposition of images. For instance, readers see the workers in a cap factory through the eyes of the newly arrived Carrie, who risks being corrupted by city life: "They were a fair type of nearly the lowest order of shop girls,—careless, rather slouchy, and more or less pale from confinement. They were not timid however, were rich in curiosity and strong in daring and slang" (25). Their physical deterioration and verbal aggressiveness exist side by side. Factory work can destroy their bodies, but seemingly nothing checks the spread of their language.

Henry Fuller's *The Cliff-Dwellers* (1893) also envisions the harmful effects of nonstandard speech. Fuller had grown up in Chicago and was one of the city's first writers to receive national recognition. Kenny J. Williams notes that, although he belonged to the generation of writers claiming "the genteel tradition" for Chicago, he was also one of the first to present it in unflattering realism (*City of Men* 171). In one scene in *The Cliff-Dwellers*, an architect tells a little girl at a party about the dollhouse he is going to build for her. When asked her opinion, she replies, with the accent that the family maid uses, "I shouldn't know whether to belave you" (93). Although the guests are amused, her mother is displeased: "'That dreadful Norah!' whimpered the poor woman. 'She must go.'" The child has caught something embarrassing, if not downright harmful, from the maid. Yet the architect responds, "Don't dismiss your *bonne* . . . she'll produce a beautiful accent in time" (94).

His opinion is born out by Cornelia McNabb, a character who acquires standard English as she makes her way from being a maid in a boardinghouse to a waitress, a secretary, and the wife of a millionaire's son. Cornelia promises new life for the Brainard family, whose patriarch, Erastus Brainard, has gained his fortune as president of a large bank and through illegal activities. The family's corruption surfaces in a son, Marcus, who stabs his father with a book knife in a drunken rage. Marcus hangs himself a few days later, and Erastus, dying from the wound, has to picture the son's suicide in his own last seconds of life. Indeed, the language in which the news is communicated practically delivers the death blow: "The word was passed from man-servant to maid-servant, and came to their master through the voice of a Swedish girl whose mind was capable of dealing with emotions only in the most primitive way, and whose imperfect command of English made her communication come with a horrible and harrowing directness" (310).

The horrible and harrowing directness of the lower classes could be deadly, but Fuller also feared the loss of vitality that went with urbanization. The character George Ogden, for instance, tries every polite, legal means to get money from his brother-in-law, who has cheated him out of his inheritance. He finally expresses his rage by smashing a chair over the man's head: "Ogden, for the first time in his life, passed completely out of himself. There fell away from him all the fetters that shackle the super-civilized man who is habitually conscious of his civilization" (298). Although not advocating violence, Fuller must have felt that, in former times or in a more rural area, Ogden would have confronted the scoundrel sooner.

The novel's metaphorical title expresses a similar ambivalence toward both modern American entrepreneurial culture and past influences not British in origin. In naming his book *The Cliff-Dwellers*, Fuller in all like lihood was drawing on the interest in Native American ruins generated by Gustaf Nordenskiold's *The Cliff Dwellers of the Mesa Verde, Southwestern Colorado*, published in the same year. The introduction to Fuller's novel comparing the city of Chicago to the dwellings of the Anasazi suggests both that civilization has not come very far since then and that it has come too far and therefore degenerated.[8] Thus, the story's immigrants both contribute to the primitive, unhealthy condition of the city and promise to renew a culture spoiled by greed and decadence. Fuller's ambivalence about the upper classes and his allusions to Native American culture hold out the possibility of assimilation and set the stage for the primitivism of later Chicago writing.

Disparagement of dialect literature and written slang, warnings against careless speech, worries about the lower classes' continued literacy, and the fear of immigrants' illiteracy all have in common the relationship between written and spoken language. Was nonstandard writing producing poor speech or vice versa? Either case threatened to introduce variability into the language, and countering that threat required a system that could both resist and withstand change. In its campaign for pure English, the *Dial* claimed sometimes that writing reflected proper pronunciation and at other times that comprehension of written English relied on visual, not phonetic, cues. Arguing against spelling reform often occasioned these formulations of the journal's linguistic concepts.

Proposals by professional societies, politicians, and educators to simplify English spelling paralleled the departure from tradition represented by dialect literature. Beginning in 1906, spelling reform was routinely attacked with the advent of a "Casual Comment" column that contained short, sometimes tongue-in-cheek editorials on current matters of interest. Topics included such ideas as the suggestion that phonograph records might be useful as an objective measure of correct pronunciation: "Like the standard metre preserved at Paris, we might have a standard pronunciation stored in a fire-proof vault of the British

Museum or the Congressional Library" ("Casual Comment" 42:363).
Although whimsical, this suggestion demonstrates the depth of the editors' desire to suppress linguistic variability. A more serious argument
for standard language grounded pronunciation in English's traditional
written form. An editorial reply to a letter written by a reader in favor
of spelling reform explains the relation between conventional spelling
and phonetics:

> The reason why we consider "program" horrible is that it inevitably leads
> to a pronunciation which accents the first syllable, and reduces the sec-
> ond to an inconsiderable caudal appendix. . . . We know of no way to
> keep the full value of the second syllable (which means preserving the
> dignity of a fine old word) without spelling it in the orthodox way. "Epi-
> gram," "monogram," and "telegram" are not cases in point, for the ex-
> cellent reason that they are *three-syllabled* words, which makes it almost
> impossible not to give the "gram" its full value in their pronunciation.
> This is so elementary that we are almost ashamed to write it. (Editorial
> Response 55:105–106)

In an editorial entitled "The Cause" and dedicated to the topic of
spelling reform, the *Dial* linked reformed spelling to dialect literature
and reiterated its opinion that simplified spelling would ruin pronunciation. Reacting to the "Simplified Spelling Bulletin" (which used the improvements it advocated), the *Dial* editors wrote: "Hitherto, we have
left this sort of license to the amateurs of dialect, who have alternately
bored and puzzled us to the limit of endurance, but we have not *had* to
read them. In the good time coming, it seems, everybody who writes will
devise for his words spellings *ad hoc,* in accordance with some occult
phonetic system of his own" (53:276). Idiosyncratic spelling was undesirable because it reflected the variability that already existed in American
English. The *Dial* frequently mocked the cause of spelling reform by
providing examples of proposed alterations, an effective strategy, given
the extreme changes some of its promoters advised. Ultimately, though,
the *Dial*'s campaign questioned who would control further development
of the language. "[A]s we scan this brief quotation . . . and try to read it
aloud, giving the letters the values that we instinctively attach to them,"
the editors wrote in response to an excerpt from the "Simplified Spelling
Bulletin," "we discover that just one-half of the deformed spellings indicate a pronunciation which is distinctly *not* that of the cultivated user of
the English language" (53:275).

Yet, some "Casual Comment" columns argued that a written system
determining standard pronunciation could never exist. Although dis-

similarities between the English spoken in different areas chagrined the editors, they pragmatically cited this variety as a stumbling block to spelling changes. "But even supposing it to be at the outset faultlessly phonetic, not only for London, but also for Boston and Indianapolis and Cape Town and Melbourne," the editors wrote, "how long would such an alphabet remain phonetic? Pronunciation is slowly but constantly changing, as we occasionally learn to our surprise in reading old poetry. The human throat itself, and the vocal chords, are not fashioned after one invariable pattern. . . . All spelling is and must be largely a matter of convention" ("Casual Comment" 41:231). When necessary for its position, then, *Dial* editorial policy marshaled pronunciation's relationship to spelling, but the impossibility of spelling ever representing the full range of pronunciation was also presented as a reason to forego change.

Readers and reviewers provided counterpoints to the *Dial*'s editorial policies on the maintenance of standard language and the predominance of British influences on American culture, but a series of circular arguments founded the journal's official philosophy on what it called "the Anglicity of the English language" ("Casual Comment" 56:91). "Anglicity" became the center of a system in which writing could not fully represent speech because the latter varied over time and from place to place. Writing needed to remain stable in order to preserve a literary heritage in English, and to do so, speech had to stay anchored in writing. In other words, to preserve tradition, language needed a center, and writing needed to stay fixed, since speech does not provide that stability. Little did the *Dial* editors know that they were trying to postpone the fragmented sense of reality that later engaged modern and postmodern writers. In a fixed structure, "the center . . . closes off the play which it opens up and makes possible," writes Jacques Derrida. "As center, it is the point at which the substitution of contents, elements, or terms is no longer possible" (*Writing* 279). Anglicity had to be the center because writing could not represent the variability of speech without speech undermining the stability of writing. In order to maintain the belief that an English heritage represented everything American, only speech that conformed to an English heritage could be represented. For that heritage to remain intelligible, writing needed to be reflective of speech or speech reflective of writing, and a convention that allowed anglicity to represent everything American accomplished these goals. Therefore, any change in conventions pointed to the failure of the Anglo-Saxon heritage to represent everything American.

In their "Casual Comment" column on anglicity, the *Dial* editors bewailed the coming separation between actual usage and great literature that changes in "[p]ronunciation, idiom, vocabulary, [and] spelling" were causing:

> An effort to postpone that evil day is put forth by the new Society for Pure English, which has recently issued its first pamphlet . . . formulating certain basic principles and urging a return to dialectic naturalness and raciness of expression. Words and idioms that smack of the soil whence they sprang are to be revived and cherished, while the artificialities of urban speech need to be repressed. Not only does the thoughtless multitude require guidance and correction in this matter, but it is probable that the educated and the careful are doing their part, often unconsciously, toward breaking up the uniformity and purity of our English tongue. The arts and sciences are flooding the dictionary with new and in many instances ill-constructed terms, journalists are familiarizing us with modes of expression not always worthy of adoption, innovators in spelling are perniciously active, and the foreign languages spoken within our borders add an alien tinge to our speech. (56:91)

This comment from 1914 covers many of the issues the *Dial* had addressed for two decades: the dangers to speech from immigrants and the uneducated and the dangers to writing from artists, journalists, scientists, and spelling reformers. All of these groups threatened to undermine the centrality of anglicity to American English. The call to preserve "dialectic naturalness and raciness of expression" sounds a relatively new note, although this idea had its basis in earlier positions.

The forces that led the *Dial* to indict both the educated and the uneducated in connection with linguistic change modified the language. The epidemic Payne believed to be "nearly spent" in 1895 had not played itself out, for instance, and the *Dial* eventually embraced such dialect creations as Mr. Dooley and George Ade's *Fables in Slang* ("Briefs" 32:207; "Briefs" 49:336). The journal also came to a qualified acceptance of common parlance in literature by conceding that certain kinds of slang were actually of Anglo-Saxon derivation.

From the beginning of the century, the *Dial* reminded readers that language shaped national character ("Three Centuries" 29:486). Like those who proclaimed the uniqueness of American literature, especially literature produced in the western half of the nation, the *Dial* editors argued that democracy and language were interdependent. While the former group claimed slang and dialect as instruments for democratic change, in literature at least, the journal subsequently reclaimed our slang heritage by asserting, "[S]ome of our raciest so-called Americanisms are nothing but survivals of old idioms that have died out in the home of their origin" ("Casual Comment" 50:149; see also "Casual Comment" 47:63). In "The Language of the Unlettered," Bicknell recommended renewing American English by restoring Anglo-Saxon colloquialisms: "Dialectic regeneration is said to be the crying need at present of our effete and anaemic language, and the attempt to restore to it some of the vigorous and racy words and expressions of a ruder age is not to be frowned upon. There is something about the unaffectedness, the directness, the rugged strength and artless picturesqueness of untutored speech that refreshes the ear wearied with the studied correctness and self-conscious refinement of cultured utterance" (56:405). Just as immigrants had the power to corrupt or to renew Chicago society in *The Cliff-Dwellers*, "folk" speech could either poison or revitalize the English language, depending on who the folk were. One group's horrible and harrowing directness was another's rugged strength and artless picturesqueness—the qualities of the legendary American language.

As early as the 1895 editorial "The Use and Abuse of Dialect," the *Dial* had distinguished between proper and improper representations of the vernacular. A quote from Professor Willis Boughton of Ohio University parallels salvage anthropology[9]: "To preserve the speech of a vanishing people, dialect literature may be justified; but to propagate such language is vicious" ([Payne] "Use and Abuse" 18:68). The editorial then defines the proper use of dialect:

> The facts of dialect speech, as distinguished from the inventions of the newspaper humorist, are of great importance to the history of language. No more important linguistic work remains to be done in this country than that of recording the thousands of local variations of our speech from what may be called standard English. To fix these colloquialisms in time and place, to trace them to their origins, to construct speech-maps embodying the salient facts of popular usage wherever it has distinctive features—these are scientific aims of the worthiest.

Payne concludes that he has done his duty if his essay "turn[s] even one misguided realist from a grinder-out of dialect 'copy' for the newspapers into an exact observer of local usage for the scientific purposes" of dialect dictionaries (18:69). If unable to fix the vernacular so that its purity was restored, "speech-maps" could at least restrict variability to its place.

This sifting of good and bad slang, dialect copy in journalism, and scientific observation left African-American speech and alleged representations of it in a complicated position, for African Americans were both native English speakers and the target of traditions mocking their usage. Even as *Dial* editorials listed them among groups of people corrupting

the language, *Dial* reviewers wrote favorably of the works of Paul Laurence Dunbar and Joel Chandler Harris ("Holiday Publications"
31:447, "Casual Comment" 45:32). The journal also reviewed books by
Booker T. Washington, W. E. B. DuBois, and Kelly Miller, with the last
two serving occasionally as contributors, but a "Casual Comment" column on Harris's death indicates that what passed for exact observation
of African-American speech and life could not be separated from paternalistic attitudes toward southern blacks: Harris's "negro dialect stories,
rich in folklore but delightfully free from the dreary dryness of much
that is published under that name, are full of laughter and sunshine and
light-heartedness. The irresponsible, happy-go-lucky son of Africa has
been with us, in abundance, for generations; but he waited for a Joel
Chandler Harris to catch and reproduce his peculiar charms and graces"
("Casual Comment" 45:32).

Sometimes African Americans were categorized with city dwellers who
were thought to be ruining the language; at other times their speech fell
into the endangered species category. Distinctions were seldom made between representation and actual practice. For example, Alexander L.
Bondurant of the State University of Mississippi marvels in a letter: "The
negro dialect, as spoken on the plantations in the South, is rich in survivals; and that a number of these are still found in England, is shown by
some examples taken from 'Lorna Doone'—a well of English undefiled."
He concludes, after listing examples of undefiled survivals, "These words
and expressions are all in common use among the negroes, and must
have come to them from Old England" (18:105). E. W. Hopkins of
Bryn Mawr College replied to Bondurant and others, insisting that their
observations proved that American material for the English Dialect Dictionary should "be sifted first in America." Hopkins reminds readers that
Bondurant's list of words "may be heard on occasion on Yankee farms or
in a Yankee schoolyard." He plants doubt about his own qualifications,
however, when he observes: "We venture to doubt whether an uneducated negro ever used exactly the expression (cited by Professor Bondurant), '*How is your* old 'oman?' Does not the darkey say always
'Howsya old?'" (18:136). Scientific observation does not appear to have
shaken the prejudices of dialect literature or to have accounted for inter-
group variability.

Several scholars of African-American literature have discussed the impression, created in part by written dialect, that Black English consists of
misused language (Gates "Dis and Dat" 105). James Weldon Johnson
wrote that a tradition of dialect writing was established to entertain white
audiences (*Book* 4). For this reason, he believed his contemporaries
needed "a form that will express the racial spirit by symbols from within

rather than by symbols from without, such as the mere mutilation of English spelling and pronunciation" (*Book* 41). J. Saunders Redding traced dialect's conventions of mutilated English to minstrel shows (53) and to such European-American writers as Harris. Redding observes, "Harris's dialect is skillful and effective misrepresentation, a made language in every sense of the word, conveying the general type impression of untaught imagination, ignorance, and low cunning with which he believed the Negro endowed" (52).

Had it been separate from other ideological concerns, the *Dial*'s call for an end to misspelled literature might have countered the problem of writers using nonstandard English to make characters seem unintelligent. A glance at George Ade's *Pink Marsh* shows that there were plenty of reasons for disliking dialect literature. A journalist and later a playwright, for over forty years Ade wrote pieces that were collected in *Fables in Slang* and sequels to that volume (Coyle 48). "Ade gave the ancient form of the fable a sharp twist," Lee Coyle writes, "by retaining the archaic form and stilted manner and by steeping it in colloquial language generously laced with slang. The result was linguistic fire" (40). The technique used in the fables evolved gradually. Ade departed from straight news reporting with his "Stories of the Streets and of the Town," sketches of life in Chicago and the rural Midwest. With a column featuring the adventures of Artie Blanchard, an imaginary, wise-cracking Chicago office boy, he began to incorporate slang. He turned to dialect in his accounts of another Chicago type, Pink Marsh, a fictional shoeshiner who later becomes a Pullman Porter. In Marsh's episodes, a professional man, "the Morning Customer," visits the shoeshine stand and flaunts his verbal superiority. In a typical scenario, Pink says of the morning customer's words, "I could n' ketch 'em boys; not 'ith a laddeh" (20).

Ade was a lifelong vaudeville fan, and his process of writing an African-American character into his early play "The County Chairman" illustrates how the conventions of minstrelsy made their way into his work. Biographer Fred C. Kelly relates that, in writing "The County Chairman," Ade was trying to alter his reputation as a facile wit who knew street language: "He deliberately laid the scenes in the early eighties to avoid the kind of speech which adorned the Fables. If asked to do so in rehearsal he could assume a horrified air and explain that it would be an anachronism to use in a play of 1880 a phrase invented many years later" (174). Yet, when Ade heard of the plight of Willis Sweatnam, an out-of-work vaudeville performer, he rewrote the part of a "ne'er-do-well white-trash character" for the actor to do in blackface. Ade's description of this process demonstrates that, for at least one European-American writer, the sound of the minstrel had been internalized: "It was easy to write dialogue for Sweatnam. All I had to do after I wrote a speech for him was to close my eyes and listen to him repeating it and if it sounded like Sweatnam I left it in" (Kelly 176). Sweatman's character and Pink Marsh, we might say, relied heavily on convention and representations of representations.

In the context of linguistic purity movements, dialect literature represented a forbidden pleasure that challenged the stuffiness of upholders of correctness. Its disruptive potential depended on the author's relationship to the materials, awareness of the representation of speech as an illusion, and positioning of the dialect voices—for instance, whether the accented speech contrasted with the voice of a seemingly superior narrator coded as standard. As Cary Nelson writes, "Dialect in the end has no essential and unchanging meaning. Even the same dialect poem can have different effects in different contexts" (118).

Chicago journalist Finley Peter Dunne's creation, the Irish-American bartender Mr. Dooley, exemplifies Nelson's point. Authorial intention seems to matter in the case of dialect literature—and to account, in part, for the changing effects writing in dialect produces. Dunne himself came from an Irish-American family, so humor arising from Mr. Dooley's ethnicity had the quality of an inside joke.

According to Charles Fanning, Dunne began working as a journalist in Chicago in 1884, when he was sixteen. Working his way up the ranks of six newspapers during the next eight years, he took charge of the editorial page at the *Evening Post,* where Mr. Dooley was born (215). Dunne's politics are hard to categorize; he was a gadfly who stung people on both sides of almost any issue. He is quoted as saying that the inspiration for Mr. Dooley came from the desire to criticize local and national figures with more freedom than his regular editorials allowed: "It occurred to me that while it might be dangerous to call an alderman a thief in English no one could sue if a comic Irishman denounced the statesman as a thief" (Bander 20).

Dunne's technique surmounted many of the problems a character such as Pink Marsh presented. For instance, Mr. Dooley spoke for himself; his words were not framed by a narrator or reported to us by someone using a prestige dialect, an effect Ade also achieved with the *Fables in Slang.* As Edward J. Bander points out, "Mr. Dooley performs on paper" (95). His language is not meant as a transcription or a parody of Irish-American speech. "Mr. Dooley's Irish brogue made no pretense to be phonetically correct," Max Eastman has observed, "it just went in for being funny. The author himself once described it to me as 'a language never heard on land or sea'" (133). Mr. Dooley's language pitted wit and departure from the standard against each other. "Dunne employed the common techniques of dialect writers: misspellings, puns, funny names," Bander writes. "He used 'dishpot' for despot, 'autymobill' to make the point that automobiles were expensive, and a James Joycian mind could detect hidden meanings in the use of words" (48). In the epigraph to this chapter, Mr. Dooley's "inthrajooce" suggests adding "juice" to a language by interjecting elements from other countries. The entire 1913 *Boston Globe* article, "Mr. Dooley on Slang," from which this passage comes, demonstrates Dunne's cognizance of the linguistic debates he was engaging by writing dialect.

As early as 1892, Dunne editorially parodied the kinds of criticism of dialect literature that were going to be found in such places as the *Dial*:

> There is no doubt that the dialect story is a very bad thing and abundantly deserves every uncomplimentary remark that anybody may find time to make about it. It has filled the magazines so full that we sometimes wonder why they do not explode, it has flooded the bookstands with its pink and yellow covers and its horrid drawings of Dakota farmers and Tennessee mountaineers; in short, it has added an immense weight to the already excessive burden of existence; but we may be pardoned if we say we think it has not perverted literary style or literary taste.
>
> That is our honest opinion of the dialect story. Of course, it might be different if we had ever heard of anybody who had succeeded in reading one. (Ellis 64)

Dunne saw beyond national debates and immediate trends to matters of speech and social status. He also commented indirectly on the imposition of European languages on other cultures. Indeed, "Mr. Dooley on Slang" begins with the bartender's reflections on a newspaper article about "a profissor at Oxfurd colledge, that's about ready to declare war on us because he says we're corruptin' th' dilect they call th' English language in England with our slang" (39). Mr. Dooley then produces a conceit based on a reversal of colonial relations between England and the United States: American productivity in vernacular commodities has led to the export of our product, and he counsels the English to be grateful for the ways in which their relationship with us has improved their quality of life. Given his use of language, Mr. Dooley's comment about mastering the language of a foreign country by introducing one's own suggests the process by which ethnic groups in America have modified the British form of the English language; in the context of imperialism, however, Mr. Dooley's observation is a cynical comment on the process by which European colonists "learned" the languages of the countries they invaded. His explanation, later in the essay, of his friend Hogan's theory of slang's dissemination—that first thieves "invint language to conceal thought fr'm th' polis" (39)—therefore becomes especially ironic. Even this tangential link between colonizers and foul-mouthed thugs offers a criticism of such rhetoric as the *Dial* employed, which opposed imperial impositions of culture but at some level also suggested that the subjected were unworthy of them.

The play that Dunne establishes between a representation of Dooley's accent and puns on standard English extends to the relationship between words and objects, signifiers and signifieds. Here Mr. Dooley explains Hogan's theory to his friends at the bar:

> "Wan iv ye'er ancesthors frightens a hen an' sees she's left somthing on th' ground. He pints at it an' exclaims in surprise 'Egg!'
>
> "He happens to be a man iv standin' in th' community, havin' kilt a lot iv people with his stone hatchet, an' a fellow who hears him an' wants to be in style cries 'Egg' ivery time he sees th' thropy, an' so it goes ontil an egg is a egg ivrywhere English is spoke. But th' Fr-rinch calls it a 'oof,' which shows that whin th' first Fr-rinchman see wan he started back in alarm an' cried 'Oof!'
>
> "'Now,' says Hogan, 'suppose ye're revered ancesthor had happened to use some other exclymation. Issintyally,' says he, 'an egg is no more entitled to be called an egg thin I am. We're used to eggs bein' called eggs, an' we think th' name describes thim, but if ol' Granpa Stone Hatchet Dooley had said 'Glub' we'd be orthrin' scrambled glubs at th' prisint minyit.'" (39)

Coming from an Irish American who has not mastered the niceties of standard English, this discussion challenges popular prejudices that "dialect" speakers are so insensitive to language that they cannot remember the right names for things. Hogan's theory also confronts an idea expressed the next year in the *Dial*, in "The Language of the Unlettered": "To a person with vigor and spontaneity unimpaired by meditation and introspection, words are, in a sense, the very things they stand for, and the application of a new name to a familiar object seems a gross absurdity, while the possibility that the same things may not have the same names the world over is hardly conceivable" (Bicknell 56:405). Mr. Dooley demonstrates that he is not romantic, primitive, or ignorant, despite his identifiably ethnic speech.

Dunne's sophistication, however, did not overcome all the ethical quandaries that dialect literature presented. Dunne got a lesson in the power relations involved in representation when he created an Irish-

American character named McNeery, a barely fictionalized Jim McGarry, who tended bar at an establishment Dunne and other journalists patronized. According to Elmer Ellis, "Jim McGarry's tolerance had limits and his personal dignity became affronted as more and more people called him McNeery and he began to think they were laughing at him" (75). Shortly afterward, McNeery was replaced by Mr. Dooley, who ran his business in a different neighborhood than McNeery or McGarry. Ellis comments, "Undoubtedly there were many levels of appreciation of Mr. Dooley. The lowest of these was the reader who found merely something comic in the fact that the saloon-keeper spoke in a quaint language, a dialect associated with unskilled laborers and household servants, and it was therefore an invitation for smiles to find it in print" (288–89). Overall, though, Dunne urged readers to overcome linguistic prejudices by calling attention to both spoken and written English and the arbitrary, sometimes violent, association between correctness and intelligence.

Despite the *Dial*'s recognition of Dunne's and Ade's talent and its revised attitude toward slang, the conservative journal was not ready for the new generation of Chicago writers as epitomized by Carl Sandburg. Sandburg, like his fellow newspapermen Ade and Dunne, worked to elevate the subject matter by which he earned his living to an art. His choice of genre helped ensure his success, for, unlike humorous sketches, poetry was unquestionably literature and was experiencing a resurgence in which "the language of contemporary speech" (Monroe and Henderson *New Poetry* xxxvi) would be valued explicitly. Like his journalism, Sandburg's free verse contained few connectives or subordinate clauses and relied instead on the dramatic juxtaposition of simple sentences. The publication of some of his *Chicago Poems* in *Poetry: A Magazine of Verse* in 1914 prompted the *Dial*'s editors, in "New Lamps for Old," to call Harriet Monroe's journal "a futile little periodical" and to "rally around the old standards," "those who stand for sanity and the acceptance of the ripe fruits of the world's experience" (56:231). In the editorial, Sandburg's poem "Chicago" is described as a "collocation of words" (56:231), "ragged lines," "unregulated word-eruptions," and "an impudent affront to the poetry-loving public" (56:232). Clearly, the form of the poem, or seeming lack thereof, caused some irritation, but its working-class content and use of the vernacular grated as well. The editorial fumed that the poem was "blurted out in such ugly fashion" and that "in these 'hog-butcher' pieces there is no discernible evidence that culture has been attained." As for the poet himself, the *Dial* suggested that "this author would be more at home in the brickyard than on the slopes of Parnassus" (56:232). Apparently, dialect writing that knew its place as humor, journalism, or local color was one thing; everyday speech that pretended to be literature was quite another.

Given the strong sentiment for linguistic purity, dialect writing forced audiences to examine the relationship between democratic and literary representation and to ask, What does American English represent? Nevertheless, by appearing to transcribe the actual speech of a particular group of people, dialect writing could create the impression that standard written English corresponded to the idiom of some other, "normal" group. Whether they were of the older generation, such as Ade, or the younger one, such as Sandburg, Chicago writers interested in employing the vernacular grew up amid popular notions about how America sounded. By recharging old conventions with idealized sentiments about an American language, these authors limited what the groups they wrote about could say for themselves. Yet they also called attention to dialect at a time when many wanted the non-British in origin to stay out of sight and sound. At their best, then, experiments with the vernacular avoided distinguishing between "standard" and "nonstandard," as Ade, Dunne, and Sandburg all learned. Perhaps for this reason, members of the Chicago group are cited as early influences on the poetry of both Langston Hughes and Sterling A. Brown (Hughes *Big Sea* 29, 212; Stuckey xxiv).

Who American English represents and what using English rather than another language means remain volatile issues in American education, literature, law, and culture. To date, twenty-two states have passed English-only laws (Headden 41). A growing number of Americans support making English the official language of the United States (38). English-only rules have been instituted in some workplaces (G. Flynn 87), and court cases addressing first amendment rights have dealt with issues relating to the use of languages other than English (Barringer 18). As we have seen, interpretations of the historical and cultural significance of American English will determine the rhetoric with which we conduct the debate. While the ability to understand the English of other centuries should remain a priority in American education, recourse to anglicity as a unifying concept clearly will no longer suffice. At the same time, using Americanness as a theme of rebellion may only serve to code nonanglicity as romantically primitive and leave unexamined our fears of variability and its spread.

2

CARL SANDBURG AND VACHEL LINDSAY
Composite Voices of the Open Road

You are white—

yet a part of me, as I am a part of you.

That's American.

—Langston Hughes, "Theme for English B," in *Montage of a Dream Deferred, 40*

• By the second decade of the twentieth century, fears about the ethnic heterogeneity of Chicago's population largely had been replaced in literature by celebrations of diversity. Chicago authors were still trying to represent the voices of the city's workers, migrants, and immigrants, but writing in dialect began to lose its primacy as a method of portraying demographic change. Carl Sandburg's and Vachel Lindsay's representations of Native Americans, African Americans, and European immigrants went beyond changing literary style; their cultural literacy projects extolling ethnic and regional diversity broadened the knowledge held in common by Americans. This shared information, in effect, was to constitute an American language necessary for unifying the populace. Like other Chicago writers experimenting with literary vocabulary, syntax, and diction, Sandburg and Lindsay simultaneously opened the way for other writers and perpetuated crippling stereotypes. Their enterprises encompassed goals shared by African-American writers and also usurped the places of black authors in the national canon.

Although their poetry differed stylistically and thematically, Sandburg and Lindsay both made travel and performance central to their work—with contrasting results during their own lifetimes.[1] Sandburg became phenomenally popular; in 1959, for example, he spoke before a joint session of Congress. Lindsay's star had begun to fade before his death in 1931. By and large, Sandburg was blessed with good health; Lindsay suffered from epilepsy (Niven 484). Both worried about money—Sandburg because he needed to provide lifelong support for two of his three daughters; Lindsay because his commitment to voluntary poverty became impractical as he grew older. Whereas Lindsay's financial anxieties eventually became an impediment to his work and health, Sandburg's concerns led him to new projects and the repackaging of old accomplishments. Biographer Penelope Niven concludes that Sandburg's talent in multiple genres (including journalism, poetry, children's stories, and biography) helped to promote his reputation (446). Lindsay often mixed genres—initially in ways that intrigued audiences but later in ways that baffled them. Both authors began their writing careers as spokesmen for organized reform movements (socialism in Sandburg's case, temperance in Lindsay's) and then put their energies into a combination of causes defined by themselves. Despite significant differences in their lives and work, both expressed their idealism in poetry whose oral qualities were at variance with modernist tendencies to write for the page.

Unifying Americans through literature meant writing in a language that celebrated their particular modes of speech as well as the democratic spirit that fostered those patterns. Though a hallmark of Chicago writing, informal language also characterized literature throughout the English-speaking world at the turn of the century. Indeed, Harriet Monroe claimed, "Great poetry has always been written in the language of contemporary speech" and that, working toward that end, modern poets were abandoning "not only archaic diction but also the shop-worn subjects of past history or legend" (*New Poetry* xxxvi). An array of poets proved her right. Although Ezra Pound's *Cantos* aimed to revive historical figures, he frequently chose forgotten, as opposed to shopworn, subjects and worked to blend tradition and modern sensibility. "Canto II," for example, begins, "Hang it all, Robert Browning," and later refers to "poor old Homer blind, blind, as a bat" (6). T. S. Eliot, though he retained rhyme, significantly altered the sound of poetry with his emphasis on the mundane, as in "Prufrock" and, later, the "Sweeney" poems. Langston Hughes followed his own advice while lobbying for an art inspired by working-class African Americans in its subject matter and style: "Their joy runs, bang! into ecstasy. Their religion soars to a shout. Work maybe a little today, rest a little tomorrow. Play awhile. Sing awhile. O, let's dance!" ("Negro Artist" 168). Monroe remembers William Butler Yeats saying to an audience in Chicago, "We wanted to get rid not only of rhetoric but of poetic diction. We tried to strip away everything that was artificial, to get a style like speech, as simple as the simplest prose, like a cry of the heart" (*New Poetry* xxxix).

The employment of ordinary language served a variety of purposes beyond jettisoning "the *deems, 'neaths, forsooths,* etc." (Monroe *New Poetry* xxxv) of conventional poetry. Pound devised his own canon of ancient history; Hughes explored African-American music and community life; Sandburg recorded folk knowledge, both urban and rural; and Lindsay combined Eastern religion, Egyptology, American history, and agrarian values. For modern writers affiliated with Chicago and New York, Eric Homberger concludes, "their enemy, the genteel, gave them a shared but insecurely based sense of cohesion" (158). Today differences are more apparent than similarities between the Chicago poets, east-coast writers (including William Carlos Williams, Marianne Moore, and Wallace Stevens), American expatriates (including Gertrude Stein, Eliot, and H. D.), and writers of the Harlem or Black Renaissance and its turn-of-the-century precursor, the New Negro Movement (including James Weldon Johnson, Alain Locke, Langston Hughes, Sterling A. Brown, and Zora Neale Hurston).[2] All along, attitudes toward the social changes that necessitated a new poetic diction differentiated these groups. According to Richard Sheppard,

> Eliot, Yeats, and Rilke seem, like Hofmannsthal, to be intent on preserving the sense of eternity which inhabits the few fragments left to them by the past, and without which, they suggest, all would be blackness, boredom and despair.
>
> This overwhelming sense of the imminence of linguistic aridity and imaginative death is an aspect of a much wider socio-cultural problem: the suppression of an aristocratic, semi-feudal, humanistic and agrarian order by one middle-class, democratic, mechanistic and urban. (324–25)

Simplification of vocabulary thus did not always facilitate an audience's comprehension or go hand in hand with populism. If Eliot and his ilk responded to the breakdown of civilization with anxiety, then Sandburg and other self-taught men of the Chicago Renaissance treated modernization as an opportunity.

Whereas the Black Renaissance could boast a Rhodes scholar, several professors, and a number of college graduates, few of Chicago's writers or editors had earned advanced degrees,[3] and several came from humble backgrounds. The need for money, for instance, initially drove Sandburg, the son of Swedish immigrants, into a variety of jobs (including shoeshine boy, milk truck driver, fireman, door-to-door salesman) and into freight cars headed for the Kansas wheat harvest (Niven 20, 25, 32, 46, 59).

Unlike Sandburg, who once marveled that his Lincoln biography was "a book about a man whose mother could not sign her name, written by a man whose father could not sign his" (Detzer 10), Lindsay grew up surrounded by books. He attended Hiram College in Ohio and, like Sandburg, almost graduated with a college degree. He then studied at the Art Institute of Chicago and in New York City under William M. Chase and Robert Henri. During this time, he received reluctant financial support from his parents and earned money teaching at the YMCA. Tiring of this life, he launched several walking tours through the South, the East, and the West and published accounts of those adventures. His poetry was beginning to appear in magazines, but his career took off after he was asked to recite "The Congo" at a *Poetry* magazine banquet in honor of Yeats (Ruggles 56, 69–70, 85, 105–108, 210, 216–18). Both Lindsay and Sandburg, especially Sandburg, welcomed the dissolution of an old order because that system would never have included them as artists.

• • •

A reevaluation of Walt Whitman coincided with the social changes brought about by industrialization and urbanization in the United States. Previously considered an aberration within American literature, Whitman—or, more importantly, what he symbolized—became negotiable during this time of cultural turmoil. As academics worked to assimilate him into a New England tradition (Baym 473-75), those writing from and about the heartland were associating him with democracy, simple language, and midwestern values. Chicago sociologist Robert Park acknowledged his debt to Whitman, explaining that, having worked as a reporter, he identified with Whitman the journalist and chronicler of urban life (Cappetti 25). Sandburg biographer Philip R. Yannella explains that Whitman was claimed by American socialists as a source of inspiration and allusions (103). Whitman's tributes to Abraham Lincoln probably made him an honorary Midwesterner at a time when various contingencies were trying to appropriate him for their own ends; furthermore, positive reappraisals of his free verse authorized what turn-of-the-century writers from the middle states were producing. According to Stanley Waterloo, a *Dial* reader writing from Chicago in 1892, the story of the American West had "nothing reflected or imitative about it. It may be sometimes crude, but it is interesting. So crude but interesting were the Norsemen's Sagas. So the force of the ragged-versed Whitman is felt in its reckless naturalness" (207). Waterloo's description—with its references to raw power, nature, crudity, and virility—says more about Whitman's reception than about his poetry, but the perception that Whitman had dispensed with artifice is also expressed later in William P. Trent's review of American literature in the *Dial*'s twentieth-anniversary issue. Trent claims that the general popularity of "our rugged chanter of the glories of democracy" presents "another proof of the democratization of our literature" (339).

Sandburg gave his first formal lecture on Whitman at the International Lyceum Association annual meeting, a talk he subsequently took on the road (Durnell 17–18). In 1904, when a trip he had planned to England had to be canceled, he went instead to Camden, where he placed a rose on Whitman's grave (Niven 81). Lindsay, too, referred often to Whitman, sometimes with an insistence on his shortcomings that only underlined his own dependence on the nineteenth-century poet's example.

New Whitmans were needed in order for the arts to continue adapting to the challenges of increasing diversity and regional identification, and the Midwest appeared to many to be the place most likely to produce modern bards. In 1903, for instance, William Dean Howells surveyed a growing "Chicago School of Fiction" and linked the Midwest with a natural expression of democracy: "The republic of letters is everywhere sufficiently republican; but in the metropolis of the Middle-West, it is so without thinking, it is so almost without feeling; and the atmospheric democracy, the ambient equality, is something that seems like the prime effect in literature of what America has been doing and saying in life ever since she first formulated herself in the Declaration" (739). H. L. Mencken made a similar observation in 1917 when he referred to Chicago as the city "most thoroughly American, at least among the big ones." He continued, "A culture is bogus unless it be honest, which means unless it be truly national—the naif and untinctured expression of a national mind and soul" (5).

New Yorkers and expatriates may have simplified and modernized their vocabulary, but Midwesterners were thought to speak for and to the entire country. Whitman's lists of different kinds of people and Twain's ability to suggest the speech of ordinary citizens converged at the turn of the century in Chicago,[4] where writers experimented with styles based on the usage of rural Americans and urban immigrants. Becoming the people's representative in the spirit of Whitman meant portraying America's diversity, and African-American culture supplied Sandburg and Lindsay with a ready means for doing so, since its speech and lore epitomized either the ultimate non-British influence or a folksy Anglo-Saxonism that white Southerners largely had lost.

The questions posed by writers of the Black Renaissance stirred the imaginations of white writers exploring ways to carry on Whitman's legacy. The study of sociology and anthropology, questions about modernity, the desire for community-building through an aesthetic that reached the general public, and what Nathan Huggins identifies as a desire to shake the effects of a colonial education (59–60) made Chicago and Harlem of interest to each other. African-American writers had lived and worked in Chicago even before the WPA Illinois Writers' Project made possible "the second phase of Negro literary awakening" (Bontemps "Famous" 46). Additionally, in Chicago Jane Addams worked with W. E. B. DuBois on the founding of the NAACP, Charles S. Johnson contributed to *The Negro in Chicago* (the massive analysis that followed the Chicago race riots of 1919), and Sherwood Anderson and Jean Toomer corresponded, as did Lindsay and Hughes. Common literary interests stemmed from shared perceptions that new kinds of voices could now enter literature.

Sandburg aspired to establish for Americans in general what Henry Louis Gates, Jr., credits Zora Neale Hurston with achieving in African-American letters—that is, producing a "voice that echoes and aspires to the status of the impersonality, anonymity, and authority of the black vernacular tradition, a nameless, selfless tradition, at once collective and compelling, true somehow to the unwritten text of a common blackness" (*Signifying* 183). Gates puts Hurston and the poet Sterling A. Brown within the context of a long debate over the best method for representing black speech (174). If Sandburg contributed to this discussion, it was because he privileged speech through content and technique and provided a stunning example of the way the vernacular could become poetry. Louis D. Rubin, Jr., credits him with combining the new images of industrial America with apt language for urban experience (184–85). According to Rubin:

> In his best poetry Sandburg *uses* vernacular language, slang even; by this I mean that in Sandburg's instance it isn't the self-conscious employment of a "low" vocabulary to call attention to commonness, a vaunting of plebeian virtue (though later in his career Sandburg was prone to do just this, ad nauseam). An expression such as "the *crack* trains of the nation" is an organic part of his vocabulary, not an affectation, and he employs the adjective because it is simply the appropriate word to image what he wishes to convey about the train. As such it provides precisely the intensification of language, the heightened awareness of the texture of experience, that the best poetry affords. (182–83)

Like many African-American writers, Sandburg believed in the transformative power of oral storytelling; he describes a world audibly engaged in communication, usually laughing or singing. His aesthetic shares with oral cultures what Walter J. Ong calls a "sense of the word as necessarily spoken, sounded, and hence power-driven" (32). "Laughing Corn" exemplifies Sandburg's references to sound, especially the human voice, as a metaphor for life. The poem describes the activities accompanying the ears' growth, celebrations that happen each summer because the wind, rain, sun, and corn "talk things over together" (87).[5] Fertile and productive, the human voice is part of nature, where even blackbirds become hoarse as the growing season peaks. Poets do not know all the names for things; instead of possessing Adamic qualities, they have learned to use their bursting ears.

Similarly, the poet's self-effacing ability to utter others' sounds has given the "I" in the poem "Under a Telephone Pole" collective status. So slight that it is hardly noticeable, the personified tele-

Carl Sandburg

phone line sings a complex song that includes the "Death and laughter of men and women passing through me, carrier of your speech" (70–71). Sandburg privileges the spoken word by depicting its extension throughout nature and via technology. By the end of his career, he was extending his own voice via phonograph records, radio, and television.

Working as a journalist compelled Sandburg to listen to the ordinary and extraordinary Chicagoans who made the news. What he heard convinced him that talk produces grassroots sentiment for change. In *The Chicago Race Riots*, a collection of his newspaper articles written just prior to the event, he lists statistics that help to explain an increase in racial conflicts in the North and then cites numbers pertaining to African-American military service in World War I. "So it is clear," Sandburg writes, "that in one neighborhood are thousands of strong young men who have been talking to each other on topics more or less intimately related to the questions, 'What are we ready to die for? Why do we live? What is democracy? What is the meaning of freedom; of self-determination?'" (8). One of the most important assignments of his journalistic career, covering the racial tensions leading up to the riots, confirmed for Sandburg that discussions among ordinary people alter group consciousness.

Coming from the town where Lincoln practiced law and was laid to rest after his assassination, Lindsay grew up steeped in questions of race. Although his writings offered fewer practical aesthetic models than did the poetry of Sandburg, his enormous popularity as a performer in all likelihood inspired black writers looking for ways to harness a tradition of oratory, music, and storytelling. As Faith Berry relates, when Langston Hughes was struggling to make ends meet, Mary McLeod Bethune (president of Bethune-Cookman College) encouraged him to go on the road and read his poetry at southern colleges (120). Lindsay was not the only poet to set a precedent by touring, but his desire to take literature directly to the people and his example of subsisting on the "profits" from poetry may have emboldened Hughes. "[I]n those Depression days," writes Berry, "when some sponsoring institutions could not afford fifty dollars, Langston spoke for twenty-five dollars, and when they could afford nothing, he spoke for free" (138).

Sometimes deliberately, sometimes not, the Chicago poets and African-American writers engaged in dialogue. Sandburg offered a preliminary technique for using vernacular language strikingly yet unobtrusively, but black writers had valued the spoken word of ordinary people as literature, collected folklore, and taken inspiration from American forms of music well before Sandburg began his career. Lindsay's example offered assurance that audiences would embrace the performative aspects of poetry. Although exploiting the possibilities of informal language endures as a legacy of the modern age, Sandburg and Lindsay also believed that the technique could create a network of shared references that would help to unify the country.

• • •

E. D. Hirsch, Jr., begins his 1987 best-seller *Cultural Literacy* by claiming that "to be culturally literate is to possess the basic information needed to thrive in the modern world" (xiii). He argues that everything from comprehension of newspapers to success in business and industry depends on the knowledge he describes. In response to Hirsch and to Allan Bloom's *The Closing of the American Mind,* Graywolf editors Rick Simonson and Scott Walker compiled an anthology, *Multi-Cultural Literacy: Opening the American Mind* (1988). The intervening years have failed to produce a consensus as to what should be taught in American schools, what learning is necessary for success, or what degree of unification or pluralism exists within the United States. Paul Gagnon reports that in the early 1990s the United States Department of Education abandoned a project to recommend national standards in several areas of the secondary curriculum. The group working on English, for example, spent $900,000 before the project was abandoned (68).

As nearly all parties to the debate about what children should learn acknowledge, the questions raised are not new; the views of Noah Webster, Horace Kallen, and William James, as well as those of Hugh Blair, Jonathan Swift, and Samuel Johnson, are sometimes examined for their historical perspective on the issue. Vachel Lindsay and Carl Sandburg are names less likely to arise, but, like Hirsch, they launched national campaigns to stress the importance of what Hirsch has termed "communally shared information" (xv). Lindsay, however, would have used different terminology, preferring the idea of "the strange composite voice of many million singing souls" (*Poetry* 1:284).[6] Thus, whether it is Hirsch listing "what every American needs to know," Richard Rodriguez remembering the Irish nuns who taught him (*Hunger of Memory*), or Vachel Lindsay traversing the country, those with strong opinions about what Americans should learn share the belief that cultural knowledge is composite in nature.

Lindsay was trying not so much to improve the schools as he was to ensure a utopian future by combining religion and aesthetics. Although his goal was national, he felt that it could best be achieved at the local level by young people's developing a commitment to their place of birth. "They should, if led by the spirit," he wrote, "wander over the whole nation in search of the secret of democratic beauty with their hearts at the same time filled to overflowing with the righteousness of God. Then they should come back to their own hearth and neighborhood and gather a little circle of their own sort of workers about them and strive to make the neighborhood and home more beautiful and democratic and holy with their special art" (*Prose* 1:158). Lindsay felt that everyone, from the local contractor to the minister, had a part to play, although the job would not be easy. In "An Editorial for the Art Student Who Has Returned to the Village," Lindsay offers the following encouragement:

Oh, all you students that I have loved, whose work I have enviously admired, who are now back home grubbing at portraits, though they are not your specialty; or designing billboards, though they are not your divine call; or acting on the committee to paper the church and buying bad paper to please them; or back on the home newspaper that will not often print your short novels; or singing in the old choir for no salary at all; or composing advertisements in the real estate office and neglecting your lyrics; or taking charge of the Sunday School orchestra and curing them of the Moody-Sankey habit—greeting, and God-speed to you! If you have any cherished beauty-enterprise, undertake it where you are. *You will find no better place in all America.* (*Prose* 1:151)

Lindsay issued his greeting based on his own experience in returning to Springfield. His localism directly contradicts Hirsch's assertion that facts of national importance should take precedence over local knowledge in the classroom (25–26). Like Wendell Berry, Lindsay hoped to slow "the unsettling of America" by urging commitment to a particular locale. Although certainly a dreamer, Lindsay recognized, unlike Hirsch or Berry, that education does not necessarily lead to success in cities (where artists and the liberally educated are in overabundance) and that going home does not necessarily lead to fulfillment. Returning from educational and geographical journeys is sometimes the only remaining option, and the towns and small cities benefit as a result. Individuals must take heart from the fact that their aesthetic and religious efforts, while not always benefiting them personally, will renew their hometowns and nation.

Sandburg's goals were less idiosyncratic than those of Lindsay. Initially, he took an unabashedly socialist approach to the education of the masses, concentrating on what John Dewey called a "socialism of the intelligence and of the spirit" (107). As a writer for the *International Socialist Review,* he used poetry to supplement his articles (Yannella 43). In "I Am the People, the Mob," his belief in the power of the spoken word is combined with the conviction that the working classes will arise: "when I, the People, use the / lessons of yesterday and no longer forget who robbed me last year / . . . then there will be no speaker in all the / world say the name: 'The People,' with any fleck of a sneer in his voice" (71). The poetry itself, accessible to the people, bolsters their confidence and encourages them to remember. The recovered knowledge is not necessarily gained in school; the people instead need an enzyme that allows them to use their experience and fragmented wisdom. Just as the people will become powerful by keeping these lessons in mind, rather than writing them down, respectful speech from those in power serves metonymically for just treatment. By listening to poetry, Sandburg's audience takes the first step in an educational process that appeals not to the artist, as did Lindsay, but to the worker in everyone.

Both poets believed that they could accomplish their social objectives by encouraging Americans to pay attention to language. Being educated should not be reduced to a matter of knowing language, but the idea of language can be expanded to involve additional competencies. Like others who discuss the process of reading, Hirsch argues that comprehension involves not just knowing the definitions of individual words but also possessing the ability to fill in their contexts and common associations. He uses an excerpt from a newspaper article as an example, explaining that in order to understand the paragraph about a federal appeals court decision one would need to comprehend, if only sketchily, the American legal system, the power of courts, the location of Missouri, and the role of the Department of Agriculture (13–14). Lindsay and Sandburg likewise address what they perceive to be deficiencies in Americans' ability to understand the nation in which they live. Their poetry is designed to improve their neighbors' means of communication by familiarizing them with American symbols, history, aphorisms, and lore.

Lindsay and Sandburg advocated a unifying American language not only by capturing Americans' speech but also by attempting to create a system of signs drawing on the nation's ethnic and regional diversity. With *The American Songbag* (1927), a collection of American folk songs, Sandburg claims in his introduction to have begun a "song history of America" that helps revise American history. A chronicle of music, he suggests, would "give the feel and atmosphere, the layout and lingo, of regions, of breeds of men, of customs and slogans, in a manner and air not given in regular history, to be read and not sung. . . . If and when such history is written it will help some on the point registered by a Yankee philosopher that there are persons born and reared in this country who culturally have not yet come over from Europe" (xii). *American Songbag* provides the materials for the cultural passage across the Atlantic. Americans not only become acquainted with America's rich history through this singable text but also begin to share each other's cultural contexts. The songs thus serve as the basis of a common literacy. Like some kind of language instructor to the nation, Sandburg encourages readers to sing America for themselves.

Lindsay's notion of a national language had more to do with a sense of mission than with representing the actual speech of the American people. Unlike Sandburg, he did not make much use of slang or the vernacular and preferred rhyming forms to free verse. Yet the spoken word informed his poetics because of his interest in American orators and the heroes of folklore (Enkvist). Despite his stylistic preferences, Lindsay included uniquely American words in Whitmanesque litanies. In "So Much the Worse for Boston," for example, his lists of place names, flora, fauna, and topographical features call attention to a distinctively American idiom. A conversation between a mountain lion and a hiker in the Rocky Mountains, the poem works on a conceit in which everything the cat has heard about Boston is actually the truth about the American West, as in this impression of Boston's lovers:

Telling to each other what the Boston Boys have done,
The lodge-pole pines go towering to the timber-line and sun.
And their whisper stirs love's fury in each pantherish girl-child,

Till she dresses like a columbine, or a bleeding heart gone wild.
Like a harebell, golden aster, bluebell, Indian arrow,
Blue jay, squirrel, meadow lark, loco, mountain sparrow. (*Poetry* 2:474)

In the essay "The Real American Language," Lindsay described American English as "a new vocabulary arranged on an old British framework" (257). Yet he was not advocating a standardized British English or a single correct form of "American." His early poem "The Airship of the Mind" had expressed a desire to escape from a country becoming too uniform in all of its parts. The airship of the mind floats above a nation obsessed with speed and "bound down from coast to coast / By one strong net of railroad iron and wire." As a result of rushing from place to place, Americans "speak one speech, endure one slavery!" (*Poetry* 1:101). In contrast, the airship of the mind consists of the forces that have resisted standardization, "all the blended songs" (102) of rural people, plants, and weather. Nature and human voices vary, but, contrary to Sandburg's vision, technology threatens both because of its reliance on invariability. Ideally, in Lindsay's view, American English is not uniform but a composite.

Hirsch uses the term *composite* to describe how national languages "overcome local and ethnic dialectal variations inside a large nation" (93). Yet, beyond a brief description of the way in which intellectuals make folklore part of learned culture (83), he does little to explain how this composite results. Indeed, he defends the anglocentricity of traditional American schooling (106–7). Lindsay, in contrast, believes that participatory art and democracy give America its compound character. Balz Engler relates Lindsay's linguistic/aesthetic theories to his Campbellite faith:

> Beyond belief in Jesus Christ and what is explicitly said in the Bible, the Disciples claim to leave everything to individual interpretation. They do not privilege the insights of, or revelations to, some people over those of others, and therefore make no distinctions between layperson and cleric. At the same time they seek to emphasize what Christians share rather than what divides them. The insights of the individual Christian therefore can only be a contribution to a shared truth. At the same time the church believes—as Lindsay did—that the partial truths revealed to individuals are not contradictory, but add up to a more general truth and eventually to universal truth. (124)

An early statement of this concept occurs in "When Bryan Speaks": "When Bryan speaks, then I rejoice. / His is the strange composite voice / Of many million singing souls / Who make world-brotherhood their choice" (*Poetry* 1:284). Lindsay likewise delivered a series of lectures at the Springfield YMCA on "composite citizenship," or the role of the nation's ethnic groups (*Poetry* 3:914). While this approach encouraged stereotyping, it nevertheless demonstrated that Lindsay's notions about poetic voice extended beyond the realm of the aesthetic.

Sandburg's poetry, too, affirms that American culture is a composite. In addition to representing ethnic diversity, the poems stress that writing owes its authority not to its transcription of speech but to the social nature of that language. The poem "Repetitions," from *Cornhuskers* (1918), for example, describes the oral response of a crowd and dramatizes the relationship between the people's speech and the poet's writing. Despite the fact that radicals were often unpopular during this period, those collected around Inez Milholland's casket "are crying salt tears." Their affection stems from the fact that "she loved open-armed" and regarded love as "a cheap thing" (102). Although Poe found the death of a beautiful woman "the most poetical topic in the world" (201), Sandburg begins the poem as if mawkishness marked the passing of the attractive feminist lawyer who had encouraged strikers, broken Vassar's baseball-throwing record, embraced pacifism, served as a war correspondent, advocated "a more natural observance of the mating instinct," and died of pernicious anemia after campaigning for the National Woman's Party and its suffragist platform (Boyer 188–90). The tone of "crying salt tears" implies that the people's grief is not a major aesthetic response but is cheap, which is also the way Milholland regarded her love. Unlike the ideal nineteenth-century woman, she did not keep love precious, and the poem refigures the idea of cheapness so that it refers to the essential elements of life owned by no individual. The title "Repetitions" may refer to Milholland's having loved repeatedly, the crowd's continuous mourning, or the poet's repetition of the crowd's response. The sense of promiscuity, of cheap reiteration, extends to the poet's writing, which seems not to create something precious but merely to repeat the reactions of others.[7] Cheap like speech but vital like Milholland, writing belongs not to the elite but to all. Men, women, activists, and average citizens all contribute to the communal rituals that give poets their reason for being. Poets, in turn, codify idealized communal beliefs and revise the process of remembering.

Debates about what children should learn and the merits of vocational training occurred at the time (Gagnon 70), but Sandburg and Lindsay did not participate directly in efforts to change school policies, even though both also wrote for children. Instead, the two poets concentrated on influencing the tastes, values, and knowledge of the adults who taught children both inside and outside the classroom. In addition to having their books published, they traveled and performed in the tradition of

Whitman the wandering bard in order to spread their ideas. While performing around the country did not succeed in reaching the public as Lindsay had envisioned, its importance to both poets' work and reputations nevertheless reveals the dynamics of how information circulates and becomes knowledge through deliberate attempts to change language.

Traditionally, Lindsay is a literary figure known for energetic poetic recitations that led to artistic and spiritual exhaustion.[8] More recently, critics have concentrated on either Lindsay's oral performances or his reliance on visual paradigms. Although he suffered from bouts of tremendous egoism, Lindsay effaced himself to the extent that critics disagree as to what really constitutes his work. In effect, he is a poet lost between his speaking and his writing. His ideas did not influence American literature as much as they represented an effort to change American literacy. In light of this goal, his efforts appear consistent, even though his own statements about his writing are contradictory.

Both recitation and print served Lindsay's educational mission. On his first walking tours, when he traded performances for meals and a night's lodging, he distributed pamphlets to underline whatever seriousness he attached to his cause,[9] to reinforce his message when he was gone, and to serve as additional payment to his hosts. After returning from the East to live with his parents in Springfield, Lindsay became a lecturer for the temperance crusade and began issuing the *Village Magazine* (1910) and the *War Bulletin* (1909), both self-publishing ventures consisting of his own poems and essays. Though printed rather than performed, these publications maintained the interactive form the walking tours had taken, as the instructions for subscribing to the *Village Magazine* demonstrate:

> The *Village Magazine* is not for sale. It is a birthday present for the chosen. Good passer-by, if you want a copy, persuade the owner of this one to write an elegant letter about you to the address below or construct your own application. The letter should contain some evidence that you have a contrite heart, also a proper sense of humor, and that you have read with rightly mixed emotions, some portion of the work. But the idea is not copyrighted. Let some better man continue the work, principally for places of one thousand inhabitants, or thereabouts. (*Poetry* 1:85)

Traveling and the circulars were thus attempts to persuade audiences to take up the cause of beauty and democracy for themselves or to define their own causes.

Though at the beginning of his career Lindsay balanced recitation and print, solitude and interaction, motion and stasis, he later came to be in such demand (and in such need of income) that he traveled almost all the

time. By 1922, he had sickened of reciting his poetry and instead emphasized his grounding in the visual arts. Haunted by his reception as a bom-
bastic entertainer, he disassociated himself from his chanting style in the
preface to the first edition of *Collected Poems,* claiming that his poetry
"should be whispered, however contradictory that may seem. All poetry is
first and last for the inner ear, and its final pleasures are for the soul, whis-
pering in solitude" (*Poetry* 3:943). He stressed that he always had been a
visual artist (3:949) in order to revise his public's perceptions of him. The
concept responsible for the reputation he came to loathe had evolved during his walking tours. He called the idea the Higher Vaudeville.

Lindsay's best-known poems today are the Higher Vaudeville pieces—
"General William Booth Enters Into Heaven" and "The Congo." Lindsay performed these with great energy, moving about the stage, gesturing
with his arms and head, sometimes chanting or singing, and employing
dramatic pauses and a wide range in volume. The text directs "General
William Booth" "to be sung to the tune of 'The Blood of the Lamb'
with indicated instrument" (*Poetry* 1:148). Lindsay explained that in
"American vaudeville . . . every line may be two-thirds spoken and one-
third sung, the entire rendering, musical and elocutionary, depending
largely upon the improvising power and sure instinct of the performer"
("Mr. Lindsay" 161). Lindsay was inspired by African-American clergy-
men as well. As James Weldon Johnson relates, African-American preach-
ers' "intoning is always a matter of crescendo and diminuendo in the intensity—a rising and falling between plain speaking and wild chanting.
And often a startling effect is gained by breaking off suddenly at the
highest point of intensity and dropping into the monotone of ordinary
speech" (*God's Trombones* 10).

Engler argues that Lindsay's career as a performer must not be evalu-
ated solely in terms of the poet's later disaffection with the strains of
travel and self-repetition (136–37); moreover, Lindsay's poetry largely
has been forgotten because printed selections ignore the context of performance and its goals (145). The point of Lindsay's performances was
to create community by involving an audience in a shared experience,
and the Higher Vaudeville was instrumental in carrying out this plan.[10]
According to Engler, "Lindsay used poems like these to 'blow ashes into
flame,' to start the process of reviving the imagination and thus of recre-
ating community" (146). He stresses that Lindsay wanted to reach an
audience similar to the one vaudeville attracted and that in order to do so
he borrowed the vaudeville convention of "the stand-up performer addressing and reacting to an audience, entertaining, usually with novelty
and still more novelty" (147) but also incorporating "familiarity, repetition, and participation" (152). When Lindsay felt that the vaudeville

techniques alone were not accomplishing his goals, he asked his audiences and handlers for advanced preparations, including reading his poems and bringing the books to the performances (Engler 155–56).

While Engler has reassessed Lindsay's work in the context of performance, Marc Chénetier has stressed his reliance on visual elements. "To Lindsay," writes Chénetier, "a poem . . . was always first and foremost a picture" ("'Free-Lance'" 499). Engler and Chénetier both discuss his oral and visual orientations but emphasize one or the other. This contrast is not surprising, since Lindsay vacillated on the relative importance of speaking, writing, and drawing to his career. At times he seemed to care little about the lasting value of his poems and instead concerned himself with their effects. For example, he invited his readers to invent their own yells (*Poetry* 3:910), and he confessed that he wanted people to steal "The Marriage of the Rose and the Lotus," his poem celebrating the construction of the Panama Canal (3:849). Lindsay believed that a poet, like a clergyman or politician, should be satisfied if his words were to endure throughout his own lifetime, notes Chénetier ("American Mythocracy" 52). Despite what he considered their oral, ephemeral nature, Lindsay revised his poems, making that process participatory as well. According to Louis Untermeyer, he brought poems in progress "to groups of listeners, to friends and strangers, to poets and business men— and he heeded every comment" (138). His openness to suggestions notwithstanding, Lindsay had fixed ideas about how his poetry should be presented. He hated the thought of anyone setting his poems to music, as editor Dennis Camp explains (*Poetry* 3:908). His penchant for illustrating his books further complicates any analysis of which medium he emphasized the most. He insisted, for example, that his volume *Going-to-the-Sun* was drawn, not written (3:955).

Like Engler, Chénetier sees Lindsay's goal as the creation of an American sense of community, but he stresses the role of images—what Lindsay called "United States Hieroglyphics" (3:949)—in this process. "His idea being to reorganize the collective unconscious, to unite and homogenize it again," writes Chénetier, "Lindsay sets out to discover and transcribe, like some sort of consecrated Champollion retracing his own steps, the hieroglyphic equivalents of American life" ("'Free-Lance'" 508). One of Lindsay's contemporaries, Schuyler Jackson, saw this goal as well: "Common images make for communal purpose; and communal purpose is common sense writ large. Lindsay's images are a help to 'naturalize' more completely every citizen in the United States" (Chénetier "'Free-Lance'" 511). Glenn Joseph Wolfe maintains that "hieroglyphic was simply Lindsay's word for symbol" (133–34), but Chénetier perceives a complicated system linking what Lindsay believed to be "the 'minute cells' of American pictorial thought, imaged particles of the collective unconscious" ("American Mythocracy" 44).[11] American hieroglyphics take the form of drawings, dance steps, ideograms, and Lindsay's own set of symbols. In Lindsay's work, the amaranth represents the flowering of culture on the prairie and also the Holy Spirit, for example. Kansas represents the best of the prairie, and Johnny Appleseed is the prairie's democratic prophet. According to Chénetier, "Lindsay pulls out of the traditional conception of poetry as a system of mere printed words and explores that of poetical creations as organized systems of signs which can assume extremely varied forms" ("'Free-Lance'" 505–6). Yet Lindsay did more than blend systems of signs; he encouraged his reading and listening audiences to perform his poetical creations and to extend the process of semiosis.

For Lindsay, an improvisational art proved Americans' linguistic competency. His poem "Babylon, Babylon, Babylon the Great" is dedicated to Sandburg in celebration of his trips to New York and Memphis and "based on the episode of 'Lincoln's Lost Speech,' too dangerous to print at the time, at Cooper Union, his first appearance in the East" (*Poetry* 2:500). Babylon stands for the eastern United States, rampant industrialization, and all the dehumanizing forces of modern society. The first stanza lists those who have "marched against the jazz"[12] of the city: Isaiah, Jeremiah, Ezekiel, Daniel, St. Paul, and St. Peter. The second stanza relates, "Lincoln at Cooper Union, improvised and chanted, / Threw away his speech, and told tales out of school, / Changed from politician to God's divine fool" (2:500). The poem's refrain, "so, keep going to the sun!" encapsulates Lindsay's previous volume of verse. Glacier National Park's Going-to-the-Sun mountain stands for the quest for beauty, a fairyland, Christmas, the ancient East, Johnny Appleseed, Swedenborg, Homer, Milton, the United States with its "whole map a temple" (*Poetry* 2:468)—in short, the obsessions of Lindsay's entire career. Untermeyer writes that Lindsay "had the metaphoric sense to such a degree that everything reminded him of something else" (132). Taken as a whole, his poetry and performances attempted to modify the English language by changing the connotation of words and adding layers of symbols that resulted from his elaborate comparisons. Lincoln, for example, was not just the sixteenth president and the abolisher of slavery but also a "tall prophet" (*Poetry* 2:502) representing the majestic natural beauty of the western states. Lindsay's audience was to complete his work by improvising, using these new signs in allusions to American texts and contexts. Combined in the effort to build community, Lindsay's performances and creation of symbols aimed to change cultural literacy. Whereas Hirsch underscores the importance of basic facts and information about American history for comprehending what one reads, Lindsay emphasizes metaphorical thinking and improvisational skills as the means of improving citizenship.

As they had for Lindsay, public performances became an integral part of Sandburg's artistic process and his reputation. In 1910 he bought a guitar (Niven 215), and eventually he accompanied himself while singing folk songs between recitations of poetry around the country. Rather than attempting Lindsay's method of allusions and symbols, Sandburg advocated an American cultural literacy by calling attention to the variety and richness of the folk songs he had collected nationwide: "*The American Songbag* is a ragbag of strips, stripes, and streaks of color from nearly all ends of the earth. The melodies and verses presented here are from diverse regions, from varied human characters and communities, and each is sung differently in different places" (xii).

Sandburg and Lindsay both attempted to get their work not just into literary anthologies and magazines but also into the homes, heads, and hearts of ordinary Americans. Sandburg compiled a book that could be used literally to hear America singing her varied carols. Attempting to make citizens not only by using images and performances but also by teaching them the American language, Lindsay sought to familiarize Americans with his favorite writers and the nation's folklore, history, and geography, thereby changing what Americans knew. He also made people, plants, and places symbolic in hopes of altering how Americans knew what they knew. Hirsch echoes many of these same themes when he writes, "Only by accumulating shared symbols, and the shared information that the symbols represent, can we learn to communicate effectively with one another in our national community" (xvii).

Sandburg affirmed America's multicultural roots. A monument to American polyphony, *The American Songbag,* for example, offered audiences a more varied tradition than was being taught in the schools. In his introduction to the 1990 reissue of the collection, Garrison Keillor notes, "When *The American Songbag* appeared in 1927, schoolteachers and school singing books showed a marked preference for sentimental songs about home and family, that taught a moral, that promoted proper values of patriotism, industry, cleanliness, and reverence for God." According to Keillor, *The American Songbag* helped change this curriculum (viii).

Rather than trying to set in motion a semiotic process whereby particular groups and regions were shown to be distinctive yet connected within a sign system, as Lindsay had, Sandburg demonstrated that this kind of intracultural communication had already occurred. "Songs are like people, animals, plants," he writes in his introduction to "Casey Jones." "They have genealogies, pedigrees, thoroughbreds, cross-breeds, mongrels, strays, and often a strange love-child" (*American Songbag* 366). Like James Weldon Johnson, whose narrator in *The Autobiography of an Ex-Coloured Man* discovers that he can convert classics into ragtime and vice versa (142), Sandburg was especially interested in the cross-breeds, mongrels, and love children. The introductions to each song, which often describe where Sandburg first learned the selection, enhance his troubadour image, but they also trace the histories of songs and credit the racial or ethnic groups that introduced them to America. These little "sales talks," as Keillor refers to them (ix), reveal the degree to which "mainstream" culture has its origins in "ethnic" contributions. Sandburg introduces the well-known "She'll Be Comin' Round The Mountain," for instance, by informing readers, "An old-time negro spiritual When the Chariot Comes was made by mountaineers into She'll Be Comin' Round the Mountain, and the song spread to railroad work gangs in the midwest in the 1890's" (372).

The American Songbag gives readers a sense of the vitality of oral traditions by mapping the ways songs change as cultures adapt and blend. Long before debates over cultural literacy began, *The American Songbag* presented a vision of what Ishmael Reed calls "the multinational society" (155). Travel, then, not only spread the knowledge that Sandburg and Lindsay felt would change the nation but also exposed them to the variability of American culture, which they believed could be held together by consolidating the wisdom of each region.

Hirsch, Sandburg, and Lindsay are convinced that the proper kind of education will empower the disenfranchised, although Lindsay does not believe that this will necessarily be true in the political or economic sense. Whether education consists of formal instruction in schools, participation at poetry readings, or conversation among those whose consciousness has been raised, all three authors see newly acquired linguistic skills bringing those on the margins into the national community. None of them worries that these new members of the literate citizenry are simply being assimilated into the culture of those in power; instead, each believes that the composite nature of American culture ensures that everyone has contributed or can participate on equal footing through schooling. Hirsch writes that "the national vocabulary [does not] reflect a coherent culture of a dominant class or other group in the same way that a local dialect does. It is primarily an instrument of communication among diverse cultures rather than a cultural or class instrument in its own right" (103–4). As exemplified by folk songs, the products of various ethnic groups do mix and spread, becoming part of general knowledge, often with the help of authors and educators. The centrality of travel to the campaigns of Sandburg and Lindsay, however, raises questions about who finds contributions valid and how they are shaped before becoming part of national culture. A melting pot metaphor seems to structure the ways in which the compositeness of cultural literacy is imagined, but Sandburg's and Lindsay's efforts show that the ingredients do not all undergo the same kinds of processing; some are heavily mashed, chopped, or seared before they are thrown into the stew.

As we have seen, both Sandburg and Lindsay established their reputations as national voices of democracy by reinventing the persona of Whitman and by featuring their sojourns across the nation in their work. Touring the country disseminated their messages and established their authority to do so. Despite the fact that Lindsay's ambulatory model was more faithful to the Whitman legend, Sandburg more successfully painted himself as a national troubadour and a man of the people. According to Michael Anania, "Sandburg the poet-performer may have been Carl Sandburg's most significant invention" (106). In contrast to Lindsay's adventures, Sandburg's early journeys taught him about persuasion and enterprise. As a young man, Sandburg had traveled as an organizer for the Wisconsin Social Democratic party, and an early writing job included composing short biographies of itinerant lecturers for the *Lyceumite* (Niven 116).[13] *The American Songbag* reads like a kind of travel diary. For instance, Sandburg introduces a song he learned at the University of Oregon: "After a recital and reception there one evening three years ago, we held a song and story session lasting till five o'clock in the morning. Nearly all nations and the seven seas were represented" (20). The songs he includes map distinct regions of the country, various ethnic groups, and different kinds of jobs, and Sandburg has traversed them all, either literally or symbolically, in all-night sessions of singing and storytelling.

Traveling allowed Lindsay and Sandburg to collect the materials—words, expressions, songs, and powerful symbols—for the national language. Although liberal and democratic on its face, gathering the pieces for a multicultural literacy had its reactionary side due to its dependence on primitivism, a movement in literature and visual art that used portrayals of tribal cultures as a counterpoint to western reality. Both Sandburg's and Lindsay's projects challenged the anglicity of American culture, but ambivalence toward nonanglicity runs throughout their own work. The previous century had ended with fears that immigrants and African Americans would destroy American culture; as the new century progressed, fear often changed to hope, in literature at least, that they would save it. This hope connects Sandburg and Lindsay to earlier literature and commentary from Chicago. Like Henry Fuller, Lindsay and Sandburg invested nonanglicity with a primitive quality. Whereas compilers of dialect dictionaries wanted to record speech variations before they died out, Sandburg and Lindsay tried to keep them alive. Their effort helped to counter calls for the standardization of language; yet the desire to revive folklore had a nostalgic side, as demonstrated by Carl S. Smith's discussion of Fuller's *With the Procession* and Frank Norris's *The Pit*. Characters in these Chicago novels strive for cosmopolitan income, status, and demeanor, but in the privacy of their own homes they sing the old folk songs, hoping to forget the emptiness of their urban ambitions (25, 68). Collecting folklore sometimes resembled Sheppard's version of high modernism, in which poets treasured the fragments of past ways of life. Sandburg and Lindsay welcomed the demise of old hierarchies but often suggested that ethnic Americans represented ancient, simple qualities worth embracing again. The American language they worked to shape would thus keep its legendary raw and natural powers.

Sandburg reproduced romantic stereotypes of African Americans, Native Americans, and swarthy European immigrants. For Katharine Newman and Werner Sollors, his characterization in "Happiness" of picnicking Hungarian Americans as the happiest people in Chicago exemplifies attempts to criticize American culture by idealizing the disenfranchised. The strategy goes back at least to Harriet Beecher Stowe's representation of Uncle Tom as the humble, ideal Christian, according to Sollors, who observes, "This tendency to use ethnicity as a positively charged antithesis has persisted, with some transformations, into the twentieth century, though, along the way, the word 'Christian' may have been replaced by 'American' or simply by 'happy'" (30).[14]

If Sandburg, despite his working-class origins, tended to romanticize the lower classes, Lindsay wanted to rescue them by rewriting folklore and infusing it with what he believed to be ancient philosophy. His idea of the saving power of hieroglyphics and Egyptology derive from what Edward Said discusses as the Romantic notion that the East could recharge the spiritually drained West (115). In Said's terms, Lindsay expresses "a bad sort of eternality" that does not account for modern Eastern nations and their possibilities for "development, transformation, human movement" (208). Poems such as "Booker T. Washington Trilogy" demonstrate that Lindsay thought African-American culture as well could reconnect all Americans to ancient truths. He likewise used jungle stereotypes to create a morality play of salvation and redemption in "The Congo."[15]

Unlike unmitigated racism, literary primitivism is an attempt to criticize one's own culture via contact with an allegedly inferior one.[16] Primitivism manifests itself in a fascination with another's art, music, language, religion, communal relations, sex life, or lack of inhibitions, for the purpose of criticizing one's own. Marianna Torgovnick writes in *Gone Primitive* that, for European Americans, "to study the primitive brings us always back to ourselves, which we reveal in the act of defining the Other" (11). This description explains why whites often reinscribe racism in the process of criticizing it; our own sense of guilt and its seemingly global significance are the focus, not ownership of responsibility or a redefinition of relations. We admit the other either for purposes of self-criticism or, in the case of paternalism, self-congratulation.[17] If primitivism consists of defining another in order to define ourselves, it also means wanting to be neither the other nor ourselves. Literary primitivists want to escape the hypocrisy of their own culture through contact but not genuine dialogue with another culture. Primitivists engage in self-criticism but retain their sense of privilege (see McIntosh).

American writers had inherited from Rousseau and others a tradition of simultaneously idealizing and deprecating non-European cultures, and elaborate conventions for coding African Americans as linguistically inauthoritative had developed long before modernism began. As Amritjit Singh notes, however, pseudo-Freudian notions about race relations, industrialization, civilization, and its discontents made primitivism particularly compelling during an era of increasing mechanization (32).

What John Cooley writes of the New York Village Bohemians' relationship to their African-American neighbors holds true for European-American Chicagoans as well: "White writers drew their materials and inspiration from the Renaissance, including a great burst of interest in Africana, and often at great expense to black life" (53). At a moment when black writers were trying to assert their own authority, white writers such as Eugene O'Neill were emphasizing "exotic settings and 'Old Negro' sources" (54). Singh argues that Carl Van Vechten's novel of Harlem life, *Nigger Heaven* (1926), "represented a real threat of preemption to young black writers if the latter refused to heed Van Vechten's advice and exploit a market ripe and eager for exotic versions of black life" (35). As John S. Wright summarizes, "In addition to artists like O'Neill and Heyward, an array of European-American exoticists, bohemians, literary radicals, philanthropists, and entrepreneurs found the 'vogue for the Negro' agreeable to their own various interests and exploited it with aesthetic and commercial success beyond that achieved by African-American artists themselves" (30).

The travels of Sandburg and Lindsay—and the primitivism informing those travels—reveal some of the contradictions inherent in emphasizing cultural literacy as a means of achieving equality. Touring the nation brought the poets into contact with a diverse population, spread their messages, and established their authority as national spokesmen. Building a reputation on travel, however, poses a similar problem to the one presented by primitivism. Just as primitivists position themselves as neither themselves nor the other, wandering American bards place themselves everywhere and yet nowhere. Using the open road as a symbol uniting a multicultural democracy proves untenable because roads and railways often encouraged uniformity, sundered neighborhoods, displaced indigenous populations, and destroyed sacred sites, sources of food, and wildlife habitat. William Boelhower writes that using the road to symbolize "[t]he building of American identity and a national culture," as Whitman did, only prolonged its identity crisis. By using such a symbol,

> the American *citoyen* exposed himself to his own nothingness. The road is a non-place, it leaves the masses no rest. He who follows the national road cannot dwell because the road annihilates place. The global strategy of the map is a strategy of deterritorialization, an aesthetic of corporeal disappearance, for one cannot be ubiquitous and still keep body and soul together. For this reason, American identity is an abstract idea; indeed, such a "nation of strangers" is a society that has lost its sense of place. Without the latter there can be no memory and no identity as these too are tied to place. (Boelhower 74–75)

Sandburg claims in his introduction to *The American Songbag* that the songs he includes "have been gathered by the compiler and his friends from coast to coast and from the Gulf to Canada" (xii). Although claiming figuratively to have gone everywhere, Sandburg reveals his symbolic position nowhere in a poem in which the speaker responds to hearing a group of singing African Americans: "I went away asking where I come from" (*Complete Poems* 108). Keillor expresses admiration for Sandburg's achievement but also reservations about his keen sense of salesmanship and self-promotion as "Man of the People." "When it came to assembling this treasury of the American Authentic," writes Keillor,

> Sandburg collected everybody's oral tradition but his own. You will find black spirituals by the score, cowboy songs, work songs, sea chanties, hobo songs, and even seven songs in Spanish, but you will search in vain for anything that comes from a clean, industrious, pious Swedish immigrant family in Galesburg, Illinois. . . . His troubadour persona had no room in it for himself, only for Sailors, Negroes, Hoboes, Prisoners, Workers, the romantic heroes of the American Left. He invented himself as carefully as Bob Dylan did, or Rambling Jack Elliott, or a lot of other people in the folk business.[18] (x–xi)

Lindsay and Sandburg both emphasized particular places—Springfield and Chicago, respectively—but they also transformed them synecdochically into all-American cities. For Lindsay, the real American language was Virginian but was found in Indiana ("Real" 257), and, as he traveled west, the Rockies became the Boston/Springfield/Kansas (that is, spiritual center) of the nation. Holding the country together through a system of signs of his own making, however, echoed the imperialist drives that repressed the differences Lindsay valued.

By staying with what he and his colleagues believe most literate Americans already know (rather than attempting to manufacture, to reorganize, or to revive that knowledge), Hirsch avoids some of the pitfalls of primitivism, but he still faces the charge that collecting information and disseminating it to American educators has more to do with establishing his own authority than with assisting the disadvantaged. Although Hirsch does not physically traverse the country to make his list of what every American needs to know, he does distribute it nationwide prior to publication (135–37). Interestingly, he uses a spatial metaphor to describe the process of deciding what to include in and what to exclude from the book's appendix:

> [W]e must draw a northerly border, above which lies specialized knowledge, and a southerly one, below which lies knowledge so obvious and widely known that its inclusion would make the list unusably long. There are also easterly and westerly borderline areas. To the east lie materials that are still too new to have passed into general currency. . . . To the west are items, like *Sherman Adams,* which have passed from view and are now known only by older generations. (138)

To map something—to measure, to record, and to render visible its dimensions—is to exert control over it, as Boelhower has discussed in his treatment of maps and their role in the conquest of American territories (46–50). By imagining knowledge spatially and then drawing boundaries within which American educators should remain, Hirsch (besides revealing his regional biases) undermines his argument that the cultural literacy he advocates has a composite nature. In other words, if everyone has been let in, why does he need the fence?

In light of the way cultures sometimes originate, Hirsch's cartographic metaphor is not surprising. As several contemporary theorists of travel have written, "[C]ultures do not just spring up ready-planted in their native soils; very often cultures are the result of transplantation—in other words, of a form of *travel*" (Arshi et al. 225). Lindsay's poem "In Praise of Johnny Appleseed" conceives of concrete relationships between traveling, planting, and spreading culture. The poem begins with a description of domesticated plants, birds, and mammals straying west during Washington's presidency and eventually becoming trees, wolves, and Native American warriors. Johnny Appleseed migrates, singing ancient songs and planting his seeds, which, with some horticultural license taken, produce apples derived from the rose and the amaranth. Johnny Appleseed, compared to monks, Hindus, Buddha, and St. Francis, becomes the American medicine man and founder of institutions: "A ballot-box in each apple, / A state capital [sic] in each apple, / Great high schools, great colleges, / All America in each apple" (*Poetry* 2:434). Although Hirsch's rhetoric is never this fantastic and his educational plan is more realistic than Lindsay's description, the poem nonetheless illustrates why calls for cultural literacy often are perceived as a form of unwelcome control by an elite few. Johnny Appleseed is a self-sacrificing hero, but clearly he is also an alter ego for Lindsay as a planter of knowledge. The image of the empty west with which the poem opens recalls the kind of imperialist transplantation in which native peoples and species are ignored, exploited, or displaced. Opponents of Hirsch likewise object to a view of students as empty fields ready for cultivation by the schools. Although "In Praise of Johnny Appleseed" imagines the blending of Asian, Native American, European, and American folk traditions, the origin of institutions in particular seeds suggests that, contrary to Lindsay's interactive poetics of walking, knowledge ultimately rests with their distributor.

The idealism of the poem, in which Johnny Appleseed communes with nature without desire or need for economic gain, is instructive concerning the stakes in promoting cultural literacy. In the poem, learning serves neither as a commodity nor as a currency that buys individual success. Yet, historically speaking, the distribution of products geographically has gone hand in hand with colonizing territory (McClintock 133). Household items, movies, music, and books all have had a role in uprooting one culture and planting another. By submerging themselves in travel and the lore of others, Lindsay and Sandburg created themselves as spokesmen for American diversity; they voiced an American language representing all walks of life. In order to preach in a common American language, they had to lose themselves in their projects. To ensure the success of their programs, however, they needed to create a demand for themselves as speakers, which they did through their literacy campaigns. As in the case of their model, Whitman, a white man appeared to be the best spokesman for an ethnically diverse nation and the best sower of its new language.

Like Hirsch, Lindsay, and Sandburg, I believe that national culture, to the extent that it exists, is composite in nature. Primitivism and racism, however, limit who can contribute and the ways in which they may do so. The paradigm of travel, moreover, suggests constraints: unequal access to thoroughfares and varying speed limits. In a theory of the production of Afro-American literature based on the blues, Houston A. Baker, Jr., says of wanderers, "The 'placeless' . . . are translators of the nontraditional. Rather than fixed in the order of cunning Grecian urns, their lineage is fluid, nomadic, transitional" (*Blues* 202). The translating powers of these wanderers, however, stem in large part from necessity; no matter what hardships Lindsay endured, he represents the oxymoronic impossibility of being voluntarily displaced. At the same time, a modern inability to feel at home anywhere, to thrive neither in the city nor the small town of his birth, must have fueled his need for a culture—locally based yet transportable—that confirmed his own spiritual worth.

Lindsay's career, which ended in mental anguish and suicide, directs us to a silence in Hirsch's work when it comes to the economic advantages of a culturally literate population. Even though Hirsch is correct about the importance of rigorous early education, his plan ignores the current capitalistic limitation of opportunity whereby prices are kept low through a surplus of laborers and general underemployment. Moreover, while individuals will certainly fail without a sound education, the possession of one does not guarantee success. Americans additionally must learn to compete and to gain an advantage over others in the marketplace, a process that complicates the achievement of democratic equality. The career of Sandburg highlights the results of marketing one's self successfully, for his products—books and poems less dreamy and more accessible than those of Lindsay—made their way into the schools and helped to bring American folklore and speech into the curriculum.

James Weldon Johnson calls our attention to the making of literary reputations in *The Autobiography of an Ex-Coloured Man,* where he illustrates the disparity between blacks' and whites' potential for successfully organizing folk materials. The narrator learns that "nothing great or enduring, especially in music, has ever sprung full-fledged and unprecedented from the brain of any master; the best that he gives to the world he gathers from the hearts of the people, and runs it through the alembic of his genius" (100). Johnson depicts the same social order that allowed for the success of some European-American artists and the discouragement of African Americans in his story of an "ex-coloured man" who ends his research in the South and allows himself to pass for white after witnessing a lynching (187–91).

By dwelling on primitivism in some of Sandburg's and Lindsay's work, I do not want to suggest that the voices of African-American writers were entirely drowned out. Neither do I wish to suggest that Sandburg and Lindsay coopted them in the same ways. The poets' respective dealings with Langston Hughes, for example, disclose differences in their plans to unite the nation by enveloping it.

Arnold Rampersad relates that Sandburg gave Lincoln University's commencement address in 1943, the year Hughes received an honorary doctorate. The university in all likelihood recognized the symbolism of having the two progressive poets on stage. Any sense of symmetry was lost, however, when Sandburg spoke for over three hours. While listening to Sandburg's poetry was meant to empower ordinary citizens, such a large dose of listening must have sent a different message to the audience. After the ceremonies, the two men exchanged only brief greetings, although Hughes esteemed Sandburg and taught his work when he lectured on modern developments in poetry (Rampersad 2:70, 128).[19]

More than Sandburg, Lindsay exhibited an elitism that separated him from the people he wished to reach and represent. Yet he also learned humility. With regard to African Americans, he was uniquely honest among Midwesterners about his own inculturated racism, observing in the first preface to *Collected Poems:*

> Mason and Dixon's line runs straight through our house in Springfield still, and straight through my heart. No man may escape his bouncing infancy. I do not expect to get ten feet from my childhood till I die. . . . Springfield is as far south as Maryland, Delaware and northern Virginia. Mason and Dixon's line goes straight east and west on Edwards Street. Lincoln's home is only two blocks north of it.
>
> And it seems to me Mason and Dixon's line runs around every country in the world, around France, Japan, Canada, or Mexico or any other sovereignty. (*Poetry* 3:952–53)

Lindsay's need to universalize kept him from pushing his observations about midwestern racism any further. Self-examination led to a generalization of his own European-American predicament. The primitivist's contradictions meant that he could refer to "fat black bucks," "tattooed cannibals," and "Mumbo-Jumbo" in "The Congo" (*Poetry* 1:174–75) but also correspond with Hughes after their meeting in Washington, D.C. Tired and ill, Lindsay, after learning more about the poet he had "discovered," wrote and offered Hughes what advice he had left in the final, disturbed years of his life.[20] Hughes wrote back to thank Lindsay and to affirm that his own experience had taught him to be "wary of lionizers" (Rampersad 1:119). He later defended Lindsay—even though other African Americans loathed "The Congo" for its primitivism—and, years after Lindsay's death, visited his sister Olive Lindsay Wakefield in Springfield (2:13, 111–12).

Not meant as a means of crowding out other voices, Lindsay's walking tours originally were conceived as a way to drop out of capitalism, its hierarchies, and the limits it placed on reaching an audience. He came to the road in a manner different from Sandburg, and he traveled it with a different attitude. "Remember, if you go a-wandering, the road will break your heart," he wrote in *A Handy Guide for Beggars* (*Prose* 1:7). He failed to profit by his career partly because he possessed fewer entrepreneurial skills than Sandburg but also partly, at least early on, as a matter of design. "There is just one way to convince citizens of the United States that you are dead in earnest about an idea," he wrote in the preface to the second edition of *Collected Poems*. "It will do no good to be crucified for it, or burned at the stake for it. It will do no good to go to jail for it. But if you go broke for a hobby over and over again the genuine fructifying wrath and opposition is terrific. They will notice your idea at least" (*Poetry* 3:967). Although he devised walking tours in order to make poetry an event rather than a product, his economic naïveté and the very ideal of an American bard prevented him from circumventing the market; he became a commodity in it rather than a purveyor of cultural wisdom. In a society where all are well educated, many are likely to create economic opportunity for themselves; Lindsay's attempts at direct marketing and self-employment demonstrate, however, that social reform cannot be a strictly individual or linguistic endeavor.

The give and take involved in the relationship between Lindsay and Hughes illustrates that, although circumstances allowed European Americans to overshadow African Americans, both groups were active participants in a continuing process of creating our culture's knowledge. For their part, African-American writers did tour, collect materials, experience class struggles among themselves, learn from Sandburg's and Lindsay's successes as performers, and persist longer than Johnson's ex-coloured man. Both Sandburg and Lindsay set out to create a literature from and for the people, but conceptions of race and ethnicity, their own ambitions, ideas about American history, the role prescribed for American artists, and an unjust social and economic system[21] thwarted projects in which all could contribute on equal footing to a composite culture.

Yet, now that Lindsay and Sandburg, no longer living speakers, are declining in importance as part of our own cultural literacy, their relationship to those they tried to represent makes them interesting. No matter how much Lindsay misunderstood African-American culture, he repeatedly revealed his own inseparability from it:

> Elegant ladies ask me hundreds of times as I come to their towns as a reciter: "How did you get your knowledge of the 'neeegro'?" . . . My father had a musical voice, and he used to read us *Uncle Remus,* and he could sing every scrap of song therein and revise every story by what some old slave had told him. He used to sing the littler children to sleep with negro melodies which he loved, and which negroes used to sing to

him, when they rocked him to sleep in his infancy. We nearly always had a black hired man and a black hired girl. My father took us to jubilee singer concerts from Fisk or Hampton, and came home rendering the songs authentically, and from boyhood memory. Moreover, our negro servants did not hesitate to sing. One-fifth of the population of the town of Springfield is colored. I played with negro boys in the Stuart School yard. I have heard the race question argued to shreds every week of my life from then till now. (*Poetry* 3:952)

Clearly, Lindsay was highly influenced by African-American culture (the songs, debates, and shoulder-to-shoulder contact), but he was in no position to speak for it (because, for instance, Joel Chandler Harris shaped his perceptions, as had employer-employee relationships and the stereotype that blacks naturally sing). Aldon Lynn Nielsen writes that, "even before Lindsay began to have significant contact with blacks, he was internalizing a primarily linguistic structure of thought about them" (30).

By criticizing the foundations of Sandburg's and Lindsay's cultural literacy campaigns and comparing them to today's educational reform movements, I do not wish to suggest that all attempts at either multiculturalism or curricular standards are misguided. I do wish, however, to warn against prescriptions devised by a handful of men or an idea of multiculturalism that coheres easily, repressing unresolvable differences among various segments of the population. If we learn anything from Sandburg's and Lindsay's successes and failures, it is that language and culture, powerful as they are in forging communal identities, cannot substitute for other political and economic reforms that enlarge opportunity and ensure justice. If future students are to understand the historical dialectic between pluralism and unity, then attempts at cultural unification will need to be part of our literacy, and two poets about to disappear behind Hirsch's generational, western border offer insights into why these efforts have been flawed and temporary. Although Lindsay and Sandburg often confused art and life and mythologized themselves, we can study their goals in relation to those of the African Americans, Native Americans, and non-English immigrants they tried to represent; their projects are necessarily incomplete unless they are put alongside, for example, the poetry of Langston Hughes, who asserted, "I, too, sing America" (*Selected Poems* 275). In this way, we can appreciate the texts that now replace their performances, assess their ramifications for the English language written in America, and examine our own efforts at multicultural literacy.

3

RENAISSANCE WOMEN, REFORMERS, AND NOVELISTS

Ordinarily I am not interested in philanthropy, and I have an absolute aversion for women who lecture.

—Willa Cather, "Jane Addams on Tolstoi," 743

• Although forgotten for the most part, Chicago's women authors contributed to the new, informal style of writing that became associated with their region. Like the men, they often wrote of urban experience, but their work has not been remembered because it also belongs to women's traditions of fiction and social reform. The women of Chicago had a strained relationship to the men's achievements in journalistic style and literary diction, in part because women long have been "cast in the role of preservers of linguistic tradition" (Baron *Grammar* 2). Sandra M. Gilbert and Susan Gubar assert that in the twentieth century "literary men and women began to wage war not only with but over words themselves" (1:121), and, while this general statement applies to Chicagoans, its writers also contended and cooperated in ways specific to their community.

When they privileged the vernacular, male Chicago writers often stressed their shared experience with working men, an approach largely unavailable to women. Although individual women received favorable reviews of their work, commentators on Chicago's developing literature frequently contrasted the new idiom with what they considered an older, effeminate literary style, implicitly assigning literary women to minor roles in the Midwest. Women writers nevertheless used several means to suggest spoken language, to represent urban experience, and to position themselves as agents of social change. Through recourse to primitivism, women working in a variety of genres employed the vernacular. Novelists, for their part, affirmed women's command of colloquial language by imagining romances between plain-looking women and plainspoken men—what I will call democracy by association—and by celebrating the oratory of women reformers. At least two of these orators, Jane Addams and Ida B. Wells, published extensively, providing examples of the wide appeal and rhetorical power of women's voices.

Through arts societies, suffrage movements, labor organizations, and social work, Chicago offered new opportunities for women, many of whom took leadership roles in cultural and political activities. For instance, Harriet Monroe made the *Poetry* office a place where poets could meet, and she found that her associate editors, Helen Hoyt and Eunice Tietjens, "were a tonic, not only to the editors but to unrecognized poets—good, bad, and indifferent—who would stray into the office for encouragement and consolation" (*Poet's Life* 324). Hull-House, the inner-city settlement project founded by Jane Addams, included a theater, "offering what every playwright needs—an experimental stage to try out his work" (*Poet's Life* 199). African-American civic organizations formed literary groups as well. Allan Spear discusses, for example, the Prudence Crandall Club, "a literary society . . . that included nearly every socially prominent Negro in the city" (67). Two socially prominent women authors, Ida B. Wells and Fannie Barrier Williams, had national reputations. In addition, scholars have noted that the University of Chicago's faculty and student body included both men and women from the start, that the wives of wealthy industrialists were active in the administration of the arts (K. Williams "Invisible" 519), and that Chicago women were making names for themselves in medicine and law (Massa 126)

Although working in the relatively new and prosperous city of Chicago put women in positions to energize one other, the local situation also hampered them in symbolic ways. Struggling for a regional literary identity, midwestern writers had begun to promote their own subject matter. In an 1892 letter to the *Dial,* for instance, Stanley Waterloo found in the tale of the western half of the United States "the swing of manhood. It will not be told in the soft, trig sentences of some distant essayist or laboring sonnet-writer" (207). Midwesterners could consider themselves superior to eastern writers by emphasizing the vigor of their own region and literature.[1] Chicago came to be represented as virile, "a tall bold slugger set vivid against the little soft cities" (Sandburg *Complete Poems* 3), and its literature celebrated the city's industrial accomplishments and the perseverance of its working people. "To whom may the laurels as laureate of this Florence of the West yet fall?," Dreiser asked in

The Titan. "This singing flame of a city, this all America, this poet in chaps and buckskin, this rude, raw Titan, this Burns of a city!" (6).

Along with the language used to characterize the city, the national reception of some of Chicago's authors attests to the unlikelihood that these laurels would fall to a woman. William Drake finds the glorification of the working man—used to dispel images of the effete intellectual—illustrated in reactions to Sandburg. Egmont Hegel Arens, who would eventually found the *New Masses,* provides a telling example of the way a Chicago writer was perceived as unabashedly male: "Your hairy fist, / Like a ton of rock, / Smashes me in the face," he praises Sandburg (Drake 147).[2] Despite a variety of styles and subject matter, Chicago literature gained a reputation for ruggedness. In 1984, for example, Maxine Chernoff said in an interview concerning the writer in Chicago, "I don't think that either [Nelson] Algren or [James] Farrell would be choices or role models for a woman writer growing up in Chicago. Many of the writers you think of as the Chicago writers are the brawling, barroom kind of writers. . . . The male tradition seems to me, in my own writing, as distant as what Carl Sandburg did in poetry, say. I would never attempt to do it now or want to follow it" (333). Whether or not Chernoff's remarks apply to all the men writing about Chicago, or even to all the work by individual writers, her dilemma illustrates the difficulty of separating actual writers from the brawny reputation of Chicago literature.

At the beginning of the century, an association between exhausted forms of civilization and femininity presented a problem for women, who had more difficulty than men in creating a literary persona in keeping with the "Tool Maker, Stacker of Wheat, Player with Railroads and the Nation's Freight Handler" (Sandburg *Complete Poems* 3). Like literary men who were looking to workers and non-Europeans to put them back in touch with their lost primal powers, however, European-American women could resort to extolling the "primitive" qualities of immigrants, Native Americans, and African Americans in order to present themselves in the spirit of the times and region. In introducing Vachel Lindsay's *The Congo and Other Poems,* for instance, Monroe writes that she sees the possibility for "a return to the healthier open-air conditions and immediate personal contacts, in the art of the Greeks and of primitive nations." She also finds these qualities "in the wonderful song-dances of the Hopis and others of our aboriginal tribes. . . . [A]lso, in a measure, in the quick response between artist and audience in modern vaudeville." Monroe's enthusiasm over "the return to primitive sympathies between artist and audience" (E. Williams 13–14) in "The Congo" keeps her from seeing the poem's racial stereotypes.

Given their inability to present themselves as laborers or to admit to certain kinds of knowledge or desires, white women found representing other races and their perceived relationship to certain themes or other ages particularly attractive. The poet Marjorie Allen Seiffert, for example, at times relied on African or tropical settings when dealing with sexuality. Eunice Tietjens wrote *Profiles from Home* (1925) in free verse, and her break from song and rhymed forms is a development in keeping with the graphic language she used in *Profiles from China* (1917). Mary Aldis wrote most colloquially in dramatic monologues spoken by working-class women. While these writers did not always create insulting representations, the need to make use of a social or racial Other in order to speak in forbidden ways became a convention during this period. Even though Addams's notions about collective memory do not seem particularly malicious (168), for instance, idealized views of other cultures as connections to a lost past only strengthen racialist notions that various racial or ethnic groups exist to serve the needs of white Americans.

Although Ida B. Wells and Marita Bonner worked to erase derogatory images of African Americans, they too occasionally resorted to stereotypes of Native Americans or Jews. The problem may be inherent in the need for "types" in representation, and such images suggest that no one escapes the ideology of her day. Reductive devices were indeed specific to the local and national discourse of the time. In the work of Chicago writers and their critics, the "primitive," the virile, and the blue-collar worker become strangely synonymous. Sherwood Anderson's *Dark Laughter,* inspired by his reading of Jean Toomer's *Cane,* illustrates these conjunctions. Anderson's protagonist, a journalist who has left his artist wife for a series of wanderings, approaches the true meaning of life through contact with African Americans and working men.[3] The example of both blacks and working-class people gives the protagonist the courage to run away with the factory owner's wife. Because such attributions of primitiveness literally cost African Americans their lives, Wells struck back at European Americans, comparing their barbarous lynchings to the tactics of Native Americans and demonstrating that even she, who well understood the dangers inherent in the notion of the primitive, could not always avoid the rhetoric.

Through primitivism, European-American women ironically reinforced a semiotic chain that contributed to their own exclusion from literary history. While working men came to symbolize American and midwestern ideals, middle- and upper-class women stood for the opposite—that is to say, the ills of wealth and capitalism. The early Chicago novel *Barriers Burned Away* (1872), for instance, portrayed a stereotypically elitist woman in its saga of two artists eventually united by the Chicago fire. The character Dennis Fleet, whom Carl S. Smith describes as "a moral

Christian and democratic American," converts Christine Ludolph, "a coldly autocratic German" (21), to a genuinely American philosophy. Similarly, Duffey notes that the last line of *The Cliff-Dwellers* reflects Henry Fuller's critique of the upper-middle-class woman, in this case the Clifton hotel owner's wife: "It is for such a woman that one man builds a Clifton and that a hundred others are martyred in it" (43–44).

Portraying women in this way appears to be congruent with Thorstein Veblen's famous concept of conspicuous consumption put forward in *The Theory of the Leisure Class* (1899), which was written while he was an instructor at the University of Chicago. Yet images of "woman" as the motive for capitalist greed reassign the cause and effect relations of Veblen's theory. According to his ideas about economic evolution, despite the wife's transition from toiler for her husband to "the ceremonial consumer of goods which he produces . . . she still quite unmistakably remains his chattel in theory; for the habitual rendering of vicarious leisure and consumption is the abiding mark of the unfree servant" (83). By applauding the accomplishments of the working classes, Chicago writers tried to subvert "[t]he concept of dignity, worth, or honour, as applied either to persons or conduct" that Veblen saw as being "of first-rate consequence in the development of classes and of class distinctions" (15). In suggesting that capitalism existed for the benefit of middle- or upper-class women, however, these writers implied that women were incapable of the sympathy with the working classes that middle-class men could feel. Women writers, therefore, only confirmed this notion when they rested their authority on romantic, exotic, or patronizing portrayals of workers, immigrants, African Americans, or "foreign" lands; primitivism, therefore, always brought the idea of democracy back to virility.

Upton Sinclair departs from this pattern when in *The Jungle* the unemployed Jurgis Rudkus is awakened to socialism by a well-dressed woman who says to him between the naps he is trying to take at a rally, "If you would try to listen, comrade, perhaps you would be interested" (357). Although Jurgis learns that she can understand his plight, it is the unlikelihood of a middle-class woman calling him "comrade" that shocks him into a recognition of the party's promise. Perhaps Sandburg most economically captures the refigured values of both working-class men and upper-middle-class women: "I won't take my religion from any man who never works except with his / mouth and never cherishes any memory except the face of the / woman on the American silver dollar" (30).

The midwestern connection between primitiveness, virility, and class included style as well as plots and images. Hugh Dalziel Duncan's assessment of the lasting contributions Chicagoans made to American literature explains the loss of women's imprint on any canon of Chicago Renaissance writers. He attributes the success of the well-known authors to the training they received locally, arguing that from the 1880s on Chicago writers depended on two kinds of institutions: studios and newspapers. The newspaper editors "recruited, trained, and sent forth into the world of letters a generation of writers who wrote a new kind of English, namely the American English of the Middle West" (152).

According to Duncan, the language of newspapers, which eventually became the new American literary standard, had to appeal to a wide reading public, whose main form of "verbal expression was oral, not written" (175). Newspaper reporting, therefore, echoed men's speech more than women's speech because for women "certain uses possessed honorific value. To speak 'properly' indicated gentility, and since proper speech was controlled by teachers trained in the New England and British tradition, it was only natural that female schooling was couched in a language alien to the common interests of the Middle-West and of men whose lives were bounded by the market place" (175–76). Duncan associates the language of the studio, the institution supporting the older generation of writers—including men such as Hamlin Garland—with women's speech because of this group's emphasis on beauty and good taste (110).

If the Chicago Renaissance became, to use Gilbert's and Gubar's metaphor, a war between men's and women's language, or, in this case, a contest over whether to preserve honorific or ordinary speech, then Duncan sees it as a just war. He emphasizes a male/female rivalry when he describes the drawbacks of the "feminized, dilettante, aesthetic-erotic atmosphere" of the Little Room, a literary organization to which many of the city's women writers belonged. Duncan believes the group "conformed to the needs of upper middle class women who wanted 'cultivated' husbands or some social life beyond that possible to them as wives of business men" (105). Sidney H. Bremer gives a different account. In her version, the Little Room supported women in their work and emphasized what we might call a feminist form of interaction. She also comments on women's "control" of the group:

> when the Little Room began to formalize its organization in 1902, a split developed between the unofficial (feminine) and official (masculine) workings of the club. Although women continued to head the "entertainment" committee and one woman joined each "class" of three elected to the Little Room's board of directors, men became the officers who called meetings and kept the money and records. Then a 1906 decision to include spouses as associate members laced the Little Room with literal family ties, confusing the status of the professional women

who were attempting an extension of familylike dynamics beyond the private home. ("Lost Chicago Sisters" 222)

Duncan's and Bremer's accounts illustrate the difficulties involved in characterizing a literary period. Duncan looks at what records remain and sees a "feminized, dilettante, aesthetic-erotic atmosphere"; Bremer sees "an extension of familylike dynamics beyond the private home." Duncan's analysis of the newspapers' styles explains why women may have found midwestern expression less "natural" than William Dean Howells (739) or H. L. Mencken (5) had, since ordinary midwestern speech was as much of a construct as was honorific speech. Duncan also shows us that critics looking back on the period discounted women's achievements (even when women were writing "the American English of the Middle West"). Bremer encourages us to take women's activities seriously rather than to dismiss them as attempts at socializing or finding husbands.

Scholars may disagree as to whether the Little Room represented masculine or feminine values, but all acknowledge that the Whitechapel Club was the domain of men. Founded in 1889 by a group of journalists that included Finley Peter Dunne, the Whitechapel Club took Jack-the-Ripper as a sort of patron saint and built a reputation for wild antics and carousing (Andrews 90, Duffey 144). Even if women had been allowed to join, which they were not (Bremer "Introduction" xii), the club's aggressively male idea of entertainment probably would not have attracted many of them. Women were barred from other press clubs as well (xii). That Ida B. Wells's investigative reporting and radical journalism did not admit her socially into her colleague's ranks indicates clearly that gender and race, rather than usage of language, determined where writers belonged institutionally and how they fit into histories of the period.

The perception that hard-nosed journalists were forging Chicago's literary style posed linguistic challenges for women. As far as the written record shows, Chicago's women did not necessarily present themselves in stereotypically feminine terms. Yet women of all generations seem to have understood that they were at a disadvantage in shaping a new American literary language based on the standards of newspapers. Although some fostered this aesthetic, they still met with difficulties in adapting to the city's literary and journalistic paradigms. Margaret Anderson, founder of the *Little Review,* recalls that, when she first began reviewing books for the *Chicago Evening Post,* editor Francis Hackett asked her to simplify her style. "I tried, but I was too proud of my vocabulary and clichés to renounce them suddenly," Anderson remembers. "When I finally woke to the horror of what I was doing I made such an effort to be simple that I lost my vocabulary forever" (*Thirty Years' War* 22).

Ironically, Anderson and others associated with the *Little Review* disliked Elia Peattie's mannerly reviews, but Peattie got the last laugh by "capturing their admiration with some free verse she published under a working-class pseudonym" (Bremer "Introduction" xiii). Hull-House cofounder Ellen Gates Starr wrote to her sister in 1890 that she had composed an article for the *Tribune* but, knowing that the language would be changed to suit the conventions of journalism, confessed that she could only hope that the content would remain accurate (19).[1] Chicago poet Florence Kiper Frank complained that, despite women's strong feelings, "Still a calm modesty we must preserve. / Still on our lips and bosoms must be snow" (30). Baron writes, "Even today women are censured and occasionally dismissed from their jobs for using obscenities or other types of *unladylike* speech that would be tolerated from the mouths of men" (*Grammar* 62).

Chicago, then, presented a paradox for women writers. They worked side by side with men in a city of nearly unprecedented opportunities for women. At the same time, the burly image of Chicago drawn by male writers captured readers' attentions, and seldom could women credibly represent the city in a similar manner. Chicago's voice also came to be perceived as male, despite women's engagement in the written and oral debates of the day. Though primitivism offered one means of creating rough portraits and language, romantic love and the oratory of women reformers presented additional options for establishing women's authority.

Given the stereotypes of and taboos on women's use of language, the development of a pattern of democracy by association with men should not be surprising in the context of Chicago's male-oriented populism. Three novels of this type will be examined here: *True Love* (1903) by Edith Wyatt, *Just Folks* (1910) by Clara Laughlin, and *The Precipice* (1914) by Elia Peattie. The main character in each of these novels becomes knowledgeable about the people of Chicago, able to communicate with a broad cross-section of that society, representative of an emerging American form of verbal expression, and respected by the ordinary—and often poverty-stricken—citizens who learn to see her as an ally. To varying degrees, the women achieve these ends through the influence of their male lovers.

A poet and journalist, Edith Wyatt belonged to Harriet Monroe's generation. Her family moved from Wisconsin to Iowa and then, when she was eleven, to Chicago, where she spent most of her life (Inglehart viii–x). For two years, she studied at Bryn Mawr College. From 1894 until 1898 she taught at a girls' school (xiii). Her short stories began to appear in magazines, and in 1900 William Dean Howells wrote to encourage her and to offer assistance in finding a publisher (xiv–xv). After the turn of the century, Wyatt's interests in sociology and politics replaced her literary ambitions (xxii). She turned her pen and organizing skills to the causes of "department store strikers, slaughter-house animals, child actors, and Afro-American news boys—one of whom she even adopted" (Bremer "Introduction" xiv). The democracy-by-association formula kept her from merely relying on paternalistic representations of lower-class characters to give her access to proscribed speech. In her novel *True Love,* she created a colloquial usage that varies with individual personalities, not strictly along family or class lines. Shades of high, middle, and low culture mix and clash through the language and preferences of the different characters.

True Love is the story of four families: the William Marshes, the Edward Marshes, the Hubbards, and the Coltons. Wyatt introduces Emily Marsh of Chicago as "a person and estate more frequent in civilisation than in story, being a young lady without remarkable beauty, talents, fortune, or degree" (3). Friends of the Marsh family, Norman Hubbard and his mother, love European culture and scorn such Americans as Walt Whitman. By contrast, Norman's brother, Fred Hubbard, hums show tunes, dresses in flashy clothes, and writes on purple stationery. Fred, who has not succeeded in the Chicago business world, works downstate in Centreville, Illinois, where, by coincidence, Emily Marsh's cousin, Inez, lives. Inez Marsh's tastes match those of Norman Hubbard. Also a resident of Centreville, Dick Colton, the self-made man born to poor farmers, whistles folk songs, has lower-class relatives, and only reads books with happy endings. Although Wyatt narrates *True Love* in a standard written English, those characters whose speech conforms most closely to this pattern speak stiltedly and behave obnoxiously. The characters represent different levels of society, but the events of the novel result in a reranking based on their ability to communicate in spite of tragedy. Through dialogue and the characters' letters, Wyatt demonstrates her capacity to write in a manner outside of genteel, honorific speech. What Bakhtin would call the heteroglossia of her novel anticipates the democratic ideal the younger generation of Chicago writers sought. This many-voiced quality incorporates the experiments of earlier American writers who attempted to represent the speech of ordinary people. Indeed, William Dean Howells saw Wyatt's writing as "the apotheosis of the democratic spirit" (735).

Wyatt's range of class differences includes mostly gradations of Northern-European Americans—significantly, she uses a rural, American-born man rather than an inner-city immigrant to represent the lower classes. At the same time, she includes city and country accents and cultured and uncultured voices in order to blend urban and rural and to reject elitism for the populism that her own biases allow. An early description contrasts Tom Marsh with Norman Hubbard: "His voice, which was very colloquial and variant in tone, was as different as possible from Norman's, rather monotonous and abrupt, with a somewhat mannered accent" (17). Inez Marsh becomes engaged to Norman, only to find that they do not have true love. Wyatt describes Inez's attraction to Norman in terms of a fascination with the sound of his voice: "Of his words she could hardly think, only of the sound of his voice, so manly, so reassuring" (43). When Inez breaks the engagement, Norman converts Fanny Colton, Dick's sister, to his exclusive ways. He receives retribution for his snobbishness, however, by becoming the subject of popular gossip. Emily Marsh affirms her democratic nature by marrying Dick, who has "a quiet, good-natured voice with rich middle-west r's loudly rolled" (195). During their courtship, her simple correspondence "spoke so truthfully to him [of] her perfect attachment that not if several sonnet-cycles had passed between them could he have felt her more certainly and profoundly his own" (278).

Emily is never explicitly acknowledged as the plainspoken woman, and Wyatt seldom juxtaposes her speech and writing with anyone else's for purposes of comparison, as frequently happens between other characters in the novel. Yet her emphasis on Emily's "perfect attachment" to Dick, who "can deal with all kinds," indicates that she shares his nature. By extension, she shares his manner of expression, despite the fact that she has not engaged in the enterprises that make Dick "unusual" in "the straight way he runs things" (287) but as "common" as "all large things are" (288). Nevertheless, like the dead Inez Milholland in Sandburg's poem "Repetitions," Emily's body (through marriage to Dick), not her speech and tastes in themselves, makes her democratic.

True Love is not *The Pit* or *The Jungle*. Indeed, Duffey finds the Austen-like style of Wyatt's novel baffling, charging that she proceeds "as though there were no essential difference between the temper of Illinois life in 1900 and that of Jane Austen's England" (63). Yet in such tales of romantic love, women found their voices—their own Chicago voices that allowed them to consider issues of gender, class, region, and national unity. Nancy Armstrong argues in her work on domestic fiction that Austen created a language that "grant[ed] priority to the verbal practices of women, women who may never carry out programs of reading literature, but who are nevertheless essential to maintaining polite relationships within the community" (150). In *True Love*, Emily, despite her lack of any kind of ambition, holds the novel and its community together by sympathizing with each of the characters and maintaining links to all of them. Although Armstrong's historically contingent analysis does not explain how someone like Wyatt could reimagine the class structure of early twentieth-century Illinois, the Austen-like comedy of manners may have given Wyatt a genre that had traditionally legitimated women's patterns of speech in the formation of group and individual identity.

Writers who got their support from artistic communities in New York, London, or Paris would have been hooted at for writing a novel such as *True Love,* but Wyatt's choice makes sense in an environment where prominent thinkers were contemplating the meaning of class strife within democracy and where women writers needed to assert their importance within the community. Other Chicago novelists would follow Wyatt's lead, and Susan Glaspell would experiment with the romance novel as a forum for advancing socialist ideas in *The Visioning* (1911).

The other two novels examined here combine the democracy-by-association pattern with the story of a social worker. As public figures and orators, Jane Addams and the women of Hull-House clearly inspired these novels. Born to a wealthy businessman and farmer in 1860, Jane Addams grew up in Cedarville, Illinois, and graduated from Rockford Female Seminary in 1881. Lacking interest in becoming a missionary, teacher, or mother, she began seeking a way to use her education (Bryan and Davis 1–2). In the fall of 1881 she briefly attended the Women's Medical College in Philadelphia (3). There she suffered for the second time a mental breakdown and was sent to S. Weir Mitchell (DeKoven 334), whose rest cure was made infamous by Charlotte Perkins Gilman's short story "The Yellow Wallpaper." Several trips to Europe followed. In June 1888, she attended the World Centennial Conference of Foreign Missions in London with her college classmate Ellen Gates Starr and became interested in social experiments there, especially Toynbee Hall, an early university settlement (Bryan and Davis 4). Addams and Starr, unknowingly taking part in a nationwide movement, went to Chicago in 1889 and founded Hull-House, the third settlement among four hundred that appeared in the United States between 1886 and 1911. The two women planned "to be neighbors to the poor" (4–5), which initially entailed sharing the arts with the Jewish, Irish, Italian, and Greek immigrants in the district. Hull-House thus gave middle-class women the chance to live communally while they used their educations and gave low-income neighbors the chance to break the dull routine of urban existence.

Becoming acquainted with the needs of the area, Hull-House residents provided a kindergarten, organized clubs, sponsored social events, allowed labor unions to meet under their roof (6), worked to pass child labor laws, established the city's first public playground, and learned methods of social research (8). One of their shortcomings was the failure to form coalitions with ethnic leaders (128). As the new century pro-

gressed, more of the residents were students seeking to become professional social workers (64). Meanwhile, Addams and several others took
up the cause of the Progressive Party, and Addams seconded the
nomination of Theodore Roosevelt at their 1912 convention (66). Although Hull-House had always drawn criticism, attacks intensified when
Addams's pacifist efforts continued through World War I (157). During
and after the war years, racial tensions increased in the neighborhood,
and, although they did not propose anything approaching equal conditions for blacks and whites, Hull-House residents took the lead among
white reformers hoping to end racially motivated violence (158–59).

In addition to emboldening women to write and to speak about matters of social policy, Addams also proved herself sensitive to the means by
which ordinary women found their voices. Addams's *The Long Road of
Woman's Memory* (1917) develops a theory of memory and women's authority, which she bases on the oral story of the Devil Baby. Addams recalls that for six weeks rumors that the settlement had taken in a profan-
ity-spewing baby with "cloven hoofs, pointed ears and diminutive tail"
brought thousands to Hull-House with variants of the tale (3). There
were two prototypes of this story: first, an Italian version in which a
woman gives birth to the Devil Baby after her atheist husband insists he
would rather see the devil than his wife's religious icons and, second, a
Jewish version in which a father of six daughters gets his wish after de-
claring he would prefer the devil to a seventh girl (3–4). Addams relates,
"During the weeks of excitement it was the old women who really
seemed to have come into their own, and perhaps the most significant result of the incident was the reaction of the story upon them. It stirred
their minds and memories as with a magic touch, it loosened their
tongues and revealed the inner life and thoughts of those who are so often inarticulate" (8). Addams believes the story empowered these old
women because it "put into their hands the sort of material with which
they were accustomed to deal. They had long used such tales in their un-
remitting efforts at family discipline, ever since they had frightened their
first children into awed silence by tales of bugaboo men who prowled in
the darkness" (8).

Although Addams discusses social activism rather than literary activity,
she offers insights into Chicago women's participation in literary culture
despite what women had come to symbolize for area writers. Like the
story of the Devil Baby for the old women, genres and styles inconsistent
with what the better-known men were writing partially restored the status of Chicago women within the community. Although the elderly
women Addams describes lost their authority again when the Devil Baby
failed to materialize, Addams's own influence extended to both literary

men and women. Smith credits her with "best defin[ing] the basic terms of the discussion of the relationship between art and life that was a central concern in Chicago literature" (15).

Addams's direct impact on Chicago literature can be found in at least twenty "settlement house novels."[5] Guy Szuberla finds that they fall into three categories: those that mock the efforts of the reformers, those that preach their message, and those that simply espouse "a common faith in the promises of sociology and progressive reform" ("Peattie's *Precipice*" 61–62). Addams's example inspired novelists Clara Laughlin and Elia Peattie, who referred to her in their fiction, based characters on her followers, and learned from her rhetorical style.[6] Although Laughlin, Peattie, Wells, Wyatt, Harriet and Lucy Monroe, and Eunice Tietjens (who served as a war correspondent) all worked as journalists (Bremer "Introduction" xii), for the most part they could not hop freights, take part in the wheat harvests, or write about the kind of vagabondage that enhanced the Chicago men's popularity. Women could, however, become social workers with their own brand of authority and knowledge of the working classes.

Chicago women's interest in social workers defies the general trend of English and American literature, where authors often scorn do-gooders, as Dickens did in *Bleak House* and Hawthorne did in *The Blithedale Romance*. In *The Bostonians,* Henry James satirized reformers in general and suffragists in particular. He went so far as to inscribe the effects of public speaking on his characters' physiognomy. One reformer "looked as if she had spent her life on platforms, in audiences, in conventions, in phalansteries, in *seances;* in her faded face there was a kind of reflection of ugly lecture-lamps; with its habit of an upward angle, it seemed turned toward a public speaker, with an effort of respiration in the thick air in which social reforms are usually discussed" (55). A less cynical portrayal of a social worker, Edith Wharton's Gerty Farish in *The House of Mirth,* nonetheless arouses pity rather than admiration.[7] Sherwood Anderson, in *Marching Men,* depicts the settlement worker Margaret Ormsby confronting the emptiness of her own soul after losing to a milliner in a competition for the affections of the labor leader Beaut McGregor (291–93). Rather than seeing social workers as hypocrites, meddlers, desperate voyeurs, or pampered women with nothing better to do, as many British and American writers did, Laughlin and Peattie imagine them as authorities on social change. Addams's own experience became their Devil Baby.

The daughter of Irish immigrants, Clara Laughlin moved to Chicago when she was in grade school (Raftery 46–47). Despite the precariousness of the family's finances, the children were sent to private tutors. Her writing career began when her father's death forced her to seek work. She served as book reviewer and then editor of two Presbyterian periodicals, *Interior* and *Continent*. Her devotion to her career made marriage an option she never pursued (47). Laughlin wrote several sentimental novels, and her advice columns appeared in *Good Housekeeping*. Conforming less to gender stereotypes in other ways, she ran a travel agency, wrote travel books, and served as an editor at *McClure's Magazine*. Her only attempt at realistic fiction (Bremer "Introduction" xii; Fanning 243), *Just Folks* (1910) portrays a probation officer and her inner-city neighbors and clients.

Filled with dialect, *Just Folks* suffers from many of the problems that plague literature where dialect is used: the overuse of apostrophes; an emphasis on the linguistic differences between the immigrants, the middle-class characters, and the "standard" narrator; and a tendency to make the impoverished sound quaint. Laughlin's piety, antilabor sentiments, conventional work ethic, and insistence on referring to the heroine as "little Beth" also may exasperate today's readers. Although not the most enjoyable of Chicago novels, *Just Folks* does illustrate a gendered struggle for the authority to represent urban experience. The character concerned with words in this novel, Beth's journalist boyfriend has protested her moving into a poor section but discovers what may prove the big break of his career there. Beth's elderly neighbor, according to the narrator, "was a real 'cracker-barrel sage' in petticoats, and Hart Ferris, with 'Mr. Dooley' in mind, was projecting a 'signed column' of Liza's wisdom for his paper." Beth remarks, "I tell you, Hart, the real things, worth writing about, are over here, and I'm glad there's something, if it's only I, that brings you over here, where the real things are" (64). Although Beth does not capture the voices of the city, she takes credit for Hart's being able to do so.

Australian novelist Miles Franklin included a similar theme in her posthumously published Chicago novel *On Dearborn Street*, begun in 1913 while she edited and contributed to *Life and Labor*, the magazine of the National Women's Trade Union League.[8] Narrated by a middle-aged, feminist bachelor, *On Dearborn Street* tells the story of his success in wooing Sybyl Penelo due to her love for his mother. Franklin's feminism becomes evident in the narration by this "new man" and in the description of Sybyl and her partner, Edna Maguire, running a stenography and ghostwriting service in the Loop. *Just Folks* reverses the metaphor of ghostwriting in that Hart writes the words of Beth's neighbors without their permission and they, not he, remain the ghosts. Yet in both novels the woman's work—either writing, uttering wisdom, or choosing where to live—goes unacknowledged in the world of urban commerce.

Despite *Just Folks's* patronizing tone and the depiction of outsiders blithely and beneficially intervening in the lives of the poor (this is no *Howard's End*), Laughlin at times criticizes Hart's use of the neighborhood for material. After struggling with whether to withhold information from the police in order to protect a boy accused of murder, Beth decides to counsel the youngster on the wisdom of confessing, for Hart has lectured to her on why women have "no business fooling with the law" (348). When she informs him that she is going to see the boy on her lunch break, Hart, whose newspaper has assigned him to the case, replies, "That is too late for our paper." Beth retorts, "[I]t is Mikey that I'm thinking of—not the paper—and not you!" (357). The conflict resolves itself when the boy proves to have a solid but embarrassing alibi, and the novel ends with Liza's sentiment that, despite what looks like a lucky break, "when you live real close t' people an' know lots about their lives, the ways o' Providence, it seems t' me, is pretty plain" (376). Beth agrees, validating her decision to live "close" rather than to report from outside (see also Bremer "Introduction"). By creating a heroine who works as a probation officer, Laughlin is able to present scenes from urban life, to use dialect and vernacular language, and to criticize the practices of male journalists—whose authority on social issues is questioned—all the while writing in a typically feminine style and genre.

Unlike Laughlin's Beth, who receives no credit in the world of writers, Elia Peattie was considered something of a literary broker. A reviewer, editor, and frequent contributor of short stories to the *Tribune*, Peattie had over one hundred stories published in magazines with a national circulation and was the author of thirty-two books, including children's and travel literature (Bremer "Introduction" xiii). She grew up in Chicago (x) and left school in the seventh grade to help her mother with the demands of the family. Marriage to Robert Peattie allowed her to pursue her dreams of reading and writing, although financial pressure frequently compelled her to turn out commercial fiction (xviii–xix). At one point, the couple moved to Omaha, where both worked for the *Omaha World Herald* and where Elia also wrote for the Populist Party; William Jennings Bryan called her "the first Bryan man" (xii–xiii).

Like Beth in *Just Folks*, Kate Barrington, the heroine of Peattie's novel *The Precipice*, also is involved with a man whose language conforms to Chicago's main literary paradigm. Unlike Beth, however, Kate achieves her own authoritative voice as well. Kate falls in love with Karl Wander, an enterprising, outdoor type from Colorado. The novel ends with their decision to work out a long-distance marriage. While Karl's name labels him as the one who undertakes journeys, Kate also travels, attending suffragist events and promoting a Children's Protective Association. Their romance begins by correspondence, and Karl writes in one letter, "Don't mind my emphatic English" (210). His cousin warns, "You'll have to make allowances for his being so Western and going right to the point in such a reckless way" (247). Kate does not mind because she cultivates an equally forthright style. She sharpens her ideas by corresponding with prominent people in her field (219), supports the Federation of Women's Clubs' agenda of "undeviating, disinterested determination to help women develop themselves" (379), and finds her writing voice by contributing to women's magazines—"brief, spontaneous, friendly articles, full of meat and free from the taint of bookishness" (91). When she begins public speaking, she captures audiences with "[h]er abrupt, picturesque way of saying things" (82). The press responds with "articles concerning the country girl who had come up to town, and who, with a simple faith and courage, had worked among the unfortunate and the delinquent, and whose native eloquence had made her a favorite with critical audiences" (185).

Women's conversations may not have set the standard for journalism, but *The Precipice* describes their oratory as unadorned speaking. Kate cannot understand the fuss over her speeches because initially "[s]he made so little effort when she spoke that she could not feel much respect for her achievement" (178). As her confidence grew, the narrator relates, "She ceased to think about herself save as the carrier of a message" (266). Not everyone, however, is pleased with her lack of artifice. Mrs. Dennison, a friend from her mother's generation, finds Kate's way of expressing herself "so very emphatic" and "quite out of taste" (231). Kate's frankness finally makes her incompatible with an on-again, off-again suitor, Ray McCrea, but fits her perfectly for the westerner Karl Wander.

Kate has not simply appropriated "masculine" speech. She rejects some of the ways in which her upbringing has socialized her to speak but adapts others. Kate's mother "moved by her well-chosen phrases; they were like rules set in a copybook for her guidance" (12). Kate, though, distances herself from such phrases when she explains herself to Mrs. Dennison: "I dare say I am getting to be rather violent and careless in my way of talking. It's a reaction from the vagueness and prettiness of speech I used to hear down in Silvertree, where they begin their remarks with an 'I'm not sure, but I think,' et cetera" (231). Another friend, however, attributes Kate's success as a speaker to her "Silvertree method" (183). Peattie explains that Kate reached audiences others could not because

> she offered not vital statistics, but vital documents. She talked in personalities—in personalities so full of meaning that, concrete as they were, they took on general significance—they had the effect of symbols. She

furnished watchwords for her listeners, and she did it unconsciously. She would have been indignant if she had been told how large a part her education in Silvertree played in her present aptitude. She had grown up in a town which feasted on dramatic gossip, and which thrived upon the specific personal episode. To the vast and terrific city, and to her portion of the huge task of mitigating the woe of its unfit, Kate brought the quality which, undeveloped, would have made of her no more than an entertaining village gossip. (179)

As Bremer notes, Kate's progress is seldom dramatized ("Introduction" xxii). Her letters, conversations, and speeches rarely are presented to readers; Peattie, using standard written English, describes them instead.

Like Lindsay's American hieroglyphics, Kate's method aims to invent new symbols for American realities, and her reliance on anecdotes corresponds to Addams's portrayal of Hull-House's neighbors, a technique for which the story of the Devil Baby serves as only one of many examples (see also Szuberla "Peattie's *Precipice*" 69–70). Addams believed that such accounts were important because she recognized the power of "those individual reminiscences which, because they force the possessor to challenge existing conventions, act as a reproach, even as a social disturber" (53). *The Precipice* explicitly acknowledges "the Addams breed of citizens" (185) in the development of Kate's rhetoric and methods:

> Yes, always, in high places and low, among friends and enemies, this sad, kind, patient, quiet woman, Jane Addams, of Hull House, had preached the indissolubility of the civic family. Kate had listened and learned. Nay, more, she had added her own interpretations. She was young, strong, brave, untaught by rebuff, and she had the happy and beautiful insolence of those who have not known defeat. She said things Jane Addams would have hesitated to say. She lacked the fine courtesy of the elder woman; but she made, for that very reason, a more dramatic propaganda. (182)

Although the text appears to be setting up Kate, her assertive speech, and her improvisations on Addams's philosophy for a fall, she stays firmly balanced on the precipice. Szuberla argues that Kate develops her voice at the expense of the immigrants she too often considers backward ("Peattie's *Precipice*" 72–74), and the novel does indeed raise sobering questions about the ethnocentricity of social workers and their plans to control the parenting of children. At the same time, the novel disturbs conventions as to the portrayal of women's speech, in part through democracy-by-association with the plainspoken man but more importantly because of the heroine's involvement with the poor, other professionals, suffragists, and audiences eager to hear her working woman's voice.

Reformer and orator Ida B. Wells-Barnett spent three decades of her career as a writer in Chicago, where she took up residence at the height of her campaign to end lynching. Wells, who was born into slavery in Mississippi in 1862, began her crusade against lynching when three black men she knew were murdered for competing with white businessmen. Her articles and editorials on the incident resulted in white residents destroying the office of the newspaper in which she was part owner and threatening her with death if she returned to Memphis. With the support of black women's clubs, Wells began a speaking tour of Great Britain. Later, after marrying Ferdinand Barnett, she became involved once again in the women's clubs; continued writing newspaper articles and books protesting lynching and discrimination; investigated the causes of riots and racial violence; served as a probation officer; established a reading room and employment service for black men; raised six children; served on a variety of citywide, state, and national commissions; and, in 1928, began her autobiography, *Crusade for Justice*, which she had not completed at the time of her death in 1931.

Wells continued her activism in Chicago after her marriage—despite her middle-class intention of remaining at home to care for their children—primarily because the experiences of the large numbers of black Americans migrating to Chicago demanded attention, protest, and action in the early decades of the century. James R. Grossman writes that Chicago attracted Southerners because, among other reasons, its meatpackers had storage buildings in the rural South, its black American Giants baseball team toured there every summer, its railways made the city easy to reach, and its *Defender*, "the most widely read newspaper in the black South, afforded thousands of prospective migrants glimpses of an exciting city with a vibrant and assertive black community" (4).

In her autobiography, Wells employed linguistic patterns deriving from oratory and journalism, a variety of devices for overcoming racial barriers, and several of the practices Peattie attributed to the fictional Kate Barrington. Wells's life story reveals as clearly as any statements by Chicago writers what achieving a simple and democratic style entails. In her role as reformer, Wells, too, could have served as a rhetorical model for Peattie's heroine, but Chicago's racial segregation prevented such a possibility. Indeed, Peattie showed her reluctance to make interracial alliances when, at the 1902 General Federation of Women's Clubs, she argued against admitting black clubs for fear that their inclusion would dissolve the coalition of Northern and Southern women working for suffrage (Bremer "Introduction" xv). Her case is but one example of what Hazel V. Carby calls "the dominant domestic ideologies and literary conventions of womanhood which excluded" black women "from the definition 'woman'" (6).

Although Wells achieved the authoritative political and literary expression Wyatt, Laughlin, and Peattie also sought, the white women's failure to form multiracial coalitions reduced her visibility in Chicago's literary history. At the same time, many women writers also went unrecognized by commentators on the Harlem Renaissance. Paula Giddings writes, "Black women were seen as having all the inferior qualities of White women without any of their virtues." Giddings quotes a commentator from *The Independent* in 1902: "I cannot imagine such a creature as a virtuous Negro woman" (82). Black women were considered promiscuous, a notion supporting the belief that black men were rapists. Allegedly, the voracious sexual appetites of black women created black men's inability to restrain themselves around white women (31). Gloria Hull maintains that, in response to such stereotypes, the burden of being "proofs of black female morals and modesty" kept women of one class and generation "outside the sensational mainstream" of the Harlem Renaissance (24–25).

Even though living at a distance from New York put black women writers at a disadvantage for literary success, Wells's life in the South and the Midwest contributed to her developing a powerful voice in protest of post-Reconstruction racism. "[O]ur American Christians," she wrote, "are too busy saving the souls of white Christians from burning in hellfire to save the lives of black ones from present burning in fires kindled by white Christians" (154–55). At a time when white American writers were celebrating the jazz age, taking a sudden interest in black culture, their fellow citizens were murdering African-American men, women, and children. The Midwest was in no way immune to this violence: there were race riots in Chicago and East Saint Louis and lynchings in other parts of the region. Spear notes, "During the East Saint Louis riots, the *Tribune* offered financial aid to Negroes who would leave Chicago" (203). Wells worked relentlessly to call attention to these outrages in an area where African Americans lacked the prominence some had gained in the Northeast and where European Americans were not adjusting well to the changing demography brought about by the migration of African Americans from South to North.

Wells found herself both highly regarded and disregarded among the city's leadership, both sought after in and squeezed out of city matters. She admired Jane Addams, comparing her own social settlement to Hull-House (356), and, for the most part, the two women enjoyed a cooperative relationship. They cosigned an appeal to the nation to celebrate Abraham Lincoln's centennial by taking action against racial injustice, and they served together on the committee that planned Chicago's observance (321–22). When the *Chicago Tribune* ran a series advocating racially segregated schools, Wells convinced Addams to form a citizens' committee that would persuade the paper to drop the matter (274–78). Yet Wells openly disagreed with an editorial Addams wrote condemning lynching. In her reply, Wells stated that she appreciated the fact that Addams had spoken out strongly against mob violence but protested her assumption that lynching victims had actually committed rape.[9]

Unfortunately for Wells, her relationship to the city's African-American leadership was also complicated. Although they were respected for their accomplishments, she and her husband were often excluded from important coalitions, due largely to their criticism of Booker T. Washington. Thomas C. Holt writes, "In all her chosen roles—clubwoman, settlement house worker, and protest leader—Wells-Barnett was thwarted by the long shadow of Tuskegee" (54). Disagreement over Washington separated Wells and fellow writer and clubwoman Fannie Barrier Williams, whose husband, S. Laing Williams, was "Washington's close personal friend and Chicago agent" (57). Holt concludes that the Barnetts' differences with the Washington camp "might best be described as strategic and tactical rather than ideological or personal." Nonetheless, they "shaped most of the critical encounters in her life vis à vis the black community: the women's club movement, the settlement house, the NAACP, and the Urban League" (59). Carby, however, cautions against interpreting Wells's career strictly in relation to such male leaders as Washington and DuBois. "No men found her easy to work with," writes Carby, "for she was a woman who refused to adopt the 'ladylike' attitudes of compromise and silence. . . . She was, to put it bluntly, an 'uppity' black woman with an analysis of the relationship among political terrorism, economic oppression, and conventional codes of sexuality and morality that has still to be surpassed in its incisive condemnation of the patriarchal manipulation of race and gender" (108). Biographer Mildred I. Thompson summarizes the prevailing attitude toward Wells as "better ignored than opposed" (9).

Sexism and racism forced Wells to be more clever than the average muckraking journalist. Despite her outspokenness, she adapted to accepted gender roles by linking protest to civic duty and the promotion of racial uplift. These activities allowed her to take a confrontational stance in her speaking tours without compromising the ideals of black womanhood.[10] Although clearly working within an African-American oratorical tradition that had long included both men and women, Wells, like the fictional Kate Barrington, claims no special skills as a speaker. In her autobiography, she recounts a conversation with Frederick Douglass in which they compare notes on stage fright. Wells reports that she does not feel anxious, but Douglass still does after fifty years of experience.

"That is because you are an orator, Mr. Douglass," Wells explains, "and naturally you are concerned as to the presentation of your address. With me it is different. I am only a mouthpiece through which to tell the story of lynching and I have told it so often that I know it by heart. I do not have to embellish; it makes its own way" (231). Wells doubtless had different reasons than Peattie for using the mouthpiece image—she almost certainly was not concerned with paradigms of midwestern literature—but both utilize the figure to underline the importance of the message and to mediate gender prescriptions. While Peattie asserts Kate's participation in the "natural" speech of the Midwest, Wells participates in an African-American tradition that often values the story over its teller.

At one point in her narrative, Wells tries to alleviate any suspicions about her personal ambitions by relating that the Slayton Lyceum Bureau had offered her a contract for a series of engagements, with the stipulation that she "leave out any talks on lynching" (226). She "positively refused to consider the proposition for a moment. I felt that having been dedicated to the cause it would be sacrilegious to turn aside in a money-making effort for myself" (227).[11] In the autobiography, we see Wells clearly in charge of decisions about her own career and mission; like the heroines created by Wyatt, Laughlin, and Peattie, however, she also presents herself as authorized by a man, though to a lesser degree than the fictionalized characters. In Wells's case, she takes pains to show the extent to which she has been mentored and approved by Frederick Douglass.

Even though Wells subordinates her own talents and aspirations to the antilynching cause by presenting herself as a plain speaker and distancing herself from the composition of oratory, she elsewhere in her narrative describes her addresses as growing out of her writing. Like the prose of the male authors that Duncan studies, Wells's style, which evidently made her a popular speaker, derived in part from journalism and the need for accessibility. Having taken a position with the *Living Way* early in her career as a writer, Wells "had an instinctive feeling that the people who had little or no school training should have something coming into their homes weekly which dealt with their problems in a simple, helpful way." She writes, "[I]n weekly letters to the *Living Way*, I wrote in a plain, common-sense way on the things which concerned our people. Knowing that their education was limited, I never used a word of two syllables when one would serve the purpose" (23–24). Although European-American journalists and authors were making money trying to represent the speech of African Americans, this African-American reporter, ironically, was conforming to the demands of popular journalism. She recalls that, at the onset of her career in public speaking, her only experience with speech-making had been "public recitations . . . committed to memory" and "talks asking for subscriptions" for the newspaper she ran. Wells's columns in the *New York Age* attracted the attention of a group of East Coast African-American women, who asked Wells to speak about the murders in Memphis at a meeting in New York. "Although every detail of that horrible lynching affair was imprinted on my memory," admits Wells, "I had to commit it all to paper, and so got up to read my story on that memorable occasion" (79).

Whether addressed to a black or white audience, Wells's compositions contained only rare instances of the vernacular. She tried to educate a wide audience through traditional rhetoric and standard written English. Relying on vernacular language would have been at odds with the goals of racial uplift. Wells needed to consider not only the most effective words to convey her message but also their value as examples to the uneducated and as ammunition for those fighting social welfare battles.

Wells's autobiographical style, then, combined elements of social reform, journalism, and oratory (including alliteration, chiasmus, and epistrophe). Like Addams and any talented speaker, though, Wells relates specific incidents in order to make a general point vivid. Wells also resembled Addams in that she wrote her autobiography to call attention to her mission rather than to the details of her personal life. Like Laughlin, she highlighted the power of journalism. Unlike the other Chicago women discussed in this chapter, though, Wells endured discrimination based on race as well as on sex, and her journalism authorized her autobiography, just as service to the race authorized her public speaking and journalism. An analysis by Houston A. Baker, Jr., of the way African Americans entered exclusionary systems of making meaning can explain some of Wells's tactics against racial prejudice. The strategy Baker calls "mastery" or "denigration of form" consists of "a necessary ('forced,' as it were) adoption of the standard that results in an effective *blackening*" (*Modernism* 85).

Wells mastered form, appropriating well-known genres for her own purposes. Many chapters of her autobiography contain or consist of her earlier work in journalism as well as newspaper accounts written about her. Baker comments that "embedded documents"—quoted compliments from European-American writers—made whites acknowledge Booker T. Washington as an effective public speaker (32), and Wells by necessity also had to inscribe official recognition by European Americans into her protests (and her retrospective account of her protesting). During a speaking tour, Wells received more publicity in the British press than she could have received at home. She relates in her autobiography that after each speaking engagement, her English sponsors "purchased not less than one hundred copies of whichever paper had the best report. The next morning's work was to gather around the table in the breakfast room and mark and address these newspapers. They were sent to the president of the United States, the governors of most of the states in the Union, the leading ministers in the large cities, and the leading newspapers of the country" (213–14).

Wells's strategy in addressing the American press involved borrowing the power other newspapers wielded, and her autobiography works in a similar manner. Its narrative includes her own journalism, which contains quotes from other writings about her; the journalism of those who have covered her addresses and who paraphrase her; and selections from or paraphrases of the addresses themselves. The structure becomes repetitious both because she makes similar speeches again and again and because she includes several accounts of the same speech. Readers get lost in the layers of representation. In one instance, she quotes a reporter who quotes her work in which she quotes remarks written about her. A stylistic convention of the time, self-promotion disguised as news also served the editors of the *Dial* and *Poetry*, who frequently reprinted compliments to themselves. In a contest to see how lynching would be represented (and how her campaign against lynching would be remembered), Wells took this practice to an extreme. Mastering a process of image-building and information circulation, she wrapped herself in a web of "blackened" journalism that constituted her authority.[12] Like Sandburg, Lindsay, Addams, and Kate Barrington, she manipulated the symbols and values of the day.

Even though *Crusade for Justice* was not published until 1970, it increases our understanding of Reconstruction and the early twentieth century, provides a context in which to read other Chicago writers, and works to dismantle the ubiquitous association between African Americans and rampant sexuality. Wells's autobiography shows deep concern for the poor, black, and oppressed who fascinated midwestern authors. Along with other female writers, she demonstrates that women, too, took an interest in the working classes and shared the men's admiration for unadorned speech, despite a preference for genteel forms or conservative morals. European-American women often displayed their primitivism and paternalism, but, when they questioned the correlation of colloquial language to men, they, like Wells, disrupted equations that made literary accessibility contingent upon male representations of workers. Rather than merely preserving an antiquated linguistic tradition, then, Chicago's women helped shape the new one and celebrated traditions of their own. Their heritage within the Chicago setting teaches the importance of geography and community for the choices women make in their writing. Women who lectured may not have been appealing everywhere, but in Chicago they were living proof of speeches' potential in the process of social and literary change.

4

"THE BEST CONVERSATION THE WORLD HAS TO OFFER"
Chicago's Women Poets and Editors

If anyone has a delicate and quick way of living it is always not so important to people as if he had a strong and heavy way of saying.

—Margaret Anderson, *My Thirty Years' War*, 250–51

• Women poets in Chicago, like their novelist counterparts, faced a specific set of challenges due to the self-conscious development of a midwestern literature dependent on vernacular language. As female voices were being devalued in the region's publications, women who wrote fiction reminded their readers of women's importance in social welfare movements. The example of women reformers/orators so important to the novelists, however, did not suggest a Chicago style to the poets. Instead, the poets found authority in relation to editors who privileged conversation as a way of doing business. Both Harriet Monroe and Margaret Anderson, founder and editor of *Poetry* and the *Little Review*, respectively, formulated the philosophies of their magazines in response to debates with others, especially women associates. In publishing magazines, they tried to capture the excitement of their own discussions about literature. The intellectual communities these two editors fostered allowed women to experiment with poetry that challenged the conventions of women's speech and its representation. Yet this newfound linguistic freedom did not produce the same results in art and in life, as barriers that had been overcome in one sphere often remained in another.

The work of the women poets and editors appears much more varied thematically and stylistically than does the work of the women novelists. The social conventions of the novel, such as the romance plot, could be forgone in both poetry and editorials. Yet the former was not always a genre where women could find their voices, as evidenced by the eclecticism in much of their production. Editorials, in contrast, almost always projected confidence; as editors, women experienced certainty about the importance of their mission. Choice of genres, then, plays a key role in what women can and cannot say and in how they will express their thoughts. Equally important is the community to which a woman poet belongs and her perception of its stimuli, constraints, and linguistic norms.

The poets discussed in this chapter—Eunice Tietjens, Alice Corbin, Mary Aldis, Florence Kiper Frank, Marjorie Allen Seiffert—challenged and confirmed stereotypes of women's language. Their literary ventures especially merit analysis at a time when feminist scholarship is weighing the benefits of community for women's work, language, and development. Such landmark studies as Nancy Chodorow's *Reproduction of Mothering* and Carol Gilligan's *In a Different Voice* have underlined the significance of women's connections to others for their sense of self and moral reasoning. In *Women's Ways of Knowing,* Belenky, Clinchy, Goldberger, and Tarule also stress the importance of "connected knowing" (Belenky et al. 101) for women's success as learners. Contrasting the results of their research on the learning processes of a diverse group of women with developmental studies done of young men at Harvard, the authors conclude, "For women, confirmation and community are prerequisites rather than consequences of development" (194). Some scholars have argued that consciousness of belonging to a community has shaped women's language, although whether this speech should be celebrated, overcome, or simply acknowledged as differing from men's language remains a subject of debate. After visiting women's colleges, reporter Margaret Talbot, writing in the *Washington Post,* remarks that the kind of conversation praised for promoting women's learning "began to feel a bit like torpor" (17). Encouraging women's development in the context of community also may create false expectations, for, according to Iris Marion Young, many visions of community are counterproductive as models of social and political organization.

In what ways, then, did Chicago's women poets benefit personally and professionally from membership in active literary communities where women held positions of authority? How, if at all, did making conversation a model for publishing inspire them to write poetry? How did they choose to represent speech in an environment that included frequent conversations with other women? How did the privileging of conversation reinforce or combat stereotypes of women's language? Discussing "men's language" and "women's language" poses the risk of overgeneralization. As do many others, Talbot worries that "[s]preading the message that traits like cooperativeness and competitiveness are gender-coded . . . is risky business. It threatens to revive old stereotypes of women as gentle, intuitive caretakers and men as tough-minded aggressors" (19, 30). Despite these dangers, research continues on "masculine" and "feminine" language, and those who work with women (teachers, therapists, and organizers, for example) still wonder how best to facilitate their interactions. This sort of reflection can help to produce conditions under which women find their own voices, but it can also lead to a limiting of women's rhetorical options if only one form of exchange is considered appropriate, ethical, empowering, or feminist. Although the example of this group of Chicago women leaves today's controversies unsettled, their poems, editorials, memoirs, and letters provide a historical precedent for debate concerning gendered forms of oral interaction.

• • •

Scholars have tended to think of modernism in terms of communities—for example, Bloomsbury, Mabel Dodge's salon, various French locations that Gertrude Stein made home, Alfred Stieglitz's gallery in New York, and gatherings hosted by Carl Van Vechten, A'lelia Walker, and Georgia Douglas Johnson. Though individual modern writers have distinguished themselves, each nevertheless remains associated with a particular city or group. According to Cary Nelson, "most poets work within a contextualized sense of what is possible rhetorically: what innovations are made available to them by the work of their contemporaries; what tendencies are to be emulated, transformed, or resisted; what issues it seems necessary (or unimaginable) to address; what cultural roles have been won over or lost for poetry" (70–71).

Eunice Tietjens, who worked for *Poetry* in several capacities and contributed to the *Little Review*, offers several clues to poetry's cultural roles in Chicago. In "A Plaint of Complexity," she describes a woman who manifests a different personality for each of the cities in which she has lived:

> And I've a modern, rather mannish self
> Lives gladly in Chicago.
> She believes
> That woman should come down from off her shelf
> Of calm dependence on the male
> And labor for her living.

She likes men,
And equal comradeship, and giving
As much as she receives.
She likes discussions lasting half the night,
Lit up with wit and cigarettes,
Of art, religion, politics and sex,
Science and prostitution. She thinks art
Deals first of all with life, and likes to write
Poems of drug clerks and machinery. (*Body* 13–14)

Actual experiences in the Windy City accounted for this portrait of the Chicago woman writer and her willingness to stay up late debating controversial subjects. Monroe, Anderson, and their associates, Alice Corbin Henderson and Jane Heap, encouraged literary discussions in an area rich in the desire for them. Early-twentieth-century Chicago's hunger for literary talk, indeed, has achieved a near-mythological status, so much so that contemporary Chicagoans look back with envy. About present-day Chicago, Joseph Epstein writes, "of literary life conceived of as writers living together in some semblance of a community, meeting with one another, talking about one another's work, discussing and arguing and, yes, backbiting about reviews, books, and ideas—of this there is almost none" ("Windy City" 37). He suggests that Chicago's reputation as a once-thriving literary center makes the lack of exchange more conspicuous than similar deficiencies in other cities (38).

Even with regional self-aggrandizement, high hopes for American literature, and nostalgia taken into consideration, turn-of-the-century Chicago appears to have been a marvelous place for European Americans to live the literary life. Membership in a series of groups, clubs, salons, and centers overlapped; for instance, participants in the Whitechapel Club, Cliff-Dwellers, or the Little Room in all likelihood also attended Chicago's "little theaters" or literary discussions at Hull-House. Members of the younger bohemian crowd, who met in Floyd Dell's and Margery Currey's studios near the old World's Fair grounds, knew each other through newspaper work, *Poetry,* or other connections and helped launch the *Little Review.* A few writers strayed into the University of Chicago poetry club. Theaters and lecture series extended Chicago's literary life beyond the circles of professional writers, and William Drake notes that Harriet Monroe took seriously her magazine's motto, "To have great poets there must be great audiences too." She and other poets often lectured to women's clubs, acting as interpreters for the new literary movements (68–72). Visiting artists were assured of a place to stay and to converse late into the night at the home of Harriet

Moody. Restauranteur, caterer, and widow of the poet William Vaughn Moody, she frequently provided visitors with advice, money, and sumptuous meals (Albertine 100).

Although the accounts are probably exaggerated, memoirs and reminiscences suggest the richness of the literary conversation going on in Chicago. Eunice Tietjens writes, "I remember Floyd Dell saying once that he had to brush a poet off his desk every day at the old *Chicago Evening Post* before he could begin work. On *Poetry* we were in a far more delightful state even than this" (*World* 23). Margaret Anderson remembered the conversation in Chicago as superior to that of New York or Paris (*Thirty Years' War* 149–50), and Jane Heap, editorially refuting Harriet Monroe from New York, defended Chicago nevertheless: "I reject all criticism of Chicago, sentimentally. I have seen some of the great cities of the world and many of the finer ones. I know Chicago to the skin and bone. And Chicago has a thrall" (Anderson *Little Review* 273).

We have seen that such institutions as Hull-House gave the women of Chicago a distinct advantage regarding authority and visibility. Having women as editors of two of the prominent literary magazines created an advantage for women as well, but traditional gender roles were also in play. Although the women encouraged each other (see W. Drake 68; Bremer "Lost Chicago Sisters" 218–19), men frequently introduced them to Chicago's literary life or served as mentors. The poet Marguerite Wilkinson befriended Tietjens as a girl (Tietjens *World* 4), but she remembers actually becoming excited about the prospect of being a poet after her first evening at Currey's and Dell's; "I took my own feeble efforts at verse to these people and asked for help. It was George Cook who said the thing that released me, as the right thing said at the right moment has the power to do" (*World* 19). No one matched another area poet, Arthur Davison Ficke, in giving her "endlessly patient" criticism. "He would put his finger with an unerring instinct on anything slack or careless in my work and drive his point home with a fastidious irony that was devastating, but salutary," Tietjens writes (*World* 58). She developed a lifelong friendship with Edgar Lee Masters as well, but nothing indicates that they exchanged works in progress. Anderson's experience was similar in that Clara Laughlin introduced her to Chicago and the process of book reviewing, but Francis Hackett, the *Chicago Evening Post*'s literary editor, gave her her first practical advice (*Thirty Years' War* 22). Marjorie Allen Seiffert, of Moline, Illinois, switched from musical composition to writing poetry, due in part to a group of friends that included Ficke, Dell, Cook, Susan Glaspell, and Harry Hansen. Tietjens remembers that when Witter Bynner and

"Arthur Ficke perpetrated that most amazing literary hoax Spectra, they took in the partnership Marjorie Allen Seiffert . . . and before long they introduced her to us" (*World* 62). Although the communities in which these women found themselves included women of different generations, which thus provided opportunities for role modeling and mentoring, men were crucial to launching the women's literary careers.

The women's memoirs indicate that men valued them as friends and colleagues. Yet, as discussed in chapter 3, the writing of midwestern men often stressed stereotypically male experience and diction, so much so that critics discredited other literature by associating it with femininity. Individuals certainly varied in their literary and actual treatment of women, and the following quotation from Dell's *Women as World Builders* (1913) exemplifies the mixture of admiration, respect, amusement, egoism, and condescension with which area men regarded new women:

> We are, to tell the truth, a little afraid that unless the struggle is one which will call upon all her powers, which will try her to the utmost, she will fall short of becoming that self-sufficient, able, broadly imaginative and healthy-minded creature upon whom we have set our masculine desire.
>
> It is, then, as a phase of the great human renaissance inaugurated by men that the woman's movement deserves to be considered. And what more fitting than that a man should sit in judgment upon the contemporary aspects of that movement, weighing out approval or disapproval! Such criticism is not a masculine impertinence but a masculine right, a right properly pertaining to those who are responsible for the movement, and whose demands it must ultimately fulfill. (20–21)

Dell tries to take feminism seriously but assumes that women are pursuing some sort of self-improvement course ultimately designed for men's benefit. He looks forward to the day when women will be smart, strong, self-sufficient, and still eager to please the opposite sex.

Monroe and Anderson, in a sense, conformed to these sorts of expectations in the literary world. Until recently, their reputations have rested largely on their publication of famous men. To a large degree, they themselves are responsible for the way they are remembered. Of the selections Anderson included in *The Little Review Anthology* (1953), for instance, critical appraisals of men or works contributed by men outnumber by far women's contributions or commentary on them. Although women fared much better in *The New Poetry* anthology (1917), Monroe never tired of promoting what Tietjens referred to as "the great middle western triumvirate Carl Sandburg, Edgar Lee Masters, and

Vachel Lindsay" (*World* 21). Yet for their sustenance and success, both editors relied on women who ultimately shared their goals while expressing disagreement at every step along the way.

Born in 1860, Monroe was part of the older generation of Chicago writers. She resided in the city of her birth for most of her life but traveled extensively. In the 1880s, she worked as a freelance writer and as a critic of music, art, and drama at the *Chicago Tribune*. Her poetry gained recognition when "Columbian Ode" was read at the 1893 World's Fair in Chicago. In 1911, Monroe sought donations in order to establish a magazine devoted exclusively to the support of poets, and in 1912, she launched *Poetry* (Blain 750–51).

Much of the energy Monroe brought to her editorship came from matching wits with other editors and poets. Anyone who expected her to be a woman fond of pleasing others would have been disappointed. Those who knew her characterized Monroe as a fighter (E. Williams 187), and she seemed to enjoy fighting not only to keep *Poetry* going but also for its own sake. In an editorial exchange with the *Dial*, prompted by its attack on Sandburg, for example, Monroe proclaimed, "Next to making friends, the most thrilling experience of life is to make enemies" (*Poet's Life* 313). She recounted in her autobiography that "a succession of clever associate editors shared my work and its rewards, and most inconsiderately their agile minds kept me scrambling for precedence" (317). Writing tongue-in-cheek about interoffice competition, Monroe nonetheless offers further descriptions of intellectual wrestling: "We women of the 'staff' and our visitors used to have lively discussions during those first years, and each new letter from Ezra Pound sharpened the edge of them. Poetic technique was an open forum, in which everyone's theories differed from everyone's else, and the poems we accepted and published were a battleground for widely varying opinions." Monroe follows with an explanation of her theory that "speech rhythm is a universal principle in the poetry of languages both classic and modern" and continues:

> This view, which I still adhere to, aroused much discussion in our office and out of it. I remember one night, after a dinner I had given for Robert Frost, when he and I argued about poetic rhythms till three o'-clock in the morning, against a background of cheers and jeers from three or four other poets who lingered as umpires, until at last Mrs. Moody called up my apartment and asked me to remind my guest of honor (her house guest) that she was waiting up for him. (*Poet's Life* 324–25)

Just as Sandburg could swap folk songs until all hours of the night, Monroe was capable of arguing metrics through the wee hours of the morning.

Harriet Monroe (c. 1905)

According to several accounts, Monroe was especially suited for verbal sparring. Tietjens recalls:

> It took time for me to realize how deeply human and warm-hearted Harriet Monroe was, beneath her often prickly exterior. She grew less austere, less prickly with time, but even to the end there were moments when she froze the blood of the unknowing. I have seen her look up over her glasses at some timid young thing who had with inward quaking offered a distilled essence of soul for her editorial consideration, and blast him, or her, with a caustic criticism so devastating that visibly the edges of his soul seared and curled, like the edges of an egg frying in too hot a pan. . . . But it was also part of Harriet that she was conscious that she did this, and I have seen her realize suddenly what she was doing and undo it swiftly with a sure sympathy that wiped out the sting completely. (*World* 25–26)

Poetry's editor, then, could exchange words in what were considered de-cidedly unfeminine ways, but she also could revert to more traditional forms of interaction.

Monroe's stinging tongue met its match in her original associate edi-tor, Alice Corbin Henderson.[1] Monroe describes Henderson as "look[ing] blandly innocent, never preparing one for the sharp wit which would flash out like a sword. She was a pitiless reader of manuscripts; nothing stodgy or imitative would get by her finely sifting intelligence, and we had many a secret laugh over the confessional 'hot stuff' or the boggy word weeds which tender-minded authors apparently mistook for poetry" (*Poet's Life* 317–18). For health reasons, Corbin Henderson moved to New Mexico in 1916 (Pearce 13). Her subsequent correspon-dence with the Chicagoans confirms Monroe's impression of her acer-bity. Remarkable for their mixture of tenderness, frankness, and occa-sional ruthlessness, Henderson's letters to and from Monroe corroborate Ellen Williams's judgment that no other associate could likewise "chal-lenge and debate Harriet Monroe as a peer" (265) or "say 'Oh, Harriet!' at the right moment" (187). On November 18, 1918, for instance, she wrote: "I am afraid, Harriet, that you are surrounded by people who are willing to say the pleasant thing and the easy thing about POETRY, in-stead of the honest thing and the hard and possibly bitter thing. You may tell me it is none of my business, if you like, but if you are satisfied with POETRY. [*sic*] *I'm* not." Henderson fills the letter with complaints, in-cluding the low rates paid to poets, the "parochial tone" reviewers have been using, the magazine's "obsession" with Midwesterners, and her own feeling of isolation.

Although Monroe never found another assistant as outspoken as Hen-derson, she did not stop searching. In discussing potential candidates for the vacancy left by Henderson's replacement, Tietjens, she wrote in a let-ter to Alice on July 3, 1917, "I want a young radical in the place." When Helen Hoyt came on board, replacing Susan Wilburs, Monroe confided in her Sante Fe correspondent in a letter on September 21, 1918, "I am going to find Helen much more helpful than Susan. She has definite opinions and fights things out with me—even as you used to. And her opinions are more in line with a progressive policy than Eunice's were." Monroe and Henderson seldom complained about a current associate editor, but they always rejoiced in the change of direction and the differ-ent demands initiated by her successor. Ellen Williams contends that by 1916 the magazine's conflicting interests had become too numerous for Monroe to handle gracefully: "If she managed to reconcile Kreymborg with Sandburg, and soothe Lowell and Fletcher about Pound's propaganda while restraining theirs, if the guarantors and the censor were both appeased, and the huge successes of Masters and Frost acknowledged but kept in proportion, if Pound was at least quiet about Lindsay, Harriet Monroe could not indefinitely continue to keep all the important elements of the pattern in balance" (199).

Yet Monroe's conversational emphasis at times must have made these balancing acts almost as pleasurable as fighting. She surrounded herself with people who disagreed and resolved situations by trying to keep everyone happy and a bit unhappy at the same time. In November 1912, for the magazine's second number, she stated her policy in an editorial entitled "The Open Door," which concluded, "The Open Door will be the policy of this magazine—may the great poet we are looking for never find it shut, or half-shut, against his ample genius! To this end the editors hope to keep free of entangling alliances with any single class or school. They desire to print the best English verse which is being written today, regardless of where, by whom, or under what theory of art it is written" (*Poet's Life* 293). Almost six years later, the door was still open to disparate poets and editors alike. On May 10, 1918, Monroe mused in response to Henderson's criticism, "Funny how you and Eunice differ. You are sure to scam poems she loved." Although such disagreements must have wearied her occasionally, Monroe enjoyed the energy generated when one advisor always found another's selections to be a scam.

Monroe made conflicts generated by the literary selections published in *Poetry* a publicity tool. Claire Badaracco writes that she used both the *Dial*'s assaults on *Poetry* and the bad press Pound received in America to generate interest in her enterprise. According to Badaracco, "Monroe distributed excerpts from the 1913 papers as if they were testimonials, on handbills and advertising flyers, sending press releases containing all attacks by the *Dial* to all local and national press. . . . Similarly, Monroe used Pound's crowd bashing to involve an American public that was by and large indifferent to poetry" (45). She foreshadowed state governments' promotions of "regional identity through the 'voice' of its native artists who celebrated their sense of place" (40). This voice, too, she left up for grabs, publishing midwestern men and women whose techniques challenged the style she most often praised.

Poetry confirms Tietjens's impression that Chicagoans (as both writers and editors) preferred poems dealing "first of all with life . . . poems of drug clerks and machinery." Yet, as a champion of the "new poetry," Monroe had a rather flexible definition of "new," printing both men and women who remained committed to old forms or subjects whose inspiration came more from ancient Europe and Asia than from the mountains, prairies, and cities of the New World. Williams finds "Monroe's greatest editorial vice" to be her publication of "[h]ighly literate, intelligent, even ambitious . . . ladies" whose "poetry fades into background music" (276). Although Williams makes a significant point, the same could be said of many of the now obscure men Monroe published, and even of the early James Joyce or D. H. Lawrence.

Monroe's practices as editor present an intriguing paradox in terms of gender roles. She stands accused of being too catholic in her tastes, including in her publication work she and the literary historians who would judge her had good reasons to abhor. *Poetry,* then, stands as a monument not to the best of modern poetry but instead to the editor's inclusiveness—her desire to link as many writers as possible in a diverse community of modern poets. At the same time, Monroe stepped out of the expectations of her gender by freely expressing her opinions, by encouraging raucous discussion, and by often ignoring others' emotions. Talbot observes that "from childhood on, women generally *are* under greater social pressure than men to hold their rhetorical fire in deference to other people's feelings" (30). Although Monroe was an editor, critic, artist, and businesswoman dealing only with highly literate people at a time when lively conversation had not largely been replaced by watching movies, television, and videos, she sets an interesting historical precedent in that she was not running a salon confined to the upper classes. In Monroe's case, contention led to the relative inclusiveness of her magazine. What effect, then, did all of this arguing—and its breaks with gender prescriptions—have on the poetry itself?

Friendly disputes encouraged experimentation, but boldness was not always happily combined with the expectations governing art in the Chicago region. In most cases, literary talk was easier for women than literary practice, where, as Alicia Ostriker writes, literary criticism often can "imply that serious poetry is more or less identical with potent masculinity" (3). Rachel Blau DuPlessis concludes that the place of woman in poetry "creates a staggering and fascinating problem for the woman writer, who is presumably a speaking subject in her work while a cultural artifact or object in the thematic and critical traditions on which she, perforce, draws" (*Pink Guitar* 150). In addition to these general concerns, women poets in Chicago faced the same problems as did the women novelists—that is, that midwestern writers were being celebrated nationally for being representative of the democracy, accessibility, and originality of American art, and these qualities were all linked to virility. Conversing with other artists in this atmosphere must have increased the

pressure to conform, or at least to disagree with others, while responding to their questions (a variation on conformity). The poets appear to
have brought more energy to conflicts about form than did the novelists, and these discussions must have muddled some poets but beneficially challenged others, providing an alternative space to the world of
journalism, on which many of the Chicagoans relied for their models of
plain, accessible language (Duncan 152).

The merits of free verse especially divided the editors of *Poetry,* and
Monroe devoted several editorials to the subject of versification. As they
argued half the night about metrics, Monroe and Frost most likely
agreed that "no absolute line can be drawn between the rhythms of
verse and prose" (*Poets* 287) and that the possibility existed for "a true
science of speech-rhythms" (*Poets* 266). Yet the dispute that kept Harriet Moody waiting must have arisen over the notion of rhythm itself.
Frost did not need free verse to capture the rhythms of speech, whereas
Monroe found that traditional concepts of metrical regularity did not do
justice to the rhythmic possibilities of the English language. She found
ineffectual the terms "iambic, trochaic, dactyllic, anapaestic, etc. . . . not
because they are entirely false but because they are inexact, and are
moreover inextricably associated with false usage" (*Poets* 287). Musical
notations for rhythm more nearly served her own purposes, which included demonstrating that pauses and syllables of varying lengths (not
just stressed or unstressed) made true free verse rhythmic in its use of
"bars" but not necessarily feet (*Poets* 269). Not surprisingly, Monroe did
not single out free verse as the only road to modernity, but she especially encouraged experimentation in selecting poetry for her magazine.
When Tietjens edited a few issues while her boss vacationed, she filled
one entire number with sonnets. She wrote Henderson to say that she
hoped Monroe would not be horrified (7/17/n.y.). Apparently, too
many traditional forms, rather than radical meters, would have assaulted
Monroe's sensibilities.

Monroe cited both Walt Whitman and Emily Dickinson as precursors
to the new poetry movement (*New Poetry* xxxvii, xlii) but gave more attention to Whitman's free verse. Women writers in general did not easily
come to terms with the national and regional fascination with Whitman,
although they themselves shared and perpetuated it. Male Midwesterners Sandburg and Lindsay styled themselves as new Whitmans, but the
nineteenth-century poet's sexual frankness and freedom of movement
were hard for women to imitate.[2] Moreover, while men's voices could
be impersonal, embodying the spirit of the vast American democracy,
women's voices were too often considered the particular voice of local

color, the strong democrat's helpmate or country cousin. How much to promote local writers, especially the archetypal "corn-fed poets of the middle states" (Henderson 11/18/18), became a matter of contention among Monroe, Henderson, and Tietjens. All three backed their male neighbors to varying degrees at different points in their careers, but none wholeheartedly followed the agenda of Sandburg, Lindsay, or Masters in her own work.

Monroe sometimes took machinery as her subject matter or wrote an occasional poem in dialect, but rarely did she use the colloquial style of her letters to Henderson. According to speculation by Ellen Williams, Monroe realized that she, too, belonged to the ranks of the many minor poets she included in her magazine. Pound's influence may have made her poetry less pompous but also more humble in the process (E. Williams 276). When her love of a struggle presents itself in her mature poetry, it does so in terms of an admiration for quiet perseverance, as in "The Water Ouzel," "The Pine at Timber-Line," and "Mountain Song" (*New Poetry* 359–60). Despite her defenses of free verse, much of Monroe's poetry conforms to conventional rhythms and/or rhyme schemes. The same would hold true for the other women poets. Free verse, perhaps because of its association with Whitman, proved difficult for them to sustain. Ostriker finds that American women poets of the modern era usually fit one of two stylistic patterns: "an extension and refinement of the traditional lyric style which concentrated on intense personal feeling" and a style that "was formally innovative and intellectually assertive but avoided autobiography" (44). The women of Chicago fall into the first group; the latter route would have alienated them from the literary conversations going on in that city. Yet Whitman's freewheeling version of the picaresque, which several of the men adopted, was not possible either. Often, these women employed rhyme and regular meter but included more trochees, spondees, phyrruses, and half-feet than typically found heretofore in English poetry. Even though Monroe's free verse consisted of an ordinary vocabulary, she never achieved the relaxed diction of her male counterparts.

Mary Aldis typifies the women poets of Chicago in that her style varied widely from one poem to the next. Her refusal to limit her formal range often resulted in awkward incongruities between style and subject matter, but as Amy Lowell observed in a review of Aldis's *Flashlights,* her dramatic monologues stand out as particularly effective, due no doubt to Aldis's experience as a playwright (318–20). Several of these monologues strikingly combine literary and social concerns. "Reason," for example, is spoken by a battered wife confined in a mental hospital.

In "Ellie," a wealthy woman recalls how her manicurist died from a regimen of "Calwell's Great Obesity Cure" (91).

Of the women Monroe published, Tietjens (1884–1944)—who was a poet, novelist, mother, journalist, and world traveler—came closest to adopting a colloquial voice, but she also wrote in rhymed verse on conventional subjects for women (love, motherhood, loneliness, nature, beauty) much of the time. Even the lightest of these lyrics, however, convey a characteristic zest, as in the description of an infant as "You merry little roll of fat! / Made warm to kiss, and smooth to pat" (*Body* 19) in "The Bacchante to her Babe." Her autobiography provides additional glimpses of the "rather mannish self" portrayed in "Plaint of Complexity." She uses, for example, the type of "strenuous" metaphor for creation preferred by the naturalists (Wilson 511) to describe her memories: "I am choked up with them as an irrigation ditch is choked with debris. For the water to flow clean again among the roots of living I must grub out the lot of them, get down in hip boots, and sweat" (*World* 1). Tietjens admired Masters's "vulgarity, in the best sense—meaning that closeness to earth and the things of the earth which is an undoubted part of every really inclusive genius" (46). In her journalism, too, her preferences flouted gender prescriptions. She remarks that as a war correspondent assigned to France by the *Chicago Daily News,* "I never was really good at the strictly women's stories I was supposed to write. . . . Confronted with the immensity of the war, and with no newspaper training behind me, I simply could not find these things important" (141). No other woman writer from Chicago, and few of the men, excelled as she did at describing a disgusting scene in graphic detail. In this sense, Tietjens anticipates what Ostriker calls "a certain hardness of tone" (12) in contemporary American women's poetry, a posture the latter sees as "a perversely exaggerated version of an acceptable style" (89). Tietjens differed from the men in her occasional overt use of dialect or malapropisms as an assertion of her own superiority, sometimes reflecting on her class-bound relationship to her subject.

If Tietjens most nearly resembled the Sandburg strain of modernism, Florence Kiper Frank came closest to Lindsay's communal aesthetic. Of the Chicago women, she wrote the most blatantly political poetry, including "A Girl Strike-Leader," "The Jewish Conscript," and protests against anti-Semitism and the war. Sidney H. Bremer asserts, "While Vachel Lindsay was popularizing 'primitive' chants in *Congo Songs* (1914), his female colleagues were developing chants as public songs of urban unity" ("Lost Chicago Sisters" 219). Frank's poems of this type include "The Song of the Women," "Speak the Women of the Warring Nations," and "An Interpretive Dance," which begins, "The dance of the mating! / Young men and women out of the morning sunlight / Sturdily advancing, with joyous, proud motion" (40). "In poetry, as in drama," Bremer observes, "Chicago's women emphasize the participatory speech, rather than objectifying description, that characterizes their novelistic style, too" ("Lost Chicago Sisters" 220).

Frank's only volume of poetry, *The Jew to Jesus and Other Poems* (1915), supplements her confident, public voice with subterfuge on the issue of whether women could achieve the stature of Whitman. "Walt Whitman" characterizes the paradigmatic American poet and the figure emulated by some of the midwestern men as "the man with the hardy body . . . whom Nature claims as her own" and "not the effeminate poet, the delicate treader of flowers" (74). The poem implies both that Frank herself is no flower-treader and that as a middle-class woman she can not follow this man who travels alone and sleeps under the stars. Similarly ambivalent, the next selection in the volume proclaims, "I sing the joy of cleanliness and strength." Although emphasizing outdoor life and sensuality, the poem does not use the sweaty imagery that distinguishes much of Tietjens's poetry. The last line concludes, "I sing the well-poised man with splendid health!" (75), but nothing excludes women. Frank, therefore, would appear to be asserting her own right to sing of bodily pleasure and experience. The poem that follows, however, calls into question whether she meant the "well-poised man" generically or not, for "The Quatrain" pleads that the reader not disregard this form despite its short length. This sort of poem does not rely on "the body's strength and grace" but on what happens "within the flashing eye" (76). Eight more quatrains follow, suggesting that the stanza Dickinson chose suits Frank better than sprawling free verse. Frank's volume extends *Poetry*'s interoffice disputes, both affirming and challenging the poetics of Monroe's favorite discoveries. *The Jew to Jesus* implies that, although women like Monroe and Frank certainly could admire Whitman, they never would quite succeed him. Frank's work enraged Henderson, who responded tersely to Monroe's publication of it: "Florence Kiper stuff is the sort that seems to me unforgivable—'*not* poetry'" (12/12/17).

A commuter to Chicago's literary haunts, Marjorie Allen Seiffert expressed an even deeper ambivalence than Frank had concerning women's relationship to language. "Interior" addresses the disparity between a man's and woman's ability to communicate. Seiffert writes, "Words curl like fragrant smoke-wreaths" from the man sitting by the stove. The other occupant of the room "has a bitter thing to learn. / His words drift over her . . . uncomforted / Her pain whirls up and twists like a scarlet thread / Among his words" (Monroe and Henderson *New Poetry* 467). Deborah Tannen's delineation of men's and women's tendencies to strive for *independence* and *intimacy* respectively when communicating helps explain Seiffert's poem (26). The man apparently defies gender socialization and seeks intimacy, but rather than reaching the woman he only increases her sense of alienation. He engages in what Tannen labels "report-talk" rather than "rapport-talk" (76–77), as evidenced by his inability to make any connection with her. The woman's inability to speak as the man does, to make her pain a fragrant wreath, implies an anxiety about making herself understood and performing literarily.

Seiffert's "Ballad of Kinfolk" implicitly addresses writers in voicing discomfort over linguistic differences:

> My forefathers had lusty flesh
>   And long, proud bones;
> Their names, a text, their birth and death,
>   Are carved on stones;
>
> I know my body came from them,
>   But nowhere can I find
> If their hearts fathered my own heart,
>   Their minds, my troubled mind. (*Ballads* 73)

Seiffert's desire to relate to her predecessors, to find their silence something other than obliviousness to her existence, anticipates Adrienne Rich's description of the woman writer looking to literature and not finding "that absorbed, drudging, puzzled, sometimes inspired creature, herself, who sits at a desk trying to put words together" (39).

Occasionally, Seiffert ventured into the "drug clerks and machinery" area but seldom as an attempt at realism. Instead, the scene usually symbolizes some other situation. "The Shop," for instance, deals with women's restricted sphere when compared with what the speaker sees as the relative freedom of working-class men. The first two stanzas describe Swedish, Norwegian, Polish, and Greek men in a blacksmith's shop, their obvious competence at their jobs, and their easy interactions. The poem continues:

> Their eyes are clean and white in their black faces;
> If they like, they are surly, can speak an ugly *no;*
> They laugh great blocks of mirth; their jokes are simple;
> They know where they stand, which way they go.
>
> If I wore overalls, lost my disguise
> Of womanhood and youth, they would call me friend,

They would see I am one of them, and we could talk
And laugh together, and smoke at the day's end. (*King* 80)

The woman feels that her speech cannot be hard, solid, simple, confident, or democratic, many of the adjectives midwestern men used to glorify workers. She is capable of speaking plainly, but womanhood disguises her abilities.

Seiffert never wrote in dialect or slang. Like Lindsay, Frank, Langston Hughes, and the Irish poet Padraic Colum, however, she worked with musical forms, which were often seen as linked to the lives of ordinary people. Alice Corbin collected, translated, and wrote songs as well. A letter to Monroe reveals her ambivalence, nevertheless, about the place of musically inspired poetry in the modern milieu. Asking Monroe's opinion of a series of New Mexican poems, Corbin mused, "Do you think this digression into folk-song and ballads reactionary—or progressive? Quien sabe!" (Henderson 5/11/17). We have seen the pertinence of her question in connection with Sandburg and Lindsay, whose application of folk sources could be both radical and nostalgic. The question of folk songs' progressiveness or retrograde status held particular significance for women, who had problems with credibility when using the vernacular. With ballads, Seiffert strived, like other modern poets, to make the old new. While the rhyming ballad casts her as the feminine singer, this form also allows her to represent sexual double standards and the psychological damage they do to women. "The Ballad of the Cougar" tells the story of a young farm wife's disappearance. We see the clues from the neighbors' perspective: "One window faces toward the wood, / Its casing scored by a pointed claw, / And here a mark that might be blood / Reveals the print of a padded paw . . . ." The bed reveals "tawny hairs from an animal's hide. / Why do they think the woman died?" (*Ballads* 93). The husband has been seen hunting at night and claims that he can not speak of what he knows. The poem ends with reports that a boy has heard the wails of a dying cougar.

The evidence does not reveal whether the cougar came in through the window and onto the bed or off the bed and out through the window. The claws, hair, and blood serve as synecdoches for an attack or a sexual act. The man may be hunting the beast that attacked his wife, or it may be that she turns into a cougar at night. Does the farmer have to kill the cougar in her? Perhaps there is no place for a woman driven to nocturnal rambling. With the ballad, Seiffert places herself within a long poetic tradition, circumvents the issue of vernacular language, and yet responds to modern themes. "The Ballad of the Cougar" works aesthetically and thematically because a cougar-woman is not inconsistent with the often supernatural and violent tone of these songs. Frequently either melancholy or witty, Seiffert's poetry at times takes a metaphysical turn, making her one of the most intellectual of Chicago's poets.

The literal and figurative conversations Monroe encouraged certainly must have stimulated women's creativity, as evidenced by their devotion to her and by the decline in American women's poetic productivity after her death (W. Drake 254). In keeping with her philosophy of the Open Door, Monroe said in the last speech she delivered, "The power and richness of our renaissance is proved not only by the ever-memorable names I have mentioned, but also by the lesser poets who crowd the twentieth-century anthologies, each with a poem or two too good to be forgotten" (*Poet's Life* 471). Her expansion of what counts as power and richness reflects her desire to see a broad swath of poets share in the success. She displays what Rich, quoting Whitman, describes as a "hunger for equals" (214). That hunger involved a sense of "righteous ecstacy" (Tompkins "Fighting" 590) that led to rhetorical posturing and self-promotion but also to the pleasure of straight-talking friendships and an ethic valuing diversity, experimentation, compromise, and perseverance. The poets who gathered around her adopted many of these values and continued their arguments with her in their poems, where they pondered the amount of freedom that language afforded women. The genre itself may have prevented some of these poets from adopting the journalistic standards favored by the men, but participating in a community that demanded they be assertive and often direct may have alleviated their need to prove themselves that way in print.

• • •

For all her love of conversation, Monroe had a magazine to distribute, and her willingness to compromise served her well in regularly meeting deadlines and expectations for quality. Despite Margaret Anderson's differing priorities, Chicagoans formed interdependent communities around both journals. Like Monroe, Anderson published Aldis, Seiffert, and Tietjens. Shari Benstock concludes that Ezra Pound pitted the two magazines against each other by becoming foreign correspondent for both (363). Although his maneuvering was divisive, and the editors criticized each other in public and private, they had key aspects in common with one another, much more so than, for instance, *Poetry* did with the *Dial*.

In 1906, Anderson left college in her third year at Oxford, Ohio's Western College for Women, and returned home. Increasingly restless with her family in Columbus, Indiana, she moved to Chicago at the age

Margaret Anderson

of twenty-two after finding a job as a reviewer (Darnell 20–21). With little in the way of funding or experience, Anderson somehow began publishing the *Little Review* in 1914. At one point, she and her sister, joined often by friends, lived in tents on a Lake Michigan beach after being evicted from their housing. For all intents and purposes, Anderson's editing career ended in 1921 after she was convicted on obscenity charges for publishing excerpts of James Joyce's *Ulysses* (21). Like Monroe, Anderson both confirms and challenges stereotypes of women and their language. Indeed, comparing the philosophies of the two editors proves just how difficult categorizing language usage can be and highlights the dilemmas posed by attempts to prescribe ethical means of speaking.

Although Anderson and Monroe published many of the same people and both admired innovation, their reasons for founding magazines differed. Monroe ultimately saw *Poetry* serving the art of poetry and poets, who, unlike visual artists and musicians, had few sources of funding (*Poet's Life* 241). The *Little Review*, in contrast, has been categorized as a "personal magazine" dependent on the force of the editor's personality (A. Johnson 351–52). Anderson, for instance, would not have troubled herself over such questions as metrics. Jane Heap summarized the magazine's philosophy of art: "TO EXPRESS THE EMOTIONS OF LIFE IS TO LIVE. TO EXPRESS THE LIFE OF EMOTIONS IS TO MAKE ART" (Anderson *Strange* 19). Anderson herself wrote, "As a touchstone, I divide my responses to Art into four categories. The first produces loss of breath; the second, tears; the third, musical reward; the fourth, mental reward" (*Strange* 43). This fourth stage should not be confused with intellectual appreciation, for Anderson also stated, "INTELLECTUALS DO NOT HAVE AESTHETIC EXPERIENCES" (*Strange* 112). She envisioned a magazine that would allow her to live by "filling it up with the best conversation the world has to offer" (*Thirty Years' War* 35). As this goal suggests, the magazine, whose first number appeared in 1914, involved its readers in an ongoing process; it appeared sporadically and with scant attention to production values, at least until Jane Heap signed on in 1916 (Blain 22, 506–7). In 1930, Anderson reflected on her first years as editor, stating, "What I needed was not a magazine but a club room where I could have informed disciples twice a week that nature was wonderful, love beautiful, and art inspired" (*Thirty Years' War* 47).

Being modeled after conversation did not mean that the *Little Review* shared *Poetry*'s enthusiasm for modern speech and diction. On the contrary, John Cowper Powys sounded a note distinguishing art from life, complaining about Dreiser's novels, "[P]eople are permitted to say those things which they actually do say in real life—things that make you blush and howl, so soaked in banality and ineptitude are they. In the true epic manner Dreiser gravely puts down all these fatuous observations, until you feel inclined to cry aloud for the maddest, the most fantastic, the most affected Osconian wit, to serve as an antidote" (Anderson *Little Review* 49). The *Little Review* could be seen as a haven for those Chicago writers with no interest in representing the spoken language of the Midwest (or anywhere else, for that matter).

Yet the magazine borrowed from spoken forms in other ways. Ellen Williams writes, "The *Little Review* seems like a live conversation, full of contradictions, unexpected allusions, and false starts." Broader than *Poetry* in the sense that it was not limited to any one genre, the *Little Review* published essays as well as fiction and poetry. In contrast to Monroe's confident, focused essays, dialogues often served as a format for criticism or editorial commentary. Williams observes, "Margaret Anderson's magazine had a vitality that kept it interesting on the brink of chaos, but the editor was in constant danger of seeming silly" (148).

The epigraph to this chapter indicates that Anderson was well aware of the dangers of her whimsical manner and had experienced scorn firsthand. For almost two decades now, the risks of sounding silly have likewise concerned feminists interested in language.[3] Polemicists such as Sally Miller Gearhart, for example, have urged women to reclaim forms of communication that traditionally have been labeled "weak" or "yielding" (201) as part of a "rejection of the conquest/conversion model of interaction" (200). Although, obviously, print provides us with the only evidence for judging how Chicago's women conducted themselves, they left clues as to the ways they confirmed or challenged these linguistic stereotypes and expectations. In her willingness to appear as the good listener, or the scatter-brained hostess to a sundry gathering of writers, Anderson makes the idea of woman as nurturing environment (Gearhart 200) a method of print communication.

Anderson would not have accepted, however, Gearhart's premise that "any intent to persuade is an act of violence" (195). Like Monroe, Anderson eclectically embraced contributors and preferred seeming disarray to dogma, but unlike her older competitor, who could sympathize with both poets and patrons, Anderson remained utterly confident that she understood everything better than almost everyone else. Her attitude toward persuasion differed fundamentally from that of Heap, whom she called "the world's best talker" (*Thirty Years' War* 103). Heap, Anderson felt, could supply all who listened with the truth. She confesses to making every effort to exhibit Heap's talents wherever people gathered, a tactic that made the two of them "much loved and even more loathed" (107).

> Jane of course didn't like it entirely.
> It's an awkward role for me. You're the buzz and I'm the sting.
> And she didn't at all share my obsession about enlightening the world.
> Why should I care what people think? They should think the way they
> do. I've nothing to say to them. And I don't want them to know what *I*
> think. I believe in silence of the people, by the people and for the people.
> This would send me into a panic. Imagine allowing the intellectuals to
> stagnate in stupidity when a word or two from her would change their
> mental life! (*Thirty Years' War* 108)

While Anderson seems to have taken fewer pains than Monroe to unify her magazine and to maintain continuity, she more adamantly desired to convert others to her elitist philosophy. Although Gearhart's model would categorize both women as violent, they manifested their desires for power differently.

Heap's refusal to attempt persuasion should not be equated with non-violence either. In answer to Hart Crane, who praised the *Little Review* but pointed out that its editorial comments too often "become merely personal" instead of tackling "the real question," Heap explained,

> I make quite an effort to miss the "real question."
> When I was little I could never see a strange cat without shying a stone at it with hoots of challenge. I like cats, I never tried to hit one; I have rescued and even wept over cats, but I like to see them run. There is something in their nature that calls for the stone. Many people call for the stone. . . . Yes, you may call us personal. We try to address our remarks to the person we have in mind rather than, as is the convention, to the (or a) literary state. (Anderson *Little Review* 284)

Here Heap describes an enjoyment of what Tannen identifies as characteristics of male interaction: self-display and vying for advantage (86). Indeed, Thomas J. Farrell writes that the "female mode" of rhetoric shuns "unnecessary antagonism" and "usually does not seek to entertain sympathizers or irritate opponents in the same delightedly deliberate manner as the male mode does" (916). Yet Heap's emphasis on the personal distinguishes the kind of dialogue she claims to like from what Nancy K. Miller describes as the behavior of a prominent male critic, who can debate with colleagues in an extremely harsh manner "and then walk off, and it's as if he'd played a squash game and then went home to take a shower" (Gallop 354). Heap's analogy between literary criticism and throwing rocks at cats shows that she does enjoy it as a game, but consequences are taken into consideration. The positions one takes in literary debates are not disinterested, disembodied, or transcendent, and, her playfulness notwithstanding, Heap refuses to pretend otherwise.

Anderson came to rely on her interaction with Heap in much the same way that conversations with Henderson had honed Monroe's sense of modern poetry. By Anderson's account, Heap believed that her friend could learn the skills needed for adversarial communication, and Anderson worked to convince Heap that talk, though valuable as an end in itself, could serve as a preliminary stage of writing, especially writing for the *Little Review*. Anderson recalls the efforts required to make her reticent partner write, including transcribing her speech in longhand (*Thirty Years' War* 109–10). Heap likewise struggled to teach Anderson about public speaking: "Our talk explored also the psychology of combat. Jane taught me new ways to defend myself, taught me to develop my powers of speech instead of placing myself guilelessly in the enemy's hands, taught me that revenges induce respect. She taught me how to gauge an audience—how to give what was desired or merited but no more—that giving too much was as bad as giving too little. I pounced on this knowledge. I assimilated it. And I have almost never been able to use it" (*Thirty Years' War* 124). Anderson wanted to persuade and did not appreciate strategy; Heap knew strategy but did not wish to persuade. Their dilemma illustrates the difficulty of categorizing masculine, feminine, feminist, or nonfeminist speech because any personal style results from complex individual combinations of knowledge, motivation, perception of audience, sense of gratification, and maybe even genetics, along with communal standards deriving from occupation, family, ethnicity, regional background, gender, class, and age. Anderson ironically makes this point in this chapter's epigraph, in which she protests the privileging of "a strong and heavy way of saying." In this excerpt from her autobiography, she frequently uses the impersonal "man" and "he" to refer to her own predicament as a female speaker, while also parodying Gertrude Stein, whose subversion of "patriarchal poetry" is now considered revolutionary (see, for example, Grahn). An individual's language use, then, easily surpasses the categories outlined by stereotypes, sociolinguists, rhetoricians, polemicists, and literary critics.

Moreover, for Chicago's women poets and editors, the medium often is not the message. Challenging prejudices in art did not always mean overcoming them in other kinds of situations, and, as Monroe's career demonstrates, aggressive speech and love of confrontation did not always produce cutting-edge poetry. Although Tietjens wrote in a direct manner that men often admired, memoirs portray her as one of the "nicest" members of the Chicago group. Monroe describes her as "a clever talker in three or four languages" but "less ruthless than Alice, more tender toward the hapless aspirants whose" poetry they could not accept (*Poet's Life* 324).[4] Tietjens herself lists as one of her tasks at *Poetry* "to soften and tone down in the visiting poets these unexpected attacks of severity that sometimes seized" Monroe (*World* 26). Her ability to write in the virile Chicago voice notwithstanding, she performed the traditionally feminine peace-making role (8/16/17).

Isolation was one of Seiffert's chief complaints as a poet, and, while her poetry eloquently criticized linguistic gender roles, she had trouble surmounting them. Her social graces, rather than any desire to "labor for her living," afforded her access to the literary life she desired, but her "hostess instincts" (Steinem 181) apparently complicated her life as a poet. As Monroe wrote of Seiffert and her friends,

> Their dinners were superlative for food and service, and for a quick fencing of witty talk among intimates intellectually up-to-date. Witter Bynner in those days could keep any party going brilliantly, and with Ficke and Marjorie (the three "Spectrists") to flash back—not to speak of other clever guests—one had need to keep one's wits sharpened. Marjorie, a round-faced red-cheeked beauty, walked into the Poetry office early in 1917, and we became close friends, dipping back and forth into each other's atmospheres. (*Poet's Life* 424–25)

Although Seiffert may have fenced with Monroe and her dinner guests, their rapport appears to have been different in kind than that between Monroe and Henderson. In the years after Monroe's death, Seiffert wrote to Masters, lamenting her sense of having been left behind. Feeling too old to fit in with the younger poets coming to prominence, even if she were to be asked to join their conversations, she confided, "I'm sure I couldn't do as well as blessed old Harriet." Her letter also suggests that, even though she matched wits with her colleagues, she remained aware of her role as hostess. "People have such a horrid habit of dying and moving away, or espousing causes and losing their talent for uncontroversial human intercourse," she complained. "And then when two get divorced, they cannot meet in peace at the same dinner table, and one hates to take sides by inviting either" (10/1/n.y.).

Such pairs as the cougar-woman from "The Ballad of the Cougar" abound in Seiffert's poetry; twins and mirror images occur repeatedly.[5] Moreover, she led something of a double life. As a wealthy mother of two residing in Moline, Illinois, she kept up her obligatory social schedule, spoke to local groups, and entertained her literary friends from the area. At the same time, she could easily travel to Chicago by train to visit Monroe and the others. Vacations also gave her the opportunity to compartmentalize her life. She spent several weeks every year in New York, meeting with publishers and friends, as described in her correspondence with Idella Purnell: "Your letter reached me here, on my annual vacation of two weeks, during which I cease being 'a gentle wife / And a tender mother' and am the remains of a poet instead" (4/16/n.y.).

Basing his analysis on an unpublished story, "Rebellion," William Drake concludes that "Seiffert conceived of her creative life in terms of gender conflict; the role of the creator is male, but it is kept in slavery . . .

by the grip of domesticity." We see her inability to "escape by uniting herself with the liberated woman of her imagination" (115) in another letter to Purnell, in which Seiffert invites her to a soiree she is throwing in New York. "And by the way," she asks, "do you know any lovely creatures of the fair sex who are pretty good poets and would accept a second-hand invitation to such a party?" She goes on to explain that they will need "a poetic cutie to help entertain the men!" (5/12/n.y.). She obviously does not consider herself a mere "poetic cutie" but nevertheless feels obligated to ensure that the men are amused, even at the cost of self-alienation.

While their exclusion from literary history has made a sense of community essential for most women writers, the need to please others also has proved debilitating. Tietjens, for instance, obviously enjoyed the camaraderie of Chicago literary life but found that working at *Poetry* made doing her own writing difficult (8/16/17). Without the support of a strong group of women, several of the poets discussed here in all likelihood would not have achieved what they did. Yet living the literary life may have substituted at times for writing literature, and the expectations of the community may have constrained individual development. That none of Chicago's female poets achieved the stylistic singularity or full-fledged poetics of a Marianne Moore, Gertrude Stein, or Sara Teasdale suggests as much.

Several writers balanced "the energy of creation and the energy of relation" (Rich 43), but no clear formula emerges. Both Harriet Monroe's stern approach and Margaret Anderson's impassioned method effectively kept *Poetry* and the *Little Review* from meeting the same fate as the *Freewoman*, which Pound and his associates took over, changing its name to the *Egoist* (Benstock 364). Writers gravitated to their disparate appropriations of the "masculine right" of "weighing out approval or disapproval." Many found Monroe's warm but prickly nature intriguing, and, as Jane Rule has written of Anderson, "Claiming to be breathless, she more often lets in great gusts of fresh air" (148). Contemporary feminists should be able to learn from their example, but drawing any general conclusions about nurturing yet nonconfining communities is difficult because, despite the differences in their goals, philosophies, and means of communicating, Monroe and Anderson produced many of the same successes and shortcomings.

Chicago's women poets responded to the opportunities and demands of their community by raising the question of prejudices toward women's language, but they found their individual measures of freedom in varying ways. Literary conversations were stimulating and potentially disenabling. Try as they might, Chicago's women could not always escape the imperatives of gender roles in the social ritual of conversation, which could demand the stereotypically feminine behaviors of accommodating others and deferring to their needs. Embracing conflict defied prohibitions but produced mixed results because, according to Tannen, "status and connection are bought with the same currency" (94). In other words, identical words can constitute either an appeal for community or an assertion of superiority, both of which in turn can incite or squelch creativity.

Henderson and Monroe exemplify this ambiguity. As long as they shared the same goal, an energetic frankness and a willingness to give and to receive criticism confirmed their friendship. When conflicts developed over the division of royalties from their anthology, *The New Poetry,* however, their verbal aggressiveness only increased the bitterness as each felt compelled to keep stating her case more and more vigorously. Even though they hired lawyers to arbitrate, they could not quit fighting. Tannen believes that what the listener hears, rather than what the speaker says, often comprises the message of a conversation; she comments, "Each of us decides whether we think others are speaking in the spirit of differing status or symmetrical connection" (37). Although Monroe and Henderson were writing rather than speaking, the deterioration of their friendship demonstrates the importance of reception in forming a sense of community and fostering creativity, for the very characteristics that first cemented their relationship eventually led them to suspect that each wanted an unfair advantage over the other.[6]

As had Monroe and Henderson in the early days of *Poetry,* Anderson and Heap heard disagreement as a form of connection, in part because they perceived it as a welcome violation of social conventions. "The result of our differences," Anderson wrote, "was—argument. At last I could argue as long as I wanted. Instead of discouraging Jane, this stimulated her. . . . I had always been confronted with people who found my zest for argument disagreeable, who said they lost interest in any subject the moment it became controversial. . . . I had never been able to understand why people dislike to be challenged. For me challenge has always been the great impulse, the only liberation" (*Thirty Years' War* 122–23). Anderson not only found arguing with Heap mentally stimulating; she also used this kind of challenge as a metaphor for their lesbian sexuality. The following account of their summer together in California discloses their deepening relationship:

> By early autumn our conversations on the ranch had attained such proportions that our physical lives had to be completely readjusted to them. There was such a spell upon us when our talk went well that it was diffi-

cult—it was destroying—to break it up by saying good-night, going to bed, and calling out from one room to the other our final intellectualizations. It seemed to me that this shock could be avoided with a little ingenuity. So I moved our beds (divans) into the living room, placing them on the floor at each side of and at right angles to the fireplace. Between them I put a low table and we dined in pajamas in order to avoid the brutality of breaking up the conversation to undress. There was nothing to do after dinner but push the table away, light another cigarette, and when we could talk no more fall off to sleep under the impression that we hadn't stopped. (*Thirty Years' War* 128–29)

Like Monroe and Henderson, Anderson and Heap cannot stop arguing, but their inability to conclude has different consequences. Today, too, some women find vigorous debate liberating while others are silenced by it, and feminists disagree about how best to prepare women to participate in public and professional life. Teresa de Lauretis posits that two different desires divide feminists: "*an erotic, narcissistic drive* that enhances images of feminism as difference, rebellion, daring, excess, subversion, disloyalty, agency, empowerment, pleasure and danger" and "*an ethical drive* that works toward community, accountability, entrustment, sisterhood, bonding, belonging to a common world of women" ("Upping the Anti" 266). Elsewhere, Lauretis argues that homophobia prevents many feminists from grasping the interrelatedness of these drives because their combination occurs necessarily in lesbian feminism (30–32). We can see the presence of both of these tendencies in Heap's and Anderson's relationship, where the element of rebelliousness makes arguing pleasurable and emancipatory but also necessitates a stronger connection, including moving beds into the same room, dining in pajamas, smoking together, and falling asleep when they can no longer talk.

Yet Anderson and Heap keep a coffee table between them, at once a sign of independence and intimacy. Although their sexual orientation helped to make disagreement erotic and friendly, they needed both community and individuality, as did the other women in Chicago. We have seen that Monroe desired both to create a worldwide community of poets and to promote *Poetry*'s own identity and status. Heap wished to establish a conversation between Europe and the United States (*Little Review* 272), but, simultaneously, Anderson refused to remain rooted in any one physical community. She moved the *Little Review* to New York in 1917 and to Paris in 1922.[7] The editors of both magazines could bring together independent thinkers because women were breaking out of old forms of socialization by smoking, giving and taking, and talking about art, religion, politics, and sex, but they were not yet in structures where "disciplinarity, professionalism, and institutionalization" (Messer-Davidow 283) could both mold and set them against one another. Even so, these groups rarely crossed boundaries of race or class; the differences over which they disagreed were not the conflicts that divide and anger people on the streets. Perhaps they could all argue freely because, unlike the novelists who focused on social questions, their common mission was largely an aesthetic one. The dependence of artistic creation on privacy certainly had been well established at the time these women wrote (see Olsen), but the shape and success of modernist communities was still being tested.

Just as the results of open disagreement depended on the attitudes of the parties listening, the appearance of challenging stereotypes or reenacting them depends on reception as well as on performance. On the one hand, metrical poetry, elevated diction, and eclecticism can confirm the poets discussed here as literary ladies; on the other hand, their emphasis on women's language, their adaptation of a masculine aesthetic, and their dissatisfaction with any one particular poetic form can be seen as challenges to stereotypes of women's speech and writing. Their projects support both kinds of reactions because prejudices created by language can never be completely undone through language, because women found some stereotypes less confining than others, and because most women combine, in varying proportions, some degree of tradition and rebellion.

Women poets and editors joined the chorus making up the Chicago literary voice by creating implied speakers, imagining poetry as public song, reflecting on women's use of language, enacting policies, and calling attention to situations where women's talk was vital. As editors, Monroe, Henderson, Tietjens, Anderson, and Heap opened avenues to other women and, based on their own needs and desires, mixed traditionally feminine and unfeminine behavior in ways that challenge distinctions between femininity and masculinity. Like Kate Barrington, the heroine of Elia Peattie's Chicago novel, *The Precipice,* these women made the dynamics of their private conversations a basis for public discourse. With a modern sense of reflexiveness, however, they referred to their literary lives, creating the impression that they conducted personal interactions as public debate. The apparent disparity between their art and their lives illustrates the tensions and diverse sources of pleasure within the need for conversation itself. The women poets' productivity, spurred by their conversations, illustrates that the "ordinary" speech favored by Chicago writers came in various forms and could be represented through a number of aesthetic preferences—or resisted altogether. Using conversation as a model for running magazines consolidated artistic communities and allowed for varied exercises of women's authority; what remains of their conversations now makes audible the splendid dissonance behind the lyric poetry of the women that Monroe, Henderson, Anderson, and Heap published.

5

FENTON JOHNSON AND MARITA BONNER
From Chicago Renaissance to Chicago Renaissance

Are there no regular drum-beats? Can't you mark your step to one drum that beats
from the rim of Eternity up through the Dark Ages—through the Middle Ages—through
Renaissances—through Wars and Remakings-of-Worlds—to the same rhythm? . . .

Or is it, after all, a new gait for every new day?

—Marita Bonner, *Frye Street and Environs,* 11

• Two African-American writers demonstrated the limits and
possibilities of Chicago's literary vernacular. Fenton Johnson
and Marita Bonner privileged speech by adapting African-
American literary traditions to a Chicago style emphasizing
everyday language. Partway through his career, Johnson
(1888–1958), a black poet, author, editor, and activist who
spent most of his life in Chicago, turned from old-fashioned
tributes and dialect verse to the "new poetry" movement.
Some of his poetry included the understated free verse, the
urban setting, and the depiction of down-and-out citizens
that were important to the first group of Chicago writers to
win fame. Other segments of his opus tapped folk traditions,
the ways of the rural South, and the African signs prized by
the writers associated with Harlem. Still other poems embraced the experimental versification, political dissent, and
racial consciousness adopted by a second major group of
Chicago writers. Bonner (1899–1971), an essayist, dramatist,
writer of fiction, teacher, and mother of three, served for a
time as an exemplar to younger aspiring writers because she
regularly collected the literary prizes offered by *Crisis* and
Opportunity, the magazines published by the NAACP and the
Urban League (J. Flynn "Marita Bonner Occomy" 222).

Some of the conventions used by other Chicago writers to represent urban life—including impoverished characters, an examination of their working conditions, and the omnipresence of the neighborhood and its influence—can be seen in Bonner's fiction. Her stories and essays likewise converse with writers, black and white, who depicted African Americans as primitives for the purpose either of debasing them or of elevating them as a means to criticize Anglo-American society.

Despite working in different genres, each of these writers has a place in the development of an African-American vernacular aesthetic. Simultaneously, both are crucial to Chicago's literary history because they link the city's early-twentieth-century writing to its Depression- and World War II–era literature. While not unique in illustrating the interdependency of the literature of Chicago and Harlem, their cases demonstrate the give-and-take between black and white authors in their various renaissances, as well as the dangers of not belonging to any one movement or school.

During the Great Depression, Chicago became a hub for talented African Americans seeking employment. Prior to that, African-American writers had some visibility in the city but were largely overshadowed by white writers who depicted black Americans and shared their interest in (and to a small degree knowledge of) black culture. Chicagoans' attention to the power of the spoken word, to ethnic diversity, and to questions of social equality encouraged them to read black authors. Thus, through the efforts of black and sometimes white authors, African-American traditions became part of Chicago's literary heritage.

African-American literature always has depended in part on traditions of music, storytelling, and oratory. J. Saunders Redding writes that the bulk of the nineteenth century was devoted to a "spoken prose literature of protest" developed by black men and women who lectured as abolitionists (21). Literary techniques for incorporating African-American innovations in music and speech, however, have varied with time and become matters of contention. Henry Louis Gates, Jr., argues that nineteenth-century authors reached a consensus and mainly wrote about racial questions. Discussions of form proved more complicated than those about content, though ultimately the two were inseparable. "By the turn of the century," Gates asserts, "a second and more subtle pole of the debate had become predominant, and that pole turned upon precisely how an authentic black voice should be represented in print" (*Signifying* 172).

Discomfort arose especially from the issue of dialect and from concerns about the kinds of characters literature should portray. Although dialect poetry made turn-of-the-century poet Paul Laurence Dunbar famous as "the first American Negro poet of real literary distinction," author and critic James Weldon Johnson saw little future for this method by the 1920s (*Book* 50). In his preface to the first edition of *The Book of American Negro Poetry,* Johnson wrote that readers would probably be surprised to see that black poets were not writing in dialect. Although he felt that "it would be a distinct loss if the American Negro poets threw away this quaint and musical folk speech as a medium of expression" (40), he emphasized the need "to break away from, not Negro dialect itself, but the limitations on Negro dialect imposed by the fixing effects of long convention" (41). Johnson knew dialect's artistic limitations from the inside because he had written dialect poetry as well as hit show tunes (Kinnamon 170–71, 175). With *God's Trombones,* however, he tried to retain the spirit of African-American speaking while at the same time writing in standard English, as had his nineteenth-century predecessor Frances Ellen Watkins Harper (Redding 39).

In Gates's view, Zora Neale Hurston and Sterling A. Brown settled the question of colloquial expression's viability within a literary tradition. These writers "mediated between . . . a profoundly lyrical, densely metaphorical, quasi-musical, privileged black oral tradition on the one hand, and a received but not yet fully appropriated standard English literary tradition on the other hand" (*Signifying* 174). Although the debate over dialect would resurface in the 1970s, critics still pointed to the achievements of these earlier writers. Stephen Henderson speculates, "Perhaps the fear of Black speech in poetry comes from a too vivid recollection of the Dunbar School and the 'minstrel' tradition which preceded it; perhaps it stems from a genuine desire not to be boxed in by the speech of any particular class. It is a groundless fear, I think, which in both poet and critic . . . ignores the technical breakthroughs of James Johnson, Langston Hughes, Sterling Brown, and others" (32).

Though not connected with Chicago in any way, Hurston and Brown made their breakthroughs during the 1930s, when the sources of funding for African-American literature changed. Support for writers was more abundant in Chicago than in Harlem, due in large part to the WPA's Illinois Writers' Project. Richard Wright, Margaret Walker, Katherine Dunham, Frank Yerby, Horace R. Cayton, and St. Clair Drake were young writers on Chicago's WPA payroll, and some of them made the acquaintance of Frank Marshall Davis through the South Side Writers' Group. Both black and white authors joined the Chicago chapter of the League of American Writers, which included Jack Conroy, Nelson Algren, Meyer Levin, and Stuart Engstrand. Gwendolyn Brooks was also living and working in the Windy City. As was the case with the Harlem Renaissance, not all the important writers of the era lived in the same locale; a new metropolis, however, had become the symbolic headquarters. According to Robert Bone, the group of Chicago writers that included

Wright "made of urban realism an esthetic mode" in American literature, much as the Ash-Can School had in American painting (*Down Home* 287). He contends elsewhere that the years 1935–1950 constitute a period "in all respects comparable to the more familiar Harlem Renaissance" ("Richard Wright" 448). As Arna Bontemps remembers, "One way or the other, Harlem got its renaissance in the middle 'twenties, centering around the Opportunity contests and the Fifth Avenue Awards Dinners. Ten years later Chicago reenacted it on WPA without finger bowls but with increased power" ("Famous" 47). Chicago's reenactment of the Black Renaissance occurred at a time when Hughes, Hurston, and Brown were ensuring that vernacular influences on African-American literature remained alive but also liberated from practices that tied them to sentimental racism. Fenton Johnson and Marita Bonner illustrate some of the intermediate phases in the process of affirming this oral aesthetic.

Compared to other African-American writers of their time, Johnson and Bonner have not received much attention, in part because of their own publishing histories but also because they fall between periods or movements. They achieved minor status, never really becoming part of the network of writers who benefited from the opportunities Chicago afforded from the turn of the century and well into the 1920s. Although Theodore Dreiser had left the city, he returned to encourage novices. Opportunities for artists to present and to discuss their work occurred at Jane Addams's Hull-House; at regional theaters; and at meetings of the Cliff-Dwellers, the Little Room, and an unnamed group of younger writers associated with Floyd Dell and Margery Currey. Edited regionally but read nationally, such Chicago journals as *Poetry*, the *Dial*, and the *Little Review* drew attention to Midwesterners, especially Vachel Lindsay, Carl Sandburg, Edgar Lee Masters, and Sherwood Anderson. Newspapers, including the award-winning *Chicago Daily News*, gave authors their start as reporters, reviewers, and humorists. Despite some literary organizations established by African Americans and the presence of journalist-activists Ida B. Wells and Fannie Barrier Williams, Johnson, Bonner, and other black writers found themselves with fewer chances for publication and critical exchange than did their white counterparts. Frank Marshall Davis, who arrived in Chicago in 1927, notes, "There was no contact with the white writers of that period; our worlds were still separate. I recall an abortive attempt to start a writer's group back in 1927. Fenton Johnson, a small, dark brown, very retiring man who had been one of the pioneers in the free verse revolution of the previous decade, was among those attending" (*Livin' the Blues* 131).

Neither Bonner nor Johnson worked full-time as artists. Bonner taught school, raised a family, and wrote in her spare time. Johnson divided his attention between literature and social reform, often viewing the former as a means to the latter. Historically, both have been hard to study because some of their work remains uncollected or was not collected until recently. Even though each could arguably be read in connection with the first Chicago Renaissance, the "Harlem" Renaissance, or the second Chicago Renaissance, questions of geography, style, literary friendships, and considerations of time and space in anthologies, critical works, and literature courses have excluded them from all three. Their residence in or representations of Chicago prevented them from playing key roles during the 1920s, when African-American literature was being funded and acclaimed, or during the subsequent scholarly construction of the Harlem Renaissance period. Moreover, the often segregated nature of Chicago life meant that they did not participate fully in the city's literary conversations, and their involvement in activities other than the arts gave them low profiles during the WPA era. Significantly, stories published during Bonner's lifetime appeared in magazines intended for African-American audiences. Her writing comments disapprovingly on irresponsible sexual mores, lax standards for motherhood, materialism among upwardly mobile blacks, and racism on the part of light-skinned African Americans—in other words, hardly the kind of fare to appeal to European-American literary patrons fascinated by the glamor of Harlem. Johnson gets lost in the process of periodization because his name does not appear in the Chicago poets' memoirs; yet some scholars did not consider him part of the Harlem Renaissance because his poetry resembled that of European-American Chicagoans. Barbara Dodds Stanford writes that Johnson "was active in literary circles, belonging more to the 'new poetry' movement of White poets than to the Negro Renaissance" (303).

Johnson was born in Chicago, attended the University of Chicago, and lived all his life there except for brief periods at Columbia University and as a teacher in the South (Bell 350). His career encompasses several nineteenth-century trends in African-American poetry, anticipates some of the successes of the Black Renaissance, and crosses the literary color line due to his association with *Poetry* and the new poetry movement. In order to understand just how he adapted the Chicago voice of the new poets to his own purposes, we first must examine his place within African-American tradition. He clearly follows nineteenth-century examples in that he composed long poems, poems on conventional subjects irrelevant to race, and poetry in dialect. Joan R. Sherman writes that antebellum poets began a tradition of writing "martial or sentimental tributes to saviors of the race" and that, after the Civil War, James Madison Bell wrote "lengthy odes [that] trace the black man's history and contributions to America in peace and war" (xxiv). In his introduction to *The Book of American Negro Poetry,* James Weldon Johnson lists a number of long nineteenth-century poems, some of which commemorate such historical events as the Emancipation Proclamation (26–27). Especially in his second volume, *Visions of the Dusk* (1915), Fenton Johnson follows in this tradition of extended tributes and histories. The time-sweeping "Ethiopia" covers the accomplishments of, among others, Toussaint l'Ouverture, Nat Turner, and W. E. B. DuBois. "Douglas" [*sic*] also continues the tribute tradition:

> He came when tyranny was ripe, a torch
> That lit the darkened avenue of hope,
> He came from cabin, ragged, poor, and starved,
> And walked among the honoured of the earth. (60)

Sherman writes that with Reconstruction, the rescinding of the 1875 Civil Rights Act, and an increasingly dangerous climate, African-American writers concentrated on creating respectable images of themselves for whites. Consequently, many poets of this era "show a decided bias for neoclassical decorum, heightened poetic diction, and technical virtuosity" (xxv–xxvi). Although his motivations for writing this way may differ from those of nineteenth-century poets, Johnson's first volume, *A Little Dreaming* (1913), includes many examples of this kind of racially neutral poetry. He demonstrates his agility with the conventional singing voice in "The Death of Love":

> Not where Morning shakes the dew
> From the sunshine of her locks;
> Not where Evening breathes her flame
> And the moon so gently rocks. (20)

Johnson further exhibits his virtuosity by writing poems addressed to women of various nationalities. "Kathleen" refers to a Scottish woman; another poem begins "Mine Rachel iss der Ghetto rose" (58); a third ponders what happens "When I speak o' Jamie, sunny lass" (62). He proved himself adaptable to trends in popular verse, including the representation of immigrants and their speech, a subject that also interested fellow Chicagoan Finley Peter Dunne.

European-American contemporaries such as George Ade tried their hand at black dialect as well, prolonging with Johnson and other black authors another nineteenth-century tradition. For readers today, this poetry proves difficult because of the sheer number of words diverging

Fenton Johnson (1915)

from standard written English. Reading phonetically becomes tiresome, as is also the case with Ade's Pink Marsh or Dunne's Mr. Dooley. The following stanza from Johnson's "Fiddlah Ike" illustrates this point:

> De houn' dawg quit his howlin' all de night,
> De lonely moon put on huh brightes' light,
> Fu' all de worl' would lak to heah de chune
> Dat Fiddlah Ike's been playin' thoo de June. (*Visions* 27)

According to Jay Saunders Redding, African-American writers at the turn of the century had to accept stereotypes of black speech. Discussing James Edwin Campbell, a predecessor of Paul Laurence Dunbar, he writes that his dialect verse typifies the writing of "dozens of now forgotten white and Negro writers from the late eighties onward. The conventions as to language and racial character-concept were well established by the time Campbell wrote. They had been sung and stammered, pantomined [*sic*] and danced home by the minstrels. Campbell translated them into rhyme. It remained now only to conform" (53). Johnson clearly continues this conformity. Indeed, the title of *A Little Dreaming* alludes to Dunbar's poem "The Sum." If Johnson modifies Dunbar's example, he does so by leaning toward the lyrical, rather than the narrative, for inspiration, a direction in keeping with the rise of imagism.

The artistic success of Johnson's dialect poems varies as much as his position in the heated debates of the Harlem Renaissance as to how African Americans best should be represented. In his introduction to *Songs of the Soil* (1916), Johnson states, "[T]here is a group within my own race who bitterly oppose[s] the writing of dialect. To that group I say that unless one gains inspiration from the crudest of his fellows, the greatest of his kind cannot be elevated" (iv). Johnson's introduction provides clues as to why his contemporaries opposed such inspiration. "No institution in American life," writes Johnson, "is more exploited than the Negro mammy. Her loyalty to Southern ideals has endeared her to every true son of Dixie. The Confederacy is dead, but Mammy lives on and on, the most glorious tradition in either race" (ii). Despite his puzzling attraction to such an overburdened icon, he demonstrates that he did not choose to write dialect out of simple admiration for all vestiges of the plantation tradition. "Nothing disgusts me more than to read in a metropolitan newspaper an interview with a colored man in which dialect is employed," wrote Johnson (ii). His own use of dialect sometimes resembles the minstrel tradition depicting slow-moving, contented slaves and at other times hints at some of the qualities Gates identifies in African-American vernacular tradition: "the concrete imagery the lines can carry" ("Dis and Dat" 110), "its capacity to carry imagery compactly" (112), and its use of "a new form to convey a new meaning, a meaning insepa rable from belief" (as in the case of the spirituals) (113).

"Washin' Day" combines a few of the best and worst features of John son's dialect poems in the sense that a defiant spirit predominates despite the formal awkwardness. The poem communicates vividly and concisely a resilient woman's sense of humor, as we can see by the first stanza:

> Weddah beats de dickens,
> Heat wid sweat am mixin';
> Pappy wants some bac'n,
> But he's sh' mistaken
>   On dis washin' day. (*Visions* 64)

The use of phonetic spelling, however, makes little sense. For example, the "ea" has been changed in the first word but not in "beats," "heat," and "sweat"; the last does not rhyme with the previous two but contains the same vowel sound as *weather.* Moreover, the apostrophe in the word *bacon* is unnecessary, since the "o" receives little emphasis no matter who is pronouncing it. Discussing the problem of "eye dialect" in general, Sylvia Wallace Holton writes, "These features are somewhat decorative, but they do not represent real dialectal features. Eye dialect calls the reader's attention to the 'difference' of the speech without really contributing to its 'realism'" (58).[1]

Johnson's experiments with dialect, though less successful than those of Hurston, Brown, or Hughes, share with the Black Renaissance (and the work of other Chicagoans) an interest in folk sources. Although the form of much of Johnson's published poetry recalled the nineteenth century, he also forecast the spirit of the twentieth century. In the preface to their anthology, Richard Long and Eugenia W. Collier state, "Fenton Johnson is included in the annals of black American poetry not only because of his poems themselves, but also because his works anticipated the Harlem Renaissance" (283). Bernard Bell writes that Johnson's use of "[l]evee songs like 'Shuffle 'Long' and 'The Song of the Fish Market' provide a sharp contrast to the plaintive note of the plantation songs and are a harbinger of the phenomenal success of the musical *Shuffle Along* (1921)" (350). Like the Black Renaissance writers, Johnson tapped the wealth of the African-American vernacular as represented in the spirituals. He helped to make them familiar to American audiences as literature when *Poetry* anthologized his versions of "The Lost Love," "How Long, O Lord!," "Who is That A-Walking In The Corn?," "A Dream," and "The Wonderful Morning."

Perhaps most interesting, Johnson resembled writers of the Black Renaissance in his application of what Wilson Jeremiah Moses calls "the poetics of Ethiopianism" (156). Moses traces African Americans' use of the Bible verse "Princes shall come out of Egypt; Ethiopia shall soon stretch out her hands unto God" (Psalm 68:31) from before the Civil War to foretell the coming glory of Africa. He explains that "the theme of the rise of Africa became a tradition of reinterpreting the Biblical passage to speak to the experiences of the Anglo-African peoples" and that along with this reinterpretation went a vision of "the decline of the West" (157–59). By the twentieth century, Ethiopianism infused the rhetoric of black nationalists and admirers of Marcus Garvey. Moses writes:

> Ethiopianism may be defined as the effort of the English-speaking black or African person to view his past enslavement and present cultural dependency in terms of the broader history of civilization. It serves to remind him that this present scientific technological civilization, dominated by Western Europe for a scant four hundred years, will go under certainly—like all the empires of the past. It expresses the belief that the

tragic racial experience has profound historical value, that it has endowed the African with moral superiority and made him a seer. (160–61)

Moses explains this mythology in connection with W. E. B. DuBois, but these ideas also help to place Johnson's poetry in the context of early-twentieth-century black nationalism (despite his emphasis on reconciliation between the races). His poem "Ethiopia" begins with an invocation that the poet might use an ancient lyre to sing of "Ethiopia the Queen" (*Visions* 42) and later describes the exile of "the men of dusk" (44). This long poem of tribute then moves through history, celebrating black heroes along the way. Predicting the ascendancy of the "sons of Libya" to the throne (48), the poet vows meanwhile to keep singing Ethiopia's song in a strange land.

In later poems, Johnson puts Ethiopianism in less mystical terms when he predicts the downfall of the West due to World War I. This transition is not surprising, since disillusionment with black citizens' low status as Americans after their sacrifices in the war became a common theme for writers of the Black Renaissance. Noteworthy characteristics of Johnson's war poems include the irony he sees in black soldiers dying for Europe's freedom—a sentiment also expressed in R. C. Jamison's "The Negro Soldiers" (J. W. Johnson *Book* 195)—combined with an apocalyptic vision of the fate of the West. Johnson writes, for instance, of African soldiers fighting in "Europe's last conflict": "Zulu, robbed of land and home, / For the robber bares his heart." Even though these men are not Christians, "the God of Calvary / Will in years unborn be just / To the men who died for men, / Victims of the war god's lust" (*Visions* 19–20). Johnson implies that Europe also will meet with the justice it deserves and he takes a more ominous tone in suggesting the price the West will pay in "Mary On August The First." Here, in reply to the question of why so much violence is occurring, the poem lists the meaningless goals of the war and describes its victors as "The laughing demons of an age whose God is sleeping, / Forgetful of the women and the little children, / And thrice forgetful of the chariot of progress" (*Visions* 60). Many poets wrote in response to World War I, but the basis of Johnson's protest in Ethiopianism clearly links him to the Black Renaissance. The war poetry and the early poetry, including tributes and dialect verse, situate Johnson within an African-American literary tradition. With the exception of poems criticizing the war, this poetry conveys the impression that Johnson was content with the fashions of popular verse and the patterns that historically had allowed black poets to publish at all. By the 1920s, his adaptation of the diction privileged by fellow Chicago poets would make him appear outside of any African-American tradition.

Bonner moved to Chicago in 1930 in order to marry, although she had begun portraying the Midwest's largest city in her fiction in the 1920s. Her writings span the years from 1925 to 1941, but Bonner's collected works, *Frye Street and Environs,* which consists of essays, plays, and short stories published mainly in *Crisis* and *Opportunity,* first reached publication in book form in 1987. As a public school teacher in Chicago, Bonner did not have the political visibility of Ida B. Wells-Barnett, but she challenged social and aesthetic conventions in ways that anticipated bold writing by African-American men and women. Her multicultural vision makes her a Chicago writer, but any claims about that city's influence must be understood in the context of her place in African-American literary tradition.

Bonner began her literary career within the inner circle of the "second echelon" writers of the Black Renaissance (Primeau 247). A Boston native and graduate of Radcliffe, she worked for eight years in Washington, D.C., where she attended Georgia Douglas Johnson's salon on S Street (J. Flynn Introduction xi–xiii). Bonner came out of "the revolutionary tradition in black drama" (E. Hill 408), and her plays foreshadow the developments during the Black Arts movement. Errol Hill locates the beginning of African-American revolutionary theater in an 1823 play dealing with the Black Caribs' struggle in St. Vincent for freedom from the British. Rebellion against American slavery became the next topic for radical black playwrights (426). Hill finds Bonner's *The Purple Flower* ahead of its time because, "instead of going to history for her plot as others had done, Bonner relied solely on her imagination, informed by personal experience." In addition, she used symbolism, not realism, and "attempted to predict the future" (419). James V. Hatch writes, "For the reader who believes that the concepts of the White Devils and Us, and the Call to Revolution have developed since the burning of Watts, *The Purple Flower,* published in *Crisis* in 1928, will be a revelation" (201).[2]

Like Johnson's poetry, Bonner's writing obviously grows from nineteenth-century roots. The moral thrust of her work suggests her indebtedness to such early African-American women writers as Harper and Anna Julia Cooper. Although cherishing far fewer romantic ideals about "the folk" than many other writers of the Black Renaissance or the Chicago Renaissance, Bonner, too, attempted to update traditional oral devices for a new brand of written art. Her fictional style, which often involves repetition of words or sentences, borrows from a tradition of African-American preaching in which the minister and congregation repeat key responses or rhetorical structures. She writes early in an essay, for example:

The Young Blood hungers.

It's an old hunger. The gnawing world hunger. The hunger after righteousness.

—I speak not for myself alone.

Do not swiftly look and think you see and swiftly say, "It is not, most certainly, a hunger for righteousness this Young Blood feels!"

But it is. It is the Hunger. (9)

Concerning the antiphonal quality of the spirituals, James Weldon Johnson notes, "If the words are read, this constant iteration and repetition are found to be tiresome" (*Book* 18). Bonner adapted the characteristic for print by mixing the rhetorical devices anaphora and epistrophe and amplifying the meaning of repeated sentences with what appears in between, as in the following example:

There is only one Frye Street. It runs from the river to Grand Avenue where the El is.

All the World is there.

It runs from the safe solidity of honorable marriage to all of the amazing varieties of harlotry—from replicas of Old World living to the obscenities of latter decadence—from Heaven to Hell.

All the World is there. (102)

Here repetition lends not only an oral quality but also an ironic one. The first "all the World is there" would seem to declare the multicultural character of the neighborhood, but the description before the repetition of the phrase draws our attention to the variation in morality. The second "all the World is there," then, announces that the inhabitants of Frye Street are just like other people and that, even though Frye Street is a poor district, it reflects the moral inconsistency of wealthier areas.

Bonner's frequent use of allegory and small sermons derives from African-American religious practice as well. While thus valuing oral traditions, Bonner also questioned folk ways, and the gritty, urban character of much of her fiction—a quality that situates her fiction within both "Chicago Renaissances"—sets her apart from other writers associated with Harlem.[3]

Both Bonner and Johnson wrote from within African-American literary traditions, especially the growing debate about representations of spoken language. Yet they merged these traditions with styles coming out of Chicago as well. Bell cites Carl Sandburg and Edgar Lee Masters as influences on Johnson's uncollected poetry (350), and, in introducing Johnson in his *Poets of America,* Clement Wood compares him to Sandburg. His similarity to Sandburg forms the basis of Wood's praise, which consists of a description of the poem "Tired" as "[i]n a mood as casually ultimate as Sandburg's better things" (108). According to Frank Marshall Davis's poem "Roosevelt Smith," such an assessment eventually became a cliché with regard to African-American poetry. Davis writes of his young poet, "At twenty-three he published his first book . . . the critics / said he imitated Carl Sandburg, Edgar Lee Masters / and Vachel Lindsay . . . they raved about a wealth of / racial material and the charm of darky dialect" (*Black* 82). Although Johnson has been classified as an imitator of Sandburg, their mutual interest in spirituals, folk songs, the spoken word, and the lives of common Chicagoans indicates the degree to which Chicago writing had been black all along.

Like the new poets of Chicago, the modernists, and the writers of the Black Renaissance, Johnson adapted folk materials to modern times. For him, the mixture began with the war poems. Robert Kerlin categorizes "The New Day" as "one of the newer methods of verse, and yet with a splendid suggestion of the old Spirituals" (102). Rather than simply echoing the old spirituals, however, Johnson incorporates a new spiritual into another form, anticipating Frank Marshall Davis's and Sterling A. Brown's use of song lyrics and changes of rhyme scheme, line length, meter, and implied audience within a single poem. After six lines of free verse describing "the happy shouting of the people" in response to "the Prince of Peace," angels enter, singing a spiritual in tetrameters:

> From the East and from the West,
> From the cities in the valley,
> From God's dwelling on the mountain,
> Little children, blow your trumpets! (Kerlin 103)

The original voice returns in free verse for six more lines before yielding to the fallen black soldiers, who speak of their sacrifices and right to liberty in a manner reminiscent of Johnson's early poems of tribute.

With "War Profiles," published in *The Crisis* in 1918, Johnson grew even more experimental in fusing his many styles. Each of its five sections consists of long lines of free verse. While the poem is written in Johnson's most modern form, it also returns to his early use of black history and Ethiopianism. Stanza by stanza, he alternates historical, biblical, and mythical characters with the more ordinary people of his Chicago portraits. The opening lines again insert a song into free verse:

> The boys of Ethiopia, khaki clad, are bidding farewell to the city of their love. They are swinging the corner to the tune of

"John Brown's body lies a-mouldering in the grave,
But his soul goes marching on." (*Crisis* 65)

The second stanza moves to Port au Prince, where Toussaint L'Ouverture rouses men to fight for France, and the third and fourth stanzas switch to State Street and the Chicago Armory:

No longer walk the merchant, lawyer, doctor, thief and toiler along the lighted path of this merry thoroughfare. The khaki makes all men one.
Old men are peddling dreams of a new Ethiopia; old women and young women long for the laughter of State Street grown sober.

Here the literary interests of Chicago and Harlem clearly overlap. In the final stanza, God hears the cries of the oppressed and declares:

"Man has grown arrogant. The beast in him is not yet dead.
"Go, thou Angel of Wrath, into the four corners of the earth and spill the seeds of discord!
"Freedom shall prevail."

The Angel of Wrath is riding the winds of the earth. Look up, Ethiopia, and be comforted! (*Crisis* 65)

In juxtaposing a number of forms and traditions, Johnson also augurs the modernist collage of Jean Toomer's *Cane.*
The "new poetry" written in the colloquial diction favored by Chicago writers divides the reception of Johnson's work into two phases. This split partially accounts for his falling through the cracks of literary history. Critics' reactions also help us to follow Johnson's unusual weaving of a black tradition and a Chicago aesthetic. Bell finds that his reputation rests on the later poetry (350), and Arna Bontemps comments that Johnson wrote in the manner of Dunbar and then "succumbed to a more rugged influence" (*American* 221). Until recently, Johnson's work has had the advantage of being discussed and anthologized more frequently than that of Bonner, but additional critical attention has not necessarily meant additional admiration. The question of despair commonly arises in connection with the later poetry. In some of the more evenhanded commentary on his work, Long and Collier write, "His poetry deals with real-life situations, which it conveys in simple, concrete language. In halting rhythms and jagged lines he portrays the chaotic world of the black man, caught in the illogic of racism. He hits existential depths more characteristic of later generations than

of his own" (283). James Weldon Johnson comments that Johnson "disregarded the accepted poetic forms, subjects, and language, adopted free verse, and in that formless form wrote poetry in which he voiced the disillusionment and bitterness of feeling the Negro race was then experiencing." He continues, "In some of this poetry he went further than protests against wrong or the moral challenges that the wronged can always fling against the wrongdoer; he sounded the note of fatalistic despair. It was his poetry written in this key that brought him recognition. The central idea of this poetry was startling. Doubtless its effect was in some degree due to the fact that it was an idea so foreign to any philosophy of life the Negro in America had ever preached or practiced" (*Book* 140).

Bell tempers this image of the despairing poet when he discusses Fenton Johnson's magazine editorships. In 1916, Johnson founded and served as editor for *The Champion Magazine,* which surveyed African-American accomplishments in sports and the arts. He folded that enterprise after only one year but began publishing *The Favorite Magazine.* For the duration of that publication's three-year existence, Johnson wrote all its contents under various pen names. In a 1921 issue, he explained that the magazine was part of "The Reconciliation Movement," which, he wrote, "is not a movement of submission. It is a movement of love, that love that reconstructs life through gentle but firm methods. . . . We are materialists, such materialists as Jesus of Nazareth was, as Abraham Lincoln was and as Toussaint L'Ouverture was" (Bell 351). Bell concludes, "The tremendous power of these later poems overshadowed Johnson's early optimistic vision and won him the misleading image as the poet of utter despair" (351).

Certainly Johnson had plenty of reasons for despair. In his essay in *The New Negro,* Charles S. Johnson explains the discrimination African Americans faced in getting jobs and housing in Chicago and describes the 1919 riots there: "Passions flamed and broke in a race riot unprecedented for its list of murders and counter-murders, its mutilations and rampant savagery; for the bold resistance of the Negroes to violence" (283). Nor did Fenton Johnson's experiences with the Reconciliation Movement give him cause for hope. "I know that I am facing ruin and starvation," he wrote in *Tales of Darkest America* (1920). "I know that my dream of a magazine is about to end in the cold gray awakening because of the heavy debt hanging over it and the lack of desire Americans seem to have for the reconciliation of the races. I know that my dream of success in literature is fading because every story I have ever offered a standard magazine has returned to my desk" (8). Despite the increasing number of reasons for Johnson to lose hope over the course of his career, his later poetry constitutes a continuation of, rather than a radical break with, his earlier work. Indeed, recurring themes and techniques make the late poetry a less dramatic shift than it first appears to be.

Like the women poets of Chicago, who each employed a wide range of forms, Johnson tried a number of techniques. A spirit of experimentation unifies his pursuits, whether he was writing dialect in defiance of his colleagues' opinions or borrowing from European-American Midwesterners and their manner of social criticism. This eclecticism, however, made him appear a misfit to critics arguing for an African-American literary tradition. In comparing Johnson's hard-hitting poems with those of Hughes, Redding admits to seeing some similarity but adds, "Essentially, Johnson was a despairing poet, stuffed with the bitterness of DuBois. The attitude of despair, common among the early 'New Negroes,' in Johnson's case is ineffectually sustained" (87). From Redding's vantage point, Johnson—aesthetically but not politically—is a remnant from an earlier literature of protest rather than a harbinger of a new urban realism.[4] To make his point, Redding chooses Johnson's poem "Tired," which begins, "I am tired of work; I am tired of building up somebody / else's civilization." The speaker suggests to his wife that they quit work and take up drinking: "Throw the children into the river; civilization has given / us too many. It is better to die than it is to grow up / and find out that you are colored" (J.W. Johnson *Book* 144–45). Redding writes that the lines about disposing of the children "are supported neither by strong emotion nor apt expression. They are false to the emotion of despair as the Negro feels it, and run counter to an essential quality of spirit" (87)

Angelina Weld Grimké's 1916 play *Rachel* (Hatch 139–72) also dealt with infanticidal feelings, so Redding's sense that "Tired" seems false must have more to do with its means of expressing despair than with the speaker's desperation-produced thoughts. Thomas Kochman has found that people living in African-American communities often feel comfortable speaking with great emotion "due to the greater freedom of assertion and expression allowed in black culture" (51). Although Kochman's analysis risks overgeneralizing and opposing black to white along the lines of emotion and restraint (in the same way that male and female have been opposed along these lines), his observations do have some application for the conventions of representing feelings and the conveying of voice in modern poetry. Compare the opening of "Tired" to the opening of Sandburg's "Mag": "I wish to God I never saw you, Mag. / I wish you never quit your job and came along with me" (*Complete Poems* 13). The implied speaker continues his litany, following the same pattern (13). Sandburg's poetry generally conveys emotion by representing its suppression. The speaker of "Mag," for instance, clearly feels loathing for their situation but voices it by wishing they had not experienced hopeful moments together (buying a wedding dress, taking vows, having children). Repetition intensifies the emotion, as discussed in connection with Bonner, but also emphasizes the flatness of its expression; Mag's husband has few ways to say what he feels, and the means of communication he does possess are distinctly unpoetic.

Fenton Johnson's late poems lack the "essential quality of spirit" to which Redding refers, insofar as they often fail to allude to the musical, oratorical, or colloquial traditions that can give African-American literature a distinctive character. Ralph Ellison, for example, would later understand Richard Wright (who would surpass Johnson's "existential depths") in terms of the blues, which he defined as "an impulse to keep the painful details and episodes of a brutal experience alive in one's aching consciousness, to finger its jagged grain, and to transcend it, not by the consolation of philosophy but by squeezing from it a near-tragic, near-comic lyricism" ("Richard Wright's Blues" 199). Decidedly unlyrical, by contrast, Johnson's vignettes portray people barely capable of feeling any longer. Unlike Masters's creations, they do not speak from the cemetery; instead, they are the living dead. In "The Minister," for example, a clergyman explains that, despite a rigorous theological background, he is replaced at Mount Moriah by Sam Jenkins, who appeals to the congregation's emotions. The poem, like the voices of those sleeping on the hill, concludes on a philosophical note:

> Sam Jenkins can tear a Bible to tatters and his congregation destroys the pews with their shouting and stamping.
> Sam Jenkins leads in the gift of raising dollar money.
> Such is religion. (Kreymborg 81)

The poem not only creates a degree of sympathy for the minister not gifted in a "folk" tradition of preaching but also eschews such devices itself.

Like Gates, Henderson has identified traditional features of "Black linguistic elegance," including "[v]irtuoso naming and enumerating" (33), "[j]azzy rhythmic effects" (35), "[v]irtuoso free-rhyming" (37), "[h]yperbolic imagery" (38), "[m]etaphysical imagery" (39), "[u]nderstatement," "[c]ompressed and cryptic imagery" (40), and "[w]orrying the line" (41). Few of these techniques are to be found in Johnson's later poetry. Critics reacting negatively to this phase of his work probably are responding to such an omission. For African-American writers looking at the landscape of modernism, Sandburg and Masters may have come closest to their own social, political, and aesthetic agendas. The white poetics, however, would have to undergo crucial transformations in sensibility in order to serve black writers, as the reaction to Johnson suggests. More sympathetic to the sort of poet/clergyman displaced in "The Minister," Dudley Randall considers Johnson's poems "marred by clichés and conventional expressions" but otherwise "new and different in their mood of frustration and despair" (220). That they could be found both conventional and new speaks to the hybrid nature of Johnson's poems. As evidenced by James Weldon Johnson's and Redding's responses, stuffing African-American "disillusionment with America" (Randall 220) into the deadpan, colloquial forms used by Sandburg and Masters certainly created a new and different, if not altogether pleasing, effect. Joseph Harrington argues that Johnson wrote at a time when genres and poetic styles were fluid. "If Johnson never reaped the benefit of the intervention he attempted," he writes, "he nevertheless may have seized a hybridized *moment* that allowed later generations of poets, including Hughes and Brooks, to slowly gain the recognition they deserve" (51).

Although, according to some critics, Johnson seems to have dropped the limiting conventions of dialect only to become a ventriloquist for what the white poets considered ordinary speech, he himself began modifying the mood of the realist sketch. Both Sandburg and Johnson, for instance, wrote poems describing washerwomen. Sandburg's "Washerwoman" "sings that Jesus will wash her sins away" (*Complete Poems* 105). Johnson begins his poem "Aunt Hannah Jackson" with her age and a description of her job. Aunt Hannah Jackson talks about the man she once loved, how he was a fool, and how women of every race, class, and creed are equal in that they are fools for having loved foolish men. The poem concludes:

> For rubbing on other people's clothes Aunt Hannah Jackson gets a dollar and fifty cents a day and a worn out dress on Christmas.
> For talking to herself Aunt Hannah Jackson gets a smile as we call her a good natured fool. (Kreymborg 78)

Instead of addressing questions of final salvation, Johnson gives the washerwoman a personal history and puts her in an economic context where the only jobs available for blacks involve doing menial service for whites. Unlike the earlier dialect poem "Washin' Day," the new poetry does not present indestructible personalities but does allow for protest. Johnson's innovation is his indictment of injustice combined with the communal spirit of his early poetry.

Johnson's rugged, despairing poetry often echoes earlier concerns. That Johnson's career did not do a complete turnaround either thematically or emotionally when he crossed the color line is indicated by the vestiges of Ethiopianism in his later work. Once more, comparison with Sandburg illustrates Johnson's methods. Sandburg writes a poem called "The Junk Man"; Johnson writes one called "The Old Repair Man." In Sandburg's words, God "gave Death a job taking care of all who are tired of living" (75). When a clock no longer works, Death tells it to join him; "How glad the clock is then, when it feels the arms of the Junk Man close / around it and carry it away" (76). Johnson writes: "God is the Old Repair Man. / When we are junk in Nature's storehouse he takes us apart." Although survivors may mourn, Johnson offers assurance: "his gentle, strong hands will mold / A more enduring work—a work that will defy Nature— / And we will laugh at the old days, the troubled days, / When we were but a crude piece of craftsmanship" (Bontemps *American* 27). Both poems deal with personal salvation, but "The Old Repair Man" has meaning for a community, whose members will see some sort of transformation, an alternative to "the old days, the troubled days" and ultimately "a more enduring work" (27). I would argue that this poem is the old Ethiopian vision put in terms of the new poetry. Johnson has infused the new form with the old rhetoric about the rise and fall of societies; the poem creates a promising vision according to which the apparently junky status of African Americans can be transformed.

Another example of Johnson's old mythology informing the new work is "Aunt Jane Allen." Johnson opens the poem: "State Street is lonely today. Aunt Jane Allen / has driven her chariot to Heaven" (Kreymborg 78). Whereas the Chicago poets responded to the spirituals, they did not mix registers in this way. With the exception of Lindsay, none of them would have put a chariot on State Street, and only Johnson's poetry, with rhetoric referring to Aunt Jane Allen's sons as "the seed of Ethiopia" (Kreymborg 79), would serve as a reminder that Chicago was a seat of black nationalism. Although Johnson's experiments with the new poetry did not exactly set younger African-American writers on fire, they too worked in free verse, drew on black history, and formulated modern Ethiopian statements, as in Davis's "What Do You Want America?" Davis concludes his chronicle of black contributions to American life with the statement that "Black eyes saw the Pharaohs rise, the Kaiser tumble into / the dust . . . where is the Rome of Caesar? / . . . what lives but the dust which covers all?" (*Black* 23). Sterling A. Brown used similar images from Ethiopianism in "Memphis Blues":

> Memphis go
> Memphis come back,
> Ain' no skin

Off de nigger's back.
All dese cities
Ashes, rust. . . .
De win' sing sperrichals
Through deir dus'. (61)

Brown found a new diction that was neither the old dialect nor the new poetry. For other writers of the 1930s (such as Wright and Davis), Marxism would replace Ethiopianism. Johnson's poetry may bear slight resemblance to the successful work that followed, but, struggling in Chicago throughout both the glamorous days of the Harlem Renaissance and the early years of the Great Depression, he foresaw the need to reconcile a vital oral and literary tradition with the harshness of urban America and the conventions available for representing it.

Johnson made the "Chicago voice" his own. His adaptations of it, however, call into question the assumption of writers and critics that such a voice "naturally" speaks for ordinary people. Johnson's own voice, in turn, became part of a Chicago chorus that, along with WPA programs and other historical circumstances, empowered a new generation of Chicago writers.

Bonner, like Johnson, merges the principles of the first Chicago Renaissance and the Black Renaissance, albeit in a rather different manner. Dealing with racism, gender roles, and the effects of poverty, her *Frye Street and Environs* includes several forms used by both black and white writers. Even though individual works appeared separately over a period of sixteen years, recurring themes and symbols (especially purple flowers and tin cans)[5] give the entire volume an aesthetic unity. As did Toomer, Anderson, Masters, Garland, Tietjens, and Sandburg, Bonner accumulates a series of portraits, sketches, or interconnecting stories in order to represent an entire community. The book's imagism, lyricism, and regional focus make it, along with works by Hughes and Hurston, one of *Cane*'s heirs. At the same time, Bonner drew on a tradition of representing Chicago and its neighborhoods as polylingual and ethnically diverse, as the following description of Frye Street demonstrates: "You know how it runs from Grand Avenue and the L to a river; from freckled-faced tow heads to yellow Orientals; from broad Italy to broad Georgia, from hooked nose to square black noses. How it lisps in French, how it babbles in Italian, how it gurgles in German, how it drawls and crawls through Black Belt dialects. Frye Street flows nicely together" (69). Nellie Y. McKay finds that *Frye Street*'s depiction of a "radically integrated" neighborhood "distinguishes it from most settings in Afro-American literature" (28). While Harlem provided black writers with a sense of community and identity, a

Chicago setting allowed Bonner to explore a disjointed modernity.

Like her fellow Chicagoans, Bonner strived for verisimilitude in representing urban speech. In achieving this aesthetic goal, however, she had to surmount restrictive gender roles and stereotypes of black language. Celebrating the virility of working people would not serve her as it had Sandburg. The dialogues she invented illustrate that she rejected, as Johnson eventually did, the heavy-handed, Dunbar method of writing dialect for a style closer to standard written English. Consider the following example from "Tin Can":

> "You better not start no fighting with some of these niggers, Jimmie Joe!" warned George. . . .
>
> Jimmie Joe drained George's flask of gin this time. "That damn fool says I ain't got the guts to go git Caroline!" he was almost sobbing as he finished.
>
> "Aw let that gal go to Hell!" George blazed. (135)

With the exception of Hurston and the blues singers, few other women of the Black Renaissance wrote such "unladylike" language. Bonner resembles African-American women of her day and earlier, though, in taking a stand on the behavior of her characters, unlike, for example, Hughes, who takes a neutral or sympathetic approach to actions outside the realm of bourgeois society. Yet Nancy Chick discusses Bonner as a trailblazer defying the censoring pressures of other black writers. Her criticism of racism, sexism, and classism "gives Bonner the pessimistic tone that sets her apart from other Harlem Renaissance writers who hoped to show the potential and promise of African Americans through writing 'race uplift' material" (23). Moreover, Bonner anticipates Gwendolyn Brooks in her representation of black women's anger.[6] As it had for Johnson, portraying life in the city of Chicago led to a heretofore unfamiliar tone in black writing.

As we have seen,[7] representing speech in such a way so as not merely to confirm linguistic prejudices usually involved an integration of colloquialisms into narration itself or into the very texture of poetry. In other words, vernacular language cannot stand out from the language of an author, narrator, or superior character. As the excerpt above shows, Bonner did not achieve this kind of synthesis. She represents, however, an interesting development in an emerging African-American vernacular aesthetic because of her variations on Steinian modernism. As discussed in chapter 2, writers throughout the English-speaking world in the modern era preferred literary diction with an affinity to the spoken word, despite what now appear to be vast differences in their poetics. Typically, critics have considered the Chicagoans' contribution to be their emphasis on urban speech, and Hugh Dalziel Duncan attributes their stylistic preferences to their experience as journalists. A number of other influences, though—including oratory, social work, romance plots, folklore, recitation, linguistic purity movements, and African-American literary tradition—enabled Chicago writers to simulate the quality of spoken language in their writing. Gertrude Stein's example also inspired several writers associated with Chicago and its urban naturalism.

Although avant-garde expatriate Stein could be considered an early and extreme American example of "writerly" poetry and prose (see Barthes), her experimental essays and fiction also appealed to the ear, conveying a sense of unrestrained talking. Chicago writer Sherwood Anderson was taken by Stein's methods, particularly her use of ordinary vocabulary. Richard Wright relates that he had enjoyed "Melanctha" but worried about how his admiration squared with Marxist philosophy until he read the story to a group of black workers. Their appreciation reassured him, confirming that "Miss Stein's struggling words made the speech of the people around me vivid" (Stein *Selected Writings* 338). Stein's influence on African-American literature also can be seen when Ralph Ellison's invisible man eulogizes Tod Clifton: "His name was Clifton and he was young and he was a leader and when he fell there was a hole in the heel of his sock and when he stretched forward he seemed not as tall as when he stood. So he died; and we who loved him are gathered here to mourn him. It's as simple as that and as short as that. His name was Clifton and he was black and they shot him" (*Invisible Man* 344). Holton calls Gertrude Stein's "Melanctha" (1909), a portrait of a young African-American woman, "radically experimental" in creating "no real discordance between an established language of narration and directly quoted dialect speech or indirectly reported thought-language" (199–200). Judy Grahn observes, "Among the more remarkable aspects of *Melanctha* is the 'whole field' use of dialect in the text. Because the author has placed herself inside the characters, completely identifying with them from the inside out, their spoken language is used in the whole landscape of text, not distanced from it as is the usual case, not isolated inside quote marks indicating that this special (and hence, 'inferior, ignorant') language, belongs only to the characters and not the (hence, 'superior, educated') author" (143).

Stein suggested speech through polysyndeton (many conjunctions), nonstandard features, and circular logic, as in this statement by Jeff Campbell to Melanctha: "It only is, I am really so slow-minded in my ways, Miss Melanctha, for all I talk so quick to everybody, and I don't like to say to you what I don't know for very sure, and I certainly don't know for sure I know just all what you mean by what you are always saying to me" (*Three Lives* 129). The sound of Stein's prose frequently called attention to the strangeness of words themselves. The following passage describes the developing relationship between Melanctha and Dr. Campbell, who has come to take care of her dying mother: "Jefferson sat there for about an hour reading, and he had really forgotten all about his trouble with Melanctha's meaning. Then 'Mis' Herbert had some trouble with her breathing. She woke up and was gasping. Dr. Campbell went to her and gave her something that would help her. Melanctha came out from the other room and did things as he told her. They together made 'Mis' Herbert more comfortable and easy, and soon she was again in her deep sleep" (130–31). Assonance gives the sentences a singsong rhythm irrelevant to their content, sundering sound and sense. Words ending in "ing" are repeated, but their grammatical function varies; they can be nouns, gerunds, or parts of verbs, even though they all occur at the ends of phrases. The writing is complex, but the sound seems disarmingly simple.

Bonner experimented with the language framing her literary portraits by sounding Steinian rather than by adopting the diction of much midwestern literature, as had Johnson. For instance, "Drab Rambles" opens in the following manner:

> I am hurt. There is blood on me. You do not care. You do not know me. You do not know me. You do not care. There is blood on me. Sometimes it gets on you. You do not care I am hurt. Sometimes it gets on your hands—on your soul even. You do not care. You do not know me.
>
> You do not care to know me, you say, because we are different. We are different you say.
>
> You are white, you say. And I am black.
>
> You are white and I am black and so we are different, you say. If I am whiter than you, you say I am black.
>
> You do not know me.
>
> I am all men tinged in brown. I am all men with a touch of black. I am you and I am myself. (92)

Bonner does not play with words by using them as different parts of speech, but, like Stein, she renders words ridiculous through repetition in varying contexts in which terms come to mean their opposites. "Care," for instance, undergoes this transformation. "White," "black," and "different" become confused as Bonner states that she and the white person confronted are different because one is white and the other is black; yet the black may be whiter, and at the same time the speaker is herself and the person addressed. How, then, can they be different? Bonner creates a world in which the white person addressed has little linguistic authority. To be sure, Bonner and Stein achieve different emotional effects. Stein's long sentences suggest passivity and emotionlessness, whereas Bonner's curt statements suggest defiance. Both, however, create a sense of estrangement.

In her portrayal of an African-American woman, Stein uses repetition in such a way that she deconstructs stereotypes. She uses the word "negro," for instance, in so many contexts that we no longer have any idea what the noun or adjective could mean. Unfortunately, while she questions stereotypes at the level of language, she reintroduces them at the level of images. For example, Melanctha's friend Rose Johnson has a baby whom she simply ignores. Paula Giddings finds this representation of a lazy, ignorant black woman, whose baby dies from neglect, in keeping with the prejudices of Stein's day (82), and William Drake comments, "The depiction of black women as bad mothers is particularly offensive, given the powerful tradition of black maternal strength and wisdom, and the deep concern of some of the black women poets for the fate of children born to a life of undeserved suffering in a white world" (231).

In contrast, Bonner's portrait of a maid in "Drab Rambles" emphasizes the sexual harassment and financial challenges black working women faced as mothers. Although stylistically avant-garde at times, Bonner's fiction also drew on traditions of urban realism and naturalism. Indeed, her exploration of the conditions faced by black workers fills in the gaps left by *The Jungle,* where Upton Sinclair systematically examined the lives of immigrant workers in the meat packing industry but portrayed black migrants as feckless strike-breakers. The other sequence in Bonner's story features Peter Jackson, a ditch-digger who has trouble getting attention for his heart problem at a segregated hospital. When a white doctor finally does agree to examine him, he blames the condition on Jackson's wild living. When Jackson explains that he has had to work very hard, the doctor ridicules him for not getting a better job. Jackson's response softens the doctor, but, by this time, Jackson has become so weak that he loses the paper on which his prescription is written, the doctor's only offer of assistance. Similarly, even though Bonner echoes Stein's language and Sinclair's questions, she does not seem to have much confidence in European-American prescriptions for African-American problems.

Instead of writing in a way familiar to white audiences, Bonner repeats the word "know" in the introduction to "Drab Rambles" to emphasize what only her black audience could know. This strategy suggests the idea of "deformation of mastery" proposed by Houston Baker, Jr., which allows the speaker to create a world in which he or she feels at home and a white audience does not: "the indigenous comprehend the territory within their own vale/veil more fully than any intruder" (*Modernism* 50–51). Bonner's repetition of "you do not know me," coupled with her insistence that "I am you and I am myself" recalls DuBois's implication that African Americans have an unusual perspective on American culture because they observe it as outsiders (vii). Baker explains that the alienating effect produced by deformation of mastery involves reference to an "African ancestral past" (56). In Bonner's case, such a reference becomes a critique of primitivism. She continues in "Drab Rambles": "I am not pure Africa of five thousand years ago. I am you—all men tinged and touched. Not old Africa into somnolence by a jungle that blots out all traces of its antiquity. I am all men. I am tinged and touched. I am colored. All men tinged and touched; colored in a brown body" (92). By juxtaposing such popular notions as pure Africa, old Africa, jungle, and blackness with the concepts of antiquity (suggesting a historical progression) and brownness (suggesting her modern, American condition), Bonner denies an aesthetic that would use her as a symbol linking the present with a timeless past.

For this reason, Bonner's work becomes important for Chicago's literary history. Even before Wright and Brooks shattered romantic stereotypes of poor African Americans, she challenged the notion that, their living conditions notwithstanding, they simply would add life to the Windy City with their songs and speech. Although many Chicago writers depicted African Americans sympathetically, the well-known literature needs to be read alongside Ida B. Wells's analysis of lynching and Bonner's questioning of artistic representations of blacks. In the story "The Hands," for instance, a young woman trying to avoid crying on the bus alternates between imagining the jungle and concentrating on the hands of a man near her, drawing conclusions about the hard, upstanding life he must lead. Joyce Flynn sees this story delineating the two ways African Americans had been presented in American literature: as exotic jungle creatures or as "dutiful, religious, excessively humble characters." Flynn views the story as an expression of Bonner's "skepticism about romantic racialism of either kind" (*Frye Street* xiv). As Fenton Johnson might have wondered after his stylistic changes, Bonner's character on the bus asks at the end of her revery, "Which game, Oh God, must I play most?" (63). For African-American women, neither game seems to have been particularly satisfying. While black men could achieve some sense of authority by means of a persona palatable to white audiences, black women seldom found such empowerment due to the interweaving of primitivism and sexism. In a 1925 essay, "On Being Young— a Woman—and Colored," Bonner asks why black women are seen as "a gross collection of desires, all uncontrolled, reaching out for their Apollos and the Quasimodos with avid indiscrimination" (5). For women, the role of exotic was fraught with too many sexual stereotypes. William Drake points to "the jungle-and-tom-tom image" used by Hughes and other male writers to explain the dilemma the women faced in attempting to reappropriate primitivist symbolism (224). He finds ambivalence about such tribal imagery on the part of some African-American women poets and reads the title of Gwendolyn Bennett's 1920s arts column in *Opportunity*, "The Ebony Flute," as "a feminine alternative to the image of the tom-tom" (227).

Bonner, however, did not produce the lyric sound of the flute but instead mocked the jungle rhythms of the tom-tom. Expressing fatigue with being considered "a feminine Caliban craving to pass for Ariel," Bonner described the existence of young African-American women as "[a] hollow re-echo" (5). Bonner's stories and sketches empty out the representations of blacks with which Americans had grown comfortable and reduce the fascination with primitive rhythms to a hollow echoing.

In addition to questioning appearances, Bonner's fiction warns about the deceptiveness of sounds—a particularly apt warning within the Chicago milieu, where writers challenged and reaffirmed linguistic stereotypes through representations of speech. For example, in the story "Tin Can," a teenage boy, Jimmie Joe, dies in the electric chair for stabbing a fellow gang member during a fight over a girl. The piece reflects themes common to Bonner's writing and black middle-class goals of racial advancement, including the need for mothers to have more time at home and youth to have more in the way of opportunity and recreation. The image of a tin can containing pebbles, with which the story begins, links it to one of Bonner's plays, in which a folk preacher warns his listeners that with God they can be pots of gold but without God they will be tin cans. Bonner emphasizes that, in cans, "[y]ou can hear each hard rattling—like undigested thoughts—hollow. Hollow" (119). This sound comes to symbolize the voices that try to warn Jimmie Joe. Bonner nicknames one of them, a self-important high school principal, the Black Bass Drum. In his attempts at guidance, he too just repeats the same old message (128). The church as well fails to turn Jimmie Joe from his self-destruction or to comfort his mother after his sentencing.

For Bonner, the image of the long-suffering, humble servant of God that Johnson, Sandburg, Lindsay, and O'Neill drew on proves hollow. The execution takes place. Days later, when Ma collapses on the street, the police officers, thinking she is drunk, "rattled off down the street with Ma" (139). Bonner mourns the inability of the oppressed to articulate their suffering but also exhibits a skepticism about the capacity of

any one discourse—from modernism to old-time religion—to bring salvation. The tom-tom alone could produce no new rhythm, only hollow
echoes. To find her own literary style, Bonner looked to Paris, Harlem,
and Chicago, merging symbols from diverse sources, as Sandburg and
Lindsay had, but also making the different modes criticize each other.
Johnson's and Bonner's careers call attention both to the continual re-
newal of the city's literary life through ideas from other parts of the
world and to the constant presence of African-American thought from
Chicago Renaissance to Chicago Renaissance.

Their ancillary positions in the Black Renaissance of the 1920s, their
invisibility within the first Chicago Renaissance (along with that of
African Americans and women in general), and the neglect of the 1930s
and 1940s as a period in African-American literature in particular and
American literature in general (Bone "Richard Wright" 466, Cappetti
6–7) suggest the unwillingness to include more than one sound for any
particular group within American literary history. The two authors discussed in this chapter changed or blended literary voices and in this sense
perhaps best represent a Chicago that included Carl Sandburg and Marjorie Allen Seiffert, Margaret Anderson and Ida B. Wells, Theodore
Dreiser and Elia Peattie. Johnson and Bonner confound the notion of literary voice as transcription of speech, essential song, or heartfelt oratory
and expose the process behind the technical development of such artistic
illusions. In trying to find "a new gait for every new day," Johnson
looked backward in form but to the future in mood; Bonner began the
Black Renaissance as a near-insider but refused to compromise her
iconoclastic style.[8] The American language forged by Sandburg, Masters,
and Lindsay, presumably consisting of the blended songs of all citizens,
did not interest to a great degree either black critics or white publishers
when first echoed by African-American writers. Especially ironic for
Chicago's literary history has been the absence of Bonner's multicultural
vision of uneasy acceptance and multiple prejudices, since she "lived in a
multi-ethnic neighborhood in Chicago, where. . . [she] would frequently
surprise her neighbors by using her fluent German" (Roses and Randolph 168). Experiments with vernacular language, then, offered avenues for writers outside a small circle of Chicago authors, but the goal
of adapting American literary language to the sounds of America's people
called for multiple singers as well as multiple songs.

Every now and then some newspaper or popular periodical attempts to discuss some

literary work and workers of Chicago, and the attempt is usually characterized by woeful

ignorance and an utter lack of perspective. We have never yet seen a published treatment

of this subject that did not defeat its own object; that did not make the subject ridiculous,

however serious the purpose of the writer.

—"Chronicle and Comment," *Dial* 13 (1892): 299

• For over a century, critics have tried to characterize the literature of Chicago, often overemphasizing one aspect of its writers' art. One time period, dubbed the Chicago Renaissance, also has dominated discussion of the city's literature. Now, however, the Chicago Renaissance refers to two different periods, virtually back-to-back, one belonging to the study of American realism, naturalism, and the new poetry, and the other belonging to the field of African-American literature. Robert Bone argues that, if we preserve the label "Harlem Renaissance" to refer to the period in African-American literary history from 1920 to 1935, then we must adopt the appellation "Chicago Renaissance" when speaking of the years 1935 to 1950 ("Richard Wright" 448).[1] Recognizing these two literary periods with the same name may be a good first step toward blurring our former images of Chicago and its writers and rethinking the representation of that city and its speech.

As we have seen with their representation of ethnic groups, the lower classes, and women, Chicago writers affirmed and confronted the linguistic stereotypes of their day. Alluding to the spoken word created new aesthetic effects but often linked them with virility, particularly in the case of

Sherwood Anderson. Most important, we are reminded by Ida B. Wells, Fenton Johnson, Marita Bonner, and the women poets and novelists that representing speech is a literary technique, not a matter of transcription. The degree to which writers could challenge stereotypes often depended on their awareness that speech never can be realistically presented. At their best, Chicago writers expanded their audience's sense of who was ordinary. Mr. Dooley, for instance, helped to convince Americans that newcomers to the nation were, in Clara Laughlin's terms, "just folks." Identifying with a dialect could make that variety of speech seem representative, as Sandburg demonstrated by his eloquent statements about the lives of workers. At its worst, Chicago literature made dialects of American English seem silly or dangerous and prepared the way for stereotypes of white Midwesterners as average, innocent, and typically American.

Descriptions of Chicago literature have depended on and disguised Chicago's multiethnic character. Addams, Sinclair, Sandburg, Laughlin, and Bonner portrayed Chicago as particularly diverse, and Lindsay proclaimed the composite nature of the United States in general. The contributions of Fenton Johnson and Ida B. Wells, dialogues with African-American thinkers, and an awareness of a literary movement associated with Harlem enriched Chicago's literary production. Yet the African-American writers were soon forgotten, and European-American writers became the spokesmen for cultural diversity.

A similar situation arose for women; they played important roles in Chicago's literary world but are now largely overlooked. The women of Hull-House often set the tone of public debate, and William Dean Howells devoted about one-third of his assessment of a Chicago School in 1903 to Edith Wyatt. Such attention might be chalked up to Howells's taste, but it accurately reflected the fact that women such as Wyatt were actively producing journalism, literary criticism, social theory, fiction, poetry, and drama addressing the questions of democracy, class, multiculturalism, and urbanization now associated with the Chicago of that era. By 1917, H. L. Mencken would give no attention to Chicago's literary women, except to mention Harriet Monroe. In 1983, Henry Regnery did the same. Joseph Epstein, however, at about the same time, wrote, "The label 'Chicago writer' suggests a certain heavy-handed realism, a slight crudity of subject matter and presentation, that is far from a clear badge of merit" ("Windy City" 43). His description indicates that the stereotypically masculine elements of the city's literature have been exaggerated to the point that they have come to stand for Chicago literature as a whole. By portraying multiethnic environments, using dialect and vernacular language, and calling attention to women's patterns of speaking, women and African Americans contributed to the literary paradigms associated with Chicago. By adapting oratory, the rhetoric of black nationalism, the discourse of social work, and the conventions for portraying romantic love, they simultaneously competed with what has become the dominant Chicago voice. Revising our impressions of this most famous period in Chicago's literary history should help us to recognize subsequent endeavors, for the definition of "Chicago literature" determines what we are able to see and to appreciate.

The writers of the Chicago Renaissance left a mixed legacy of dealing with the questions of region, race, gender, and class that have dominated twentieth-century literature. Like those of other realists, naturalists, and modernists of their day, their attempts to define the nature of their reality do not answer our questions but do provide clues as to why we are still asking them. These Chicago writers' meditations on language remain part of our social and cultural milieu. Many citizens still challenge the representation of racial minorities and their speech in television shows, films, popular music, and textbooks. We confront fears about linguistic differences in "English Only" campaigns and debates over bilingual education. We shudder at the way women sound in the popular media, especially in advertisements, and marvel at the way social class is made to seem nonexistent on television. Those of us who teach wonder about the most effective ways to disseminate knowledge as we consider national standards, assessment strategies, and questions about what constitutes our history.

In addition to giving us perspective on the fervor of today's debates, considering contemporary questions in relation to the Chicago Renaissance allows us to disengage from some of the clichés about Chicago's literature—that it is plain, simple, all-American, and democratic. The writers discussed here are American voices not because they conform to expectations about Midwesterners' naturalness and normalcy but because they struggle with issues of equality and difference and how to represent them. My goal has been to expand—in one time and place—what counts as an American voice. Fenton Johnson, Marita Bonner, Harriet Monroe, Margaret Anderson, Elia Peattie, Clara Laughlin, Ida B. Wells, Carl Sandburg, Vachel Lindsay, Henry Fuller, William Morton Payne, and Sherwood Anderson are all American voices. Their every word need not be claimed with pride; American voices always have been embedded in the prejudices of their day.

Indeed, the ambiguous legacy of 1900 to 1930 is perhaps best acknowledged by emphasizing that the city's literary history does not stop there. By endorsing the notion of two Chicago Renaissances, I do not wish to suggest that the literature of a region naturally coheres or that a linear progression can be readily traced. Writers benefit from what is going on around them, however, and their own sense of place is shaped by what they read. Both Chicago Renaissances are multiethnic, often urban in sensibility, and created by both newcomers and natives. Realism and naturalism are strong strains in each, and elevated diction does not typify either. Although such poets as Gwendolyn Brooks demonstrate that not all writers of the second Chicago Renaissance felt compelled to represent speech, working for the WPA kept many authors writing in an accessible style. By that time, too, a southern migrant to Chicago spoke for himself. Pink Marsh and Sandburg's black singers prepared American audiences for Bigger Thomas's residence in Chicago, but Richard Wright transcended these romantic stereotypes. The portrayal of exotics by most writers ground to a halt. In Chicago, "the myth of primitivism," writes Bone, "proved unable to survive the harshness of the Great Depression" ("Richard Wright" 467). "The Congo," if you will, is eventually replaced by Saul Bellow's "Looking for Mr. Green" and Wright's *American Hunger*.

Since the *Dial*'s pronouncement on discussions of Chicago's literary history, the city's contribution to literature has grown, as has the quality of criticism on the topic. By embracing the Chicago Renaissance as the name for two literary periods, however, I wish to uphold the tradition of making the subject "ridiculous," for lack of a better term, because potshots, catcalls, vociferous objections, and loud disagreement have often led to the Windy City's literature.

NOTES

INTRODUCTION

1. For the history of Chicago, I have relied on Mayer and Wade's *Chicago: Growth of a Metropolis* and Masters's *The Tale of Chicago*.

2. Barbara Johnson's essay discusses similarities and differences between Derrida (in particular, *Of Grammatology, Speech and Phenomena,* and *Writing and Difference*) and Gates (in particular, *"Race," Writing, and Difference*).

3. Native American, Chicano, and Asian-American authors have often prized the role of an oral tradition within their communities as well, despite a wariness about the spoken word on the part of lawmakers, historians, and, more recently, literary theorists.

4. Masters had, for all intents and purposes, left Chicago by 1924.

1: DIALECT IS A VIRUS

1. By discussing confrontations that occurred among Chicago writers, I replicate Duffey's division of the Chicago Renaissance into a "genteel protest" and a "liberation" (51, 125). In emphasizing the similarities of some of their underlying assumptions, I depart from this pattern.

2. Today proponents of making English the official language of the United States argue that non-English speakers have no way to understand American notions of freedom. See, for example, Cannon.

3. Today, liberals and conservatives can agree that literacy in English is essential for advancement in the United States; making standard English more accessible and palatable to immigrants and the economically disadvantaged would help to reduce social inequalities. Accessibility would involve more courses in language skills, English as a Second Language classes, and tutors than are currently available. Accessibility would also mean offering classes at affordable prices and at convenient times for low-income wage earners. Consider the following example. In 1993 five hundred people participated in a lottery that would determine which fifty immigrants would be allowed to register for free English classes at New York City's Riverside Church (Sontag 29). It takes immigrants from four months to three years to get into free classes throughout the city (34). Children of non-English-speaking immigrants throughout the state sometimes find themselves placed in special education classes because of the lack of other alternatives in their school systems (Schemo 27). Palatability would mean not deprecating dialects considered nonstandard, languages other than English, or the cultures that speak them and acknowledging the physical and psychological violence that traditionally has accompanied efforts to assimilate non-English-speaking people into American culture.

4. Payne worked as a high school science teacher. The story of his education is worth noting. Payne's family was financially unable to send him to college, so when his friend Paul Shorey went to Harvard, Payne received detailed information about the curriculum there and completed the same reading at the Chicago Public Library that Shorey was doing at Harvard (Mosher 181).

5. References to the *Dial* will be cited with a volume and page number.

6. Because the lead editorial in each number of the *Dial* was typically not signed, I usually do not attribute these pieces to any individual. In his work at the Newberry Library, Mosher found that associate editor William Morton Payne wrote a large share of the editorials. When Mosher has attributed a particular column to Payne or when an essay from the *Dial* appears in Payne's *Little Leaders,* I also refer to Payne as its author. Mosher stresses the degree of agreement between Payne and founding editor Francis F. Browne (343) and Browne's desire for a unified philosophy for the magazine (342).

7. See also Payne, "The Future of American Speech," 14:234.

8. For an account of degeneration, see Pick.

9. Marcus and Fischer write that "the main motif that ethnography as a science developed was that of salvaging cultural diversity, threatened with global Westernization, especially during the age of colonialism. The ethnographer would capture in writing the authenticity of changing cultures, so they could be entered into the record for the great comparative project of anthropology, which was to support the Western goal of social and economic progress" (24).

2: CARL SANDBURG AND VACHEL LINDSAY

1. Today they also share the status of largely forgotten poets. Rachel Blau DuPlessis refers to Lindsay as "now an anomalous backwater of poetry" ("'Hoo, Hoo, Hoo'" 668). Reflecting on Sandburg, Joseph Epstein asserts, "Now his work is quite as inert as he" ("People's Poet" 52). T. R. Hummer concludes that Lindsay, Sandburg, and other practitioners of "popular modernism" "increasingly are dead foot soldiers, burnt-out tanks" from "one of the bloodiest poetry wars the world has ever known" (88).

2. For a discussion of the various names "the first fully self-conscious cultural movement among African-Americans" has gone by, see Wright, 14. *A New Negro for a New Century* (Washington et al.) represents an early example of New Negro philosophies.

3. Alain Locke was a Rhodes scholar, Sterling A. Brown and W. E. B. DuBois taught college, and Langston Hughes, Zora Neale Hurston, and Jessie Fauset all had post-secondary degrees. Edgar Lee Masters was one of the few prominent Chicago writers to have graduated from college.

4. The times called for "a new *literary* language" similar to what Mark Twain had achieved but based on urban usage, Duncan maintains, and Chicago sports writers of the 1890s set the tone for the new trend (178).

5. All quotations of Sandburg's poetry are from *Complete Poems.*

6. All quotations from Lindsay, except those from the essays "The Real American Language" and "Mr. Lindsay on 'Primitive Singing'" are to the Spoon

River Poetry Press editions.

7. Philip R. Yannella writes of Sandburg's early poetry, "[A] reader with expectations that poetry was a means of being transported to other worlds, other states of consciousness, would have been mightily disappointed, if not thoroughly outraged" (64).

8. Edgar Lee Masters put forward this version of Lindsay's career in an early biography (*Lindsay* viii).

9. According to Michael Wentworth, Lindsay's tours at the beginning were "naively self-centered and inscribed by his own puckish personality and imagination." Taking part in the Kansas wheat harvests, however, changed the focus of his tours. At that point, according to Wentworth, "Lindsay's reaping assumes a public dimension. Part of a confederacy of fellow tramps who, if only temporarily, are joined by a common enterprise and, at least in Lindsay's estimation, a common purpose. Lindsay, through his involvement in one of the most basic, and even archetypal, of human activities, now reaps for the benefit of the larger community" (37).

10. Engler devotes the first half of the book to models of social change and questions of reception and the second half to an application of these theories to Lindsay's work.

11. Lindsay was not alone in this regard. Pound, too, became interested in signs that would facilitate cultural blending (although his context was not the United States but the world). He encouraged readers to "arrive at meaning by the authority of their own perceptions" as they contemplated the juxtaposition of Chinese ideograms (Froula 7–8).

12. The question of what Lindsay meant by the term *jazz* is complicated. He often used it to symbolize chaos, especially in urban settings, and he hated being labeled "the Jazz Poet." It is difficult to know whether he considered jazz an African American form of music or whether he was referring to popular European-American adaptations of it. Lindsay may have been trying to distance his ideas about American speaking from African-American culture or he may have been rebelling against a label that he felt trivialized his objectives.

13. Gentile explains that the Lyceum began in 1826 as a discussion series involving local speakers and by the middle of the century had evolved into "a professional booking organization" for lecture appearances around the country (18–19). The Chataqua movement began near New York's Chataqua Lake in 1874 with a permanent site for outdoor summer education, and Lyceum performers frequently spoke there (37–39). Chataqua sites spread, and in 1904 Keith Vawter and Roy J. Ellison commercialized the concept, creating a circuit of tent Chataquas (68). As desire for profit increased, quality decreased; the tent Chataquas lost popularity during the 1920s as a result (91). The Lyceum fared better and was gradually replaced by the public programs of colleges and universities (94).

14. Several other critics have commented on the limitations of Sandburg's multicultural vision. See Doreski's analysis of paternalism in Sandburg's newspaper coverage prior to the 1919 Chicago race riots (643–47) and Nielsen's discussion of Sandburg's use of stereotypes and white discourse (34–37).

Yannella offers the following interpretation of how Sandburg's poetry dealt with ethnic stereotypes: "First, very often, Sandburg began by stating the typical grounds, the ethnic slur or the political caricature, for example, upon which the individual was dehumanized in ordinary discourse. . . . After that was done, he provided his own substitute images of the characters, humanizing them, ennobling them, rescuing them from the stereotypes to which they had been consigned (and, arguably, creating substitute stereotypes)" (65).

15. Several critics have discussed how, despite Lindsay's good intentions, "The Congo" manifested the condescending attitudes of his day toward African Americans. See Hummer 64–67; DuPlessis "'Hoo, Hoo, Hoo'" 676–77, 694; and Nielsen 29–34.

16. This relationship often reverses expected hierarchies, as in Melville's "Benito Cereno" or Conrad's *Heart of Darkness*. Lindsay's story "The Golden-Faced People," in which a Chinese man, a Greek, and an African American are lynched, criticizes race prejudice but also plays on racial fears. In a dream sequence, the narrator imagines that the Chinese have taken over and are treating others the way they have been treated in the United States (*Prose* 1:85–93). The story condemns racism but arouses thoughts that the Chinese could indeed conquer America if their numbers were to grow. The critique, therefore, undercuts itself, as do all recourses to primitivism.

17. Price observes that exhibitions of "primitive" art are "customarily heralded with . . . expressions of warmth and pride" resulting from an "unstated premise that such events come about through an enormously commendable broadmindedness and largesse on the part of the host culture." She detects the same dynamic at work in advertising and philanthropic campaigns that stress the equality of races and cultures: "The 'equality' accorded to non-Westerners (and their art), the implication goes, is not a natural reflection of human equivalence, but rather the result of Western benevolence" (25–26).

18. Keillor's efforts suffer from the opposite problem. As Wallace discusses, the homogenous town of Lake Wobegon has come to stand in the national imagination for all of Minnesota, leaving those who are not Scandinavian-American or German-American out of the picture (170–71).

19. Perhaps Sandburg's need to withdraw from admirers had only increased since the days when he left Chicago for a Michigan farm, in part to avoid the stream of schoolchildren who came to his doorstep seeking the author of "Fog" (Detzer 143–44). Maybe the important people he had cozied up to while researching the Lincoln biography had dampened his democratic tendencies (Durnell 35). From 1926 on, Sandburg was invited to write more prefaces and to speak at more engagements than he could possibly manage (Niven 447), so perhaps he did not want to make any additional literary acquaintances. Maybe years of self-promotion simply had turned to self-involvement.

20. Hughes, already a published poet and working as a busboy in a Washington, D.C., hotel, had given Lindsay copies of some of his poems when the latter happened to dine there. Lindsay announced at his reading that evening that he had discovered a busboy-poet. The press took up the story, and Hughes received nationwide publicity (Rampersad 1:116–17).

21. Van Wienen compares Sandburg's "radically innovative and

oppositional" early poetry with the "moderate populism of his later career" (89). Van Wienen's research describes the process by which literary criticism recuperated or caused Sandburg to compromise his social agenda. Yannella argues that Sandburg's socialist commitment and activities persisted longer than biographers have previously acknowledged. I emphasize how the terms of Sandburg's project itself made for enormous contradictions in promoting social equality.

3: RENAISSANCE WOMEN, REFORMERS, AND NOVELISTS

1. This regional emphasis on strength overlaps with what Wilson describes as an "ideological crux" of the naturalists, many of whom were identified with Chicago: "Literature was now visualized as a form of labor. Writing was associated with the outdoors, with strenuous exertion, with the world of men" (512). See also Miller for an analysis of the realists' ambivalence toward the feminine and Engel for a discussion of the "strenuosity" theme in midwestern literature.

2. While there may be enough machismo in Sandburg's writing to inspire such a response, his children's stories and poems about women, including those addressed to Adelaide Crapsey, Inez Milholland, and his daughters, have not entered popular consciousness in the same way.

3. For a discussion of Toomer's influence on Anderson (especially *Dark Laughter*), see Dickerson.

4. On another occasion, though, the perceived propriety of her speech worked to the activist's advantage. Stebner relates that Starr, who often was arrested while walking picket lines with striking workers, once was released because a policeman testified to her having exclaimed, "Leave them girls be." Her lawyer successfully argued that his socially well-connected client never would have used such grammar (89–90).

5. In his article on *The Precipice*, Szuberla discusses Andrews's analysis of twelve "social service and settlement novels" and adds that eight or more additional novels fit his definition of the genre (60). See Raftery for a discussion of three settlement novels.

6. For mention and discussion of Chicago women novelists not included here, see Andrews; Bremer "Lost Chicago Sisters"; and Bremer "Introduction."

7. See Gilbert and Gubar (2:145–46) for an analysis of Gerty Farish's role in the novel.

8. For more on Franklin's Chicago period, see Coleman's biography.

9. See Aptheker's collection, in which she includes Addams's editorial and Wells's rejoinder.

10. See Moses's chapter "Black Bourgeois Feminism versus Peasant Values: Origins and Purposes of the National Federation of Afro-American Women" (*Golden Age* 103–31) for an examination of the role of women's clubs and the theme of racial uplift.

11. In a gloss on "Race Men," Drake and Cayton report that Chicagoans tended to trust a race woman more than they did a race man because she did not "capitalize on her activities" (394). Some residents, though, felt that these women were not likely to affect the opinions of whites (395).

12. Braxton writes, "The quotes authenticate both the text and the author's image of self, as they signal the historical intention in Well's [sic] autobiographical impulse. Unfortunately, they also contribute to the eclectic quality and choppiness of form that characterize the text as a whole" (105).

4: "THE BEST CONVERSATION THE WORLD HAS TO OFFER"

1. She went by Alice Corbin Henderson in her role as editor and Alice Corbin in her role as poet.

2. Ostriker notes that, when Ella Wheeler Wilcox's *Poems of Passion* appeared in 1881, shocked critics protested that she could "out-Swinburne Swinburne and out-Whitman Whitman" (43). By the time *Poetry* was founded, however, Whitman had been even further outdone, in ways that women could not adopt.

3. In 1975, Robin Lakoff's *Language and Woman's Place* presented what the author believed to be the usual characteristics of women's speech. Politeness, ultra-correctness, uncertainty, and humorlessness were some examples (A. Hill 10). Although her methods and findings have been all but rejected, "[i]n her intent to be a goad to future research," writes Alette Olin Hill, "Lakoff has been wildly successful" (18). Ensuing studies have grouped "women's language" with "powerless language" or that of disadvantaged people in general (O'Barr and Atkins). Others have foregone assessments of effectiveness or ineffectiveness while seeking to understand men's and women's conversational styles (Tannen).

4. Being liked for clever talk may have depended on compensatory, non-threatening qualities. Monroe was older than most of the poets with whom she dealt, Henderson was cherubic-looking, and Tietjens was tactful. Few, in contrast, found Amy Lowell's verbal assertiveness endearing. Being a large Easterner put her at a disadvantage whenever she came to Chicago.

5. Ostriker discusses the idea of the monstrous in contemporary women's poetry (74) and observes that "to be a creative woman in a gender-polarized culture is to be a divided self" (60).

6. Monroe and Henderson began the correspondence about royalties in October 1921 and were still airing their differences in August 1922. See their letters in the Alice Corbin Henderson Collection, the Harry Ransom Humanities Research Center, The University of Texas at Austin.

7. Later, Anderson and Heap studied under George Gurdjieff. *The Fiery Fountains* alludes to a breakup with Heap and describes Anderson's relationship with singer Georgette LeBlanc. Anderson writes that adopting Gurdjieff's philosophies was extremely difficult initially, but the book is mainly a testimony to her new outlook. Her relationship to LeBlanc is characterized by harmony and unspoken agreement. Perhaps relationships based on argument cannot endure, or maybe the intense pressure Anderson experienced while studying with Gurdjieff produces this kind of accord.

5: FENTON JOHNSON AND MARITA BONNER

1. For additional examples of the formal analysis of dialect as song and

poetry, see Furia 26–28 and 35–36, and Gates, "Dis and Dat," 110–11.

2. For further discussion of *The Purple Flower*, see Abramson, who calls it a "revolutionary poem of a play" (11), and Chick.

3. See Bone, *Down Home*, for a discussion of pastoralism and the Harlem Renaissance.

4. In response to an earlier version of this essay, Harrington writes that "Redding goes on to paint Johnson as a kind of John the Baptist of African American poetry, wandering in the wilderness of 1903–17. . . . Thus Redding . . . locates Johnson as belonging to a period of 'adjustment'" (49). He adds that both Redding and Kreymborg see Johnson as a radical (50).

5. See Chick for a systematic examination of the purple flowers theme in Bonner's work.

6. Bonner did not write the story from which I have quoted dialogue until 1934; milder language characterizes earlier stories. She is nevertheless unusual for her generation of women with respect to street language. Like Brooks's Maud Martha, she had a sister favored by the family and considered beautiful by the day's standards (which usually meant Caucasian ones) (Roses and Randolph 166). Both Brooks and Bonner denounced color-consciousness within African-American communities. For analysis of Brooks's anger and portrayal of dark-skinned women, see O'Neale 152–53 and Washington.

7. See chapter 1 and Gates's "Zora Neale Hurston and the Speakerly Text" in *The Signifying Monkey* (170–216).

8. Roses and Randolph argue that seeking an audience beyond the readers of *Opportunity* and *The Crisis* would have meant adjusting her style. "The unpublished stories, left languishing in their cardboard notebook for some thirty years in a musty attic in Chicago," they write, "are testimony to her unwillingness to relinquish control of her voice and her vision" (180–81).

CONCLUSION

1. Bone prefers "Harlem School" and "Chicago School" but concedes to the prevailing use of "renaissance" (448).

WORKS CITED

Abramson, Doris E. "Angelina Weld Grimké, Mary T. Burrill, Georgia Douglas Johnson, and Marita O. Bonner: An Analysis of Their Plays." *Sage* 2.1 (1985): 9–13.

Adams, Henry. *The Education of Henry Adams.* 1918. Boston: Houghton Mifflin, 1961.

Addams, Jane. *The Long Road of Woman's Memory.* New York: Macmillan, 1917.

Ade, George. *Pink Marsh.* Chicago: Herbert S. Stone, 1897.

Aldis, Mary. *Flashlights.* New York: Duffield, 1916.

Albertine, Susan. "Cakes and Poetry: The Career of Harriet Moody." *A Living of Words: American Women in Print Culture.* Ed. Susan Albertine. Knoxville: U of Tennessee P, 1995. 94–114.

"An American Literature." Editorial. *Dial* 58 (1915): 37–38.

Anania, Michael. "Poetry in Motion." *Chicago* Oct. 1991: 105–6.

Anderson, Margaret, ed. *The Little Review Anthology.* New York: Hermitage House, 1953.

Anderson, Margaret. *The Fiery Fountains.* New York: Rider, 1953.

———. *My Thirty Years' War.* New York: Covici, Friede, 1930.

———. *The Strange Necessity.* New York: Horizon, 1969.

Anderson, Sherwood. Introduction. *Geography and Plays.* By Gertrude Stein. Boston: Four Seas, 1922. 5–8.

———. *Marching Men.* 1917. New York: B. W. Huebsch, 1921.

———. *Mid-American Chants.* New York: B. W. Huebsch, 1918.

———. *Sherwood Anderson's Notebook.* 1926. Mamaroneck, NY: Paul P. Appel, 1970.

———. *Winesburg, Ohio.* 1919. New York: Modern Library-Random House, 1947.

Andrews, Clarence A. *Chicago in Story: A Literary History.* Iowa City: Midwest Heritage, 1982.

Aptheker, Bettina. *Lynching and Rape: An Exchange of Views.* By Jane Addams and Ida B. Wells. New York: American Institute for Marxist Studies, 1977.

Armstrong, Nancy. *Desire and Domestic Fiction: A Political History of the Novel.* New York: Oxford UP, 1987.

Arshi, Sunpreet, Carmen Kirstein, Riaz Naqvi, and Falk Pankow. "Why Travel?: Tropics, En-tropics, and Apo-tropaics." *Travellers' Tales: Narratives of Home and Displacement.* Ed. George Robertson, Melinda Mash, Lisa Tickner, Jon Bird, Barry Curtis, and Tim Putnam. London: Routledge, 1994. 225–41.

Badaracco, Claire. "Writers and Their Public Appeal: Harriet Monroe's Publicity Techniques." *American Literary Realism, 1870–1910* 23.2 (1991): 35–51.

Baker, Houston A., Jr. *Blues, Ideology and Afro-American Literature*. Chicago: U of Chicago P, 1984.

———. *Modernism and the Harlem Renaissance*. Chicago: U of Chicago P, 1987.

Bakhtin, M. M. *The Dialogic Imagination*. Ed. Michael Holquist. Trans. Caryl Emerson and Michael Holquist. Austin: U of Texas P, 1981.

Bander, Edward J. *Mr. Dooley and Mr. Dunne: The Literary Life of a Chicago Catholic*. Charlottesville, VA: Michie, 1981.

Baron, Dennis. *The English-Only Question: An Official Language for Americans?* New Haven: Yale UP, 1990.

———. *Grammar and Gender*. New Haven: Yale UP, 1986.

———. "The Legal Status of English in Illinois: Case Study of a Multilingual State." *Not Only English: Affirming America's Multilingual Heritage*. Ed. Harvey A. Daniels. Urbana, IL: National Council of Teachers of English, 1990. 13–26.

Barringer, Felicity. "For 32 Million Americans, English is a Second Language." *New York Times* 28 April 1993: A18.

Baym, Nina. "Early Histories of American Literature: A Chapter in the Institution of New England." *American Literary History* 1 (1989): 459–88.

Barthes, Roland. *S/Z*. Trans. Richard Miller. New York: Hill and Wang, 1974.

Belenky, Mary Field, Blythe McVicker Clinchy, Nancy Rule Goldberger, and Jill Mattuck Tarule. *Women's Ways of Knowing: The Development of Self, Voice, and Mind*. New York: Harper Collins, 1986.

Bell, Bernard W. "Fenton Johnson." *Dictionary of American Negro Biography*. Ed. Rayford W. Logan and Michael R. Winston. New York: Norton, 1982. 350–51.

Benstock, Shari. *Women of the Left Bank: Paris, 1900–1940*. Austin: U of Texas P, 1986.

Berry, Faith. *Before and beyond Harlem: A Biography of Langston Hughes*. New York: Wings-Random House, 1995.

Berry, Wendell. *The Unsettling of America: Culture and Agriculture*. San Francisco: Sierra Club, 1977.

Bicknell, Percy F. "Conversational English." *Dial* 21 (1896): 107–8.

———. "The Language of the Unlettered." *Dial* 56 (1914): 405–7.

Blain, Virginia, Isobel Grundy, and Patricia Clements. *The Feminist Companion to Literature in English*. New Haven: Yale UP, 1990.

Boelhower, William. *Through a Glass Darkly: Ethnic Semiosis in American Literature*. New York: Oxford UP, 1987.

Bondurant, Alexander L. Letter. "Dialect in the United States." *Dial* 18 (1895): 104–5.

Bone, Robert. *Down Home: Origins of the Afro-American Short Story*. 1975. New York: Columbia UP, 1988.

———. "Richard Wright and the Chicago Renaissance." *Callaloo* 9 (1986): 446–68.

Bonner, Marita. *Frye Street and Environs*. Ed. Joyce Flynn and Joyce Occomy Stricklin. Boston: Beacon, 1987.

Bontemps, Arna. *American Negro Poetry*. New York: Hill and Wang, 1974.

———. "Famous WPA Authors." *Negro Digest* 8.8 (1950): 43–47.

Boyer, Paul S. "Inez Milholland Boissevain." *Notable American Women, 1607–1950.* Ed. Edward T. James, Janet Wilson James, and Paul S. Boyer. Vol. 1. Cambridge: Belknap, 1971. 3 vols.

Braxton, Joanne M. "Crusader for Justice: Ida B. Wells." *African American Autobiography.* Ed. William L. Andrews. Englewood Cliffs: Prentice Hall, 1993. 90–112.

Bremer, Sidney H. Introduction. *The Precipice.* By Elia W. Peattie. Urbana: U of Illinois P, 1989. ix–xxvi.

———. "Willa Cather's Lost Chicago Sisters." *Women Writers and the City: Essays in Feminist Literary Criticism.* Ed. Susan Merrill Squier. Knoxville: U of Tennessee P, 1984. 210–29.

"Briefs on New Books." *Dial* 32 (1902): 204–8.

———. *Dial* 49 (1910): 335–38.

Brown, Sterling A. *Southern Road.* 1932. Boston: Beacon, 1974.

Bryan, Mary Lynn McCree, and Allen F. Davis, eds. *One-Hundred Years at Hull-House.* Bloomington: Indiana UP, 1990.

Cannon, Ilvi J. Letter. *New York Times* 30 Nov. 1995: A28.

Cappetti, Carla. *Writing Chicago: Modernism, Ethnography, and the Novel.* New York: Columbia UP, 1993.

Carby, Hazel V. *Reconstructing Womanhood: The Emergence of the Afro-American Woman Novelist.* New York: Oxford UP, 1987.

"Casual Comment: The Anglicity of the English Language." *Dial* 56 (1914): 91.

"Casual Comment: A Bit of Boston-Made Slang." *Dial* 47 (1909): 62–63.

"Casual Comment: Mr. Howell's Plea for Spelling Reform." *Dial* 41 (1906): 231.

"Casual Comment: The Passing of 'Uncle Remus.'" *Dial* 45 (1908): 32.

"Casual Comment: Phonographic Canned Tongue." *Dial* 42 (1907): 362–63.

"Casual Comment: Why There Is Yet No American Literature." *Dial* 50 (1911): 149.

Cather, Willa. *The World and the Parish: Willa Cather's Articles and Reviews, 1893–1902.* Ed. William M. Curtin. Vol. 2. Lincoln: U of Nebraska P, 1970.

"The Cause." Editorial. *Dial* 53 (1912): 275–76.

Chénetier, Marc. "'Free-Lance in the Soul-World': Toward a Reappraisal of Vachel Lindsay's Works." *Prospects: An Annual of American Cultural Studies* 2 (1976): 496–512.

———. "Vachel Lindsay's American Mythocracy and Some Unpublished Sources." *The Vision of This Land.* Ed. John E. Hallwas and Dennis J. Reader. Western Illinois U, 1976. 42–54.

Chernoff, Maxine, Cyrus Colter, Stuart Dybek, Reginald Gibbons, and Fred Shafer. "The Writer in Chicago: A Roundtable." *Triquarterly* 60 (Spring/Summer 1984): 325–47.

Chick, Nancy. "Marita Bonner's Revolutionary Purple Flowers: Challenging the Symbol of White Womanhood." *Langston Hughes Review* 13.1 (Fall 1994/Spring 1995): 21–32.

Chodorow, Nancy. *The Reproduction of Mothering.* Berkeley: U of California P, 1978.

"Chronicle and Comment." *Dial* 13 (1892): 299.

Claridge, Henry. "Chicago: 'The Classical Center of American Materialism.'" *The American City: Literary and Cultural Perspectives*. Ed. Graham Clarke. New York: St. Martin's, 1988. 86–104.

Coleman, Verna. *Miles Franklin in America: Her Unknown (Brilliant) Career*. London: Angus and Robertson, 1981.

Cooley, John. "In Pursuit of the Primitive: Black Portraits by Eugene O'Neill and Other Village Bohemians." *The Harlem Renaissance Re-examined*. Ed. Victor A. Kramer. New York: AMS, 1987. 51–64.

Corrothers, James D. *In Spite of the Handicap*. New York: Doran, 1916.

———. *The Black Cat Club: Negro Humor and Folklore*. New York: Funk and Wagnalls, 1902.

Coyle, Lee. *George Ade*. New York: Twayne, 1964.

Daniels, Harvey A. "The Roots of Language Protectionism." *Not Only English*. Ed. Harvey A. Daniels. Urbana, IL: National Council of Teachers of English, 1990. 3–12.

Darnell, Don. "Martie." *Chicago Tribune Magazine* 20 Jan. 1991: 20–23.

Davis, Frank Marshall. *Black Man's Verse*. Chicago: Black Cat, 1935.

———. *Livin' the Blues: Memoirs of a Black Journalist and Poet*. Ed. John Edgar Tidwell. Madison: U of Wisconsin P, 1992.

DeKoven, Marianne. "'Excellent Not a Hull House': Gertrude Stein, Jane Addams, and Feminist-Modernist Political Culture." *Rereading Modernism: New Directions in Feminist Criticism*. Ed. Lisa Rado. New York: Garland, 1994. 321–50.

de Lauretis, Teresa. "The Essence of the Triangle, or Taking the Risk of Essentialism Seriously: Feminist Theory in Italy, the U.S., and Britain." *Differences* 1.2 (1989): 3–37.

———. "Upping the Anti (sic) in Feminist Theory." *Conflicts in Feminism*. Ed. Marianne Hirsch and Evelyn Fox Keller. New York: Routledge, 1990. 255–70.

Dell, Floyd. *Women as World Builders: Studies in Modern Feminism*. Chicago: Forbes, 1913.

Derrida, Jacques. *Of Grammatology*. 1974. Trans. Gayatri Chakravorty Spivak. Baltimore: Johns Hopkins UP, 1976.

———. *Writing and Difference*. Trans. Alan Bass. Chicago: U of Chicago P, 1978.

Detzer, Karl. *Carl Sandburg: A Study in Personality and Background*. New York: Harcourt, Brace and Company, 1941.

Dewey, John. "The School as Social Center." *Proceedings of the National Education Association* 1902: 374–83. Rpt. in *One Hundred Years at Hull-House*. Ed. Mary Lynn McCree Bryan and Allen F. Davis. Bloomington: Indiana UP, 1990. 103–8.

"The Dial, 1880–1900." Editorial. *Dial* 28 (1900): 327–28.

Dickerson, Mary Jane. "Sherwood Anderson and Jean Toomer: A Literary Relationship." *Studies in American Fiction* 1 (1973): 163–75.

Doreski, C. K. "From News to History: Robert Abbott and Carl Sandburg Read the 1919 Chicago Riot." *African American Review* 26 (1992): 637–50.

Drake, St. Clair, and Horace R. Cayton. *Black Metropolis: A Study of Negro Life in a Northern City.* New York: Harcourt, Brace, 1945.

Drake, William. *The First Wave: Women Poets in America, 1915–1945.* New York: MacMillan, 1987.

Dreiser, Theodore. *Sister Carrie.* 1900. U of Pennsylvania P, 1981.

———. *The Titan.* 1914. Cleveland: World Publishing, n.y.

DuBois, W. E. B. *Darkwater: Voices from within the Veil.* 1921. Millwood, NY: Kraus-Thomson, 1975.

Duffey, Bernard. *The Chicago Renaissance in American Letters.* Michigan State College P, 1954.

Duffield, Pitts. Letter. "The Use and Abuse of Slang." *Dial* 15 (1893): 86.

Duncan, Hugh Dalziel. *The Rise of Chicago as a Literary Center from 1885 to 1920: A Sociological Essay in American Culture.* Totawa, NJ: Bedminster P, 1964.

Dunne, Finley Peter. "Mr. Dooley on Slang." *Boston Globe* 3 Aug. 1913: 39.

DuPlessis, Rachel Blau. "'Hoo, Hoo, Hoo': Some Episodes in the Construction of Modern Whiteness." *American Literature* 67 (1995): 667–700.

———. *The Pink Guitar: Writing as Feminist Practice.* New York: Routledge, 1990.

During, Simon. "New Historicism." *Text and Performance Quarterly* 11 (1991): 171–89.

Durnell, Hazel. *The America of Carl Sandburg.* UP of Washington, D.C., 1965.

Eastman, Max. *Enjoyment of Laughter.* New York: Simon and Schuster, 1936.

Editorial Response to Letter. *Dial* 55 (1913): 105–6.

Eby, Clare Virginia. "Domesticating Naturalism: The Example of *The Pit.*" *Studies in American Fiction* 22 (1994): 149 68.

Eliot, T. S. *Poems, 1909–1925.* 1925. London: Faber and Faber, 1933.

Ellis, Elmer. *Mr. Dooley's America: A Life of Finley Peter Dunne.* New York: Knopf, 1941.

Ellison, Ralph. *Invisible Man.* 1947. New York: Random House, 1952.

———. "Richard Wright's Blues." *The Antioch Review* 5 (1945): 198–211.

Engel, Bernard F. "Muscular Innocence in the Midwestern Work Ethic." *MidAmerica: The Yearbook of the Society for the Study of Midwestern Literature* 10 (1983): 38–53.

Engler, Balz. *Poetry and Community.* Tubingen: Stauffenburg-Verlag, 1990.

Enkvist, Nils Erik. "The Folk Elements in Vachel Lindsay's Poetry." *English Studies* 32 (1951): 241–49.

Epstein, Joseph. "'The People's Poet.'" *Commentary* 93.5 (1992): 47–52.

———. "Windy City Letters." *The New Criterion* 2.5 (1984): 37–46.

Erickson, Peter. "Rewriting the Renaissance, Rewriting Ourselves." *Shakespeare Quarterly* 38 (1987): 327–37.

Fanning, Charles. *The Irish Voice in America: Irish-American Fiction from the 1760s to the 1980s.* Lexington: UP of Kentucky, 1990.

Farrell, Thomas J. "The Female and Male Modes of Rhetoric." *College English* 40 (1979): 909–21.

Flynn, Gillian. "English-only Rules Can Cause Legal Tongue Ties." *Personnel Journal* Nov. 1995: 87–91.

Flynn, Joyce. Introduction. *Frye Street and Environs: The Collected Works of Marita Bonner.* By Marita Bonner. Ed. Joyce Flynn and Joyce Occomy Stricklin. Boston: Beacon, 1987. xi–xxvii.

———. "Marita Bonner Occomy." *Afro-American Writers from the Harlem Renaissance to 1940.* Ed. Trudier Harris. Detroit: Gale Research, 1987. 222–28. Vol. 51 of *The Dictionary of Literary Biography.* 194 vols. to date. 1978–1998.

Ford, Thomas W. "*The American Rhythm*: Mary Austin's Poetic Principle." *Western American Literature* 5 (1970): 3–14.

Frank, Florence Kiper. *The Jew to Jesus and Other Poems.* New York: Mitchell Kennerley, 1915.

Franklin, Miles. *On Dearborn Street.* St. Lucia: U of Queensland P, 1983.

Frick, Elizabeth. "Metaphors and Motives of Language-Restriction Movements." *Not Only English.* Ed. Harvey A. Daniels. Urbana, IL: National Council of Teachers of English, 1990. 27–35.

Froula, Christine. *A Guide to Ezra Pound's Selected Poems.* New York: New Directions, 1983.

Fuller, Henry. *The Cliff-Dwellers.* New York: Harper, 1893.

Furia, Philip. *The Poets of Tin Pan Alley.* New York: Oxford UP, 1990.

Gagnon, Paul. "What Should Children Learn?" *Atlantic Monthly* Dec. 1995: 65–78.

Gallop, Jane, Marianne Hirsch, and Nancy K. Miller. "Criticizing Feminist Criticism." *Conflicts in Feminism.* Ed. Marianne Hirsch and Evelyn Fox Keller. New York: Routledge, 1990. 349–69.

Gates, Henry Louis, Jr. "Dis and Dat: Dialect and the Descent." *Afro-American Literature: The Reconstruction of Instruction.* Ed. Dexter Fisher and Robert B. Stepto. New York: Modern Language Association of America, 1979. 88–119.

———. *Figures in Black: Words, Signs, and the "Racial" Self.* New York: Oxford UP, 1989.

———. *The Signifying Monkey: A Theory of African-American Literary Criticism.* New York: Oxford UP, 1988.

———. "Writing 'Race' and the Difference It Makes." *"Race," Writing, and Difference.* Ed. Henry Louis Gates, Jr. Chicago: U of Chicago P, 1986. 1–20.

Gearhart, Sally Miller. "The Womanization of Rhetoric." *Women's Studies International Quarterly* 2 (1979): 195–201.

Gentile, John S. *Cast of One: One-Person Shows from the Chautauqua Platform to the Broadway Stage.* Urbana: U of Illinois P, 1989.

Giddings, Paula. *When and Where I Enter: The Impact of Black Women on Race and Sex in America.* New York: Bantam, 1985.

Gilbert, Sandra M., and Susan Gubar. *No Man's Land: The Place of the Woman Writer in the Twentieth Century.* 3 vols. to date. New Haven: Yale UP, 1988–1994.

Gilligan, Carol. *In a Different Voice: Psychological Theory and Women's Development.* Cambridge: Harvard UP, 1982.

Gilman, Sander L. *Difference and Pathology: Stereotypes of Sexuality, Race, and*

Madness. Ithaca: Cornell UP, 1985.

Glaspell, Susan. *The Visioning*. New York: Stokes, 1911.

Grahn, Judy. *Really Reading Gertrude Stein*. Freedom, CA: Crossing Press, 1989.

Grossman, James R. *Land of Hope: Chicago, Black Southerners, and the Great Migration*. Chicago: U of Chicago P, 1989.

Harrington, Joseph. "A Response to Lisa Woolley." *Langston Hughes Review* 14.1–2 (1996): 49–51.

Hatch, James V., ed. *Black Theater, U.S.A.: Plays by African Americans, 1847 to Today*. New York: Macmillan, 1974.

Headden, Susan et al. "One Nation, One Language?" *U.S. News and World Report* 25 Sept. 1995: 38–42.

Henderson, Alice Corbin. Letter to Harriet Monroe. 11 May 1917. Alice Corbin Henderson Collection. The Harry Ransom Humanities Research Center, The University of Texas at Austin.

———. Letter to Harriet Monroe. 12 December 1917. Alice Corbin Henderson Collection. The Harry Ransom Humanities Research Center, The University of Texas at Austin.

———. Letter to Harriet Monroe. 18 November 1918. Alice Corbin Henderson Collection. The Harry Ransom Humanities Research Center, The University of Texas at Austin.

Henderson, Stephen. *Understanding the New Black Poetry: Black Speech and Black Music as Poetic References*. New York: William Morrow, 1973.

Hill, Alette Olin. *Mother Tongue, Father Time: A Decade of Linguistic Revolt*. Bloomington: Indiana UP, 1986.

Hill, Errol. "The Revolutionary Tradition in Black Drama." *Theatre Journal* 38 (1986): 408–26.

Hirsch, E. D., Jr. *Cultural Literacy: What Every American Needs to Know*. Boston: Houghton Mifflin, 1987.

"Holiday Publications." *Dial* 31 (1901): 442–49.

Holt, Thomas C. "The Lonely Warrior: Ida B. Wells-Barnett and the Struggle for Black Leadership." *Black Leaders of the Twentieth Century*. Ed. John Hope Franklin and August Meier. Urbana: U of Illinois P, 1982. 39–61.

Holton, Sylvia Wallace. *Down Home and Uptown: The Representation of Black Speech in American Fiction*. Rutherford: Fairleigh Dickinson UP, 1984.

Homberger, Eric. "Chicago and New York: Two Versions of American Modernism." *Modernism*. Ed. Malcolm Bradbury and James McFarlane. New York: Penguin, 1976. 151–61.

Hopkins, E. W. Letter. "Dialect Study in America." *Dial* 18 (1895): 136.

Howells, William Dean. "Certain of the Chicago School of Fiction." *North American Review* 176 (1903): 734–46.

Huggins, Nathan Irvin. *Harlem Renaissance*. London: Oxford UP, 1973.

Hughes, Langston. *The Big Sea*. 1940. New York: Thunder's Mouth, 1986.

———. *Montage of a Dream Deferred*. New York: Henry Holt, 1951.

———. "The Negro Artist and the Racial Mountain." *The Black Aesthetic*. Ed. Addison Gayle, Jr. Garden City, NY: Doubleday, 1972. 167–72.

———. *Selected Poems of Langston Hughes*. New York: Knopf, 1966.

Hull, Gloria. *Color, Sex, and Poetry: Three Women Writers of the Harlem Renaissance.* Bloomington: Indiana UP, 1987.

Hummer, T. R. "Laughed Off: Canon, *Kharakter,* and the Dismissal of Vachel Lindsay." *Kenyon Review* 17.2 (1995): 56–96.

"Idiom and Ideal." Editorial. *Dial* 27 (1899): 305–7.

Inglehart, Babette. Introduction. *True Love.* By Edith Wyatt. Urbana: U of Illinois P, 1993. vii–liii.

James, Henry. *The Bostonians.* 1886. London: Penguin Books, 1984.

———. *The Question of Our Speech and The Lesson of Balzac.* Boston: Houghton Mifflin, 1905.

Johnson, Abby Ann Arthur. "The Personal Magazine: Margaret C. Anderson and the *Little Review,* 1914–1929." *The South Atlantic Quarterly* 75 (1976): 351–63.

Johnson, Barbara. "Writing." *Critical Terms for Literary Study.* Ed. Frank Lentricchia and Thomas McLaughlin. Chicago: U of Chicago P, 1990. 39–49.

Johnson, Charles S. "The New Frontage on American Life." *The New Negro.* Ed. Alain Locke. 1925. New York: Antheneum, 1986. 278–98.

Johnson, Fenton. *A Little Dreaming.* 1913. College Park, MD: McGrath, 1969.

———. *Songs of the Soil.* 1916. New York: AMS, 1975.

———. *Tales of Darkest America.* 1920. Freeport, NY: Books for Libraries P, 1971.

———. *Visions of the Dusk.* New York: Trachtenberg, 1915.

———. "War Profiles." *The Crisis* 16 (June 1918): 65.

Johnson, James Weldon, ed. *The Book of American Negro Poetry.* San Diego: Harcourt Brace Jovanovich, 1959.

Johnson, James Weldon. *The Autobiography of an Ex-Coloured Man.* 1927. New York: Knopf, 1979.

———. *God's Trombones: Seven Negro Sermons in Verse.* 1927. New York: Penguin, 1976.

Johnson, W. H. "The Deterioration of College English." *Dial* 22 (1897): 271–72.

Kazin, Alfred. *An American Procession.* New York: Knopf, 1984.

Keillor, Garrison. "Introduction to the 1990 Edition." *The American Songbag.* By Carl Sandburg. San Diego: Harcourt Brace Jovanovich, 1990. vii–xi.

Kelly, Fred C. *George Ade, Warmhearted Satirist.* Indianapolis: Bobbs-Merrill, 1947.

Kerlin, Robert T. *Negro Poets and Their Poems.* Washington, D.C.: Associated Publishers, 1935.

Kinnamon, Keneth. "James Weldon Johnson." *Afro-American Writers from the Harlem Renaissance to 1940.* Ed. Trudier Harris. Detroit: Gale Research, 1987. 168–82. Vol. 51 of *The Dictionary of Literary Biography.* 194 vols. to date. 1978–1998.

Kochman, Thomas. *Black and White: Styles in Conflict.* Chicago: U of Chicago P, 1981.

Kramer, Dale. *Chicago Renaissance: The Literary Life in the Midwest, 1900–1930.* New York: Appleton-Century, 1966.

Kreymborg, Alfred, ed. *Others for 1919.* New York: Nicholas L. Brown, 1920.

Lakoff, Robin. *Language and Woman's Place.* New York: Harper and Row, 1975.

Laughlin, Clara E. *Just Folks.* New York: Macmillan, 1910.

Lawton, William Cranston. "Local Color and Eternal Truth." *Dial* 25 (1898): 38–39.

Lewis, Sinclair. *Babbitt.* 1922. New York: New American Library, 1980.

Lindsay, Vachel. "Mr. Lindsay on 'Primitive Singing.'" *Poetry* 4 (1914): 161–62.

———. *The Poetry of Vachel Lindsay.* Ed. Dennis Camp. 3 vols. Peoria: Spoon River Poetry Press, 1984–1986.

———. *Prose of Vachel Lindsay.* Ed. Dennis Camp. Peoria: Spoon River Poetry Press, 1988.

———. "The Real American Language." *The American Mercury* 13 (1928): 257–65.

Long, Richard A., and Eugenia W. Collier, eds. *Afro-American Writing: An Anthology of Prose and Poetry.* Vol. 1. New York: New York UP, 1972. 2 vols.

Lowell, Amy. "Modern Monologues." *Poetry* 8 (1916): 318–21.

McClintock, Anne. "Soft-soaping Empire: Commodity Racism and Imperial Advertising." *Travellers' Tales.* Ed. George Robertson et al. London: Routledge, 1994. 131–54.

McIntosh, Peggy. "White Privilege: Unpacking the Invisible Knapsack." *Peace and Freedom* (July/August 1989): 10–12.

McKay, Nellie Y. "Renaissance Woman." *Women's Review of Books* 5.10–11 (1988): 27–28.

Marcus, George E., and Michael M. J. Fischer. *Anthropology as Cultural Critique.* Chicago: U of Chicago P, 1986.

Markels, Julian. "Dreiser and the Plotting of Inarticulate Experience." *Critical Essays on Theodore Dreiser.* Ed. Donald Pizer. Boston: G. K. Hall, 1981. 186–99.

Massa, Ann. "Form Follows Function: The Construction of Harriet Monroe and *Poetry, A Magazine of Verse.*" *A Living of Words: American Women in Print Culture.* Ed. Susan Albertine. Knoxville: U of Tennessee P, 1995. 115–31.

Masters, Edgar Lee. Letter to Alice Corbin Henderson. 14 February 1927. The Harry Ransom Humanities Research Center, The University of Texas at Austin.

———. *Spoon River Anthology.* New York: Macmillan, 1915.

———. *The Tale of Chicago.* New York: G. P. Putnam's Sons, 1933.

———. *Vachel Lindsay: A Poet in America.* 1935. New York: Biblo and Tannen, 1969.

Mayer, Harold M., and Richard C. Wade. *Chicago: Growth of a Metropolis.* Chicago: U of Chicago P, 1969.

Mencken, H. L. "Civilized Chicago." *Chicago Sunday Tribune* 28 Oct. 1917, sec. 8: 5.

Messer-Davidow, Ellen. "Know-How." *(En)Gendering Knowledge: Feminists in Academe.* Ed. Joan E. Hartman and Ellen Messer-Davidow. Knoxville: U of Tennessee P, 1991. 281–309.

Miller, Elise. "The Feminization of American Realist Theory." *American Literary Realism, 1870–1910* 23.1 (1990): 20–41.

Milroy, James, and Lesley Milroy. *Authority in Language: Investigating Language*

Prescription and Standardisation. London: Routledge, 1985.

Monroe, Harriet, and Alice Corbin Henderson, eds. *The New Poetry: An Anthology of Twentieth-Century Verse in English.* 2nd ed. New York: Macmillan, 1923.

Monroe, Harriet. Letter to Alice Corbin Henderson. 3 July 1917. Alice Corbin Henderson Collection. The Harry Ransom Humanities Research Center, The University of Texas at Austin.

———. Letter to Alice Corbin Henderson. 10 May 1918. Alice Corbin Henderson Collection. The Harry Ransom Humanities Research Center, The University of Texas at Austin.

———. Letter to Alice Corbin Henderson. 21 September 1918. Alice Corbin Henderson Collection. The Harry Ransom Humanities Research Center, The University of Texas at Austin.

———. *Poets and Their Art.* New York: Macmillan, 1926.

———. *A Poet's Life.* 1938. New York: AMS, 1969.

Moody, William Vaughn. *Poems.* Boston: Houghton, Mifflin, 1901.

Moses, Wilson Jeremiah. *The Golden Age of Black Nationalism, 1850–1925.* Hamden, CN: Archon Books, 1978.

Mosher, Fredric John. "Chicago's 'Saving Remnant': Francis Fisher Browne, William Morton Payne, and the *Dial* (1880–1892)." Diss. U of Illinois, 1950.

Nelson, Cary. *Repression and Recovery: Modern American Poetry and the Politics of Cultural Memory, 1910–1945.* Madison: U of Wisconsin P, 1989.

"New Lamps for Old." Editorial. *Dial* 56 (1914): 231–33.

Newton, Judith. "History as Usual?: Feminism and the 'New Historicism.'" *Cultural Critique* 9 (1988): 87–121.

Nielsen, Aldon Lynn. *Reading Race: White American Poets and the Racial Discourse in the Twentieth Century.* Athens: U of Georgia P, 1988.

Niven, Penelope. *Carl Sandburg: A Biography.* New York: Scribner's, 1991.

Nordenskiold, Gustaf. *The Cliff Dwellers of the Mesa Verde, Southwestern Colorado: Their Pottery and Implements.* 1893. Trans. D. Lloyd Morgan. New York: AMS, 1973.

O'Barr, William M., and Bowman K. Atkins. "'Women's Language' or 'Powerless Language'?" *Women and Language in Literature and Society.* Ed. Sally McConnell-Ginet, Ruth Borker, and Nelly Furman. New York: Praeger, 1980. 93–110.

Olsen, Tillie. *Silences.* New York: Laurel-Dell, 1978.

O'Neale, Sondra. "Inhibiting Midwives, Usurping Creators: The Struggling Emergence of Black Women in American Fiction." *Feminist Studies, Critical Studies.* Ed. Teresa de Lauretis. Bloomington: Indiana UP, 1986. 139–56.

Ong, Walter J. *Orality and Literacy.* 1982. London: Routledge, 1989.

Ostriker, Alicia Suskin. *Stealing the Language: The Emergence of Women's Poetry in America.* Boston: Beacon, 1986.

Payne, William Morton. *Little Leaders.* Chicago: A. C. McClurg, 1902.

[Payne, William Morton]. "The Future of American Speech." Editorial. *Dial* 14 (1893): 233–35.

———. "The Literary West." Editorial. *Dial* 15 (1893): 173–75.

———. "The Use and Abuse of Dialect." Editorial. *Dial* 18 (1895): 67–69.

Pearce, T. M. *Alice Corbin Henderson*. Austin: Steck-Vaughn, 1969.

Peattie, Elia W. *The Precipice*. Boston: Houghton Mifflin, 1914.

Pick, Daniel. *Faces of Degeneration: A European Disorder*. Cambridge: Cambridge UP, 1989.

Poe, Edgar Allan. *The Complete Works of Edgar Allan Poe*. Ed. James A. Harrison. 2nd ed. Vol. 14. New York: AMS, 1979. 17 vols.

Pound, Ezra. *The Cantos of Ezra Pound*. London: Faber and Faber, 1954.

Price, Sally. *Primitive Art in Civilized Places*. Chicago: U of Chicago P, 1989.

Primeau, Ronald. "Frank Horne and the Second Echelon Poets of the Harlem Renaissance." *The Harlem Renaissance Remembered*. Ed. Arna Bontemps. New York: Dodd, Mead, 1972. 247–67.

Raftery, Judith. "Chicago Settlement Women in Fact and Fiction." *Illinois Historical Journal* 88 (1995): 37–58.

Rampersad, Arnold. *The Life of Langston Hughes*. 2 vols. New York: Oxford UP, 1986–1988.

Randall, Dudley. "The Black Aesthetic in the Thirties, Forties, and Fifties." *The Black Aesthetic*. Ed. Addison Gayle, Jr. Garden City, NY: Doubleday, 1971. 212–21.

Redding, J. Saunders. *To Make a Poet Black*. 1939. Ithaca: Cornell UP, 1988.

Reed, Ishmael. "America: the Multinational Society." *Multi-Cultural Literacy*. St. Paul: Graywolf, 1988. 155–60.

Regnery, Henry. "Chicago and Its Authors." *Modern Age* 27 (1983): 256–66.

Rich, Adrienne. *On Lies, Secrets, and Silence*. New York: Norton, 1979.

Riggio, Thomas P. "Theodore Dreiser: Hidden Ethnic." *M.E.L.U.S.* 11.1 (1984): 53–63.

Rodriguez, Richard. *Hunger of Memory: The Education of Richard Rodriguez*. Toronto: Bantam, 1988.

Roe, E. P. *Barriers Burned Away*. 1872. New York: Dodd, Mead, 1882.

Roses, Lorraine Elena, and Ruth Elizabeth Randolph. "Marita Bonner: In Search of Other Mothers' Gardens." *Black American Literature Forum* 21 (1987): 165–83.

Rubin, Louis D., Jr. "Not to Forget Carl Sandburg . . ." *The Sewanee Review* 85 (1977): 181–89.

Ruggles, Eleanor. *The West-going Heart: A Life of Vachel Lindsay*. New York: Norton, 1959.

Rule, Jane. *Lesbian Images*. Garden City, NY: Doubleday, 1975.

Said, Edward. *Orientalism*. New York: Vintage Books, 1979.

Sandburg, Carl. *The American Songbag*. 1927. San Diego: Harcourt, Brace, Jovanovich, 1990.

———. *The Chicago Race Riots: July, 1919*. 1919. New York: Harcourt, Brace and World, 1969.

———. *The Complete Poems of Carl Sandburg*. New York: Harcourt Brace Jovanovich, 1969.

Schemo, Diana Jean. "Education as a Second Language." *New York Times* 25

July 1992, late ed., sec.1: 27.

Seiffert, Marjorie Allen. *Ballads of the Singing Bowl.* New York: Scribner's Sons, 1927.

———. *The King with Three Faces and Other Poems.* New York: Scribner's Sons, 1929.

———. Letter to Idella Purnell. 16 April, no year. The Harry Ransom Humanities Research Center, The University of Texas at Austin.

———. Letter to Idella Purnell. 12 May, no year. The Harry Ransom Humanities Research Center, The University of Texas at Austin.

———. Letter to Edgar Lee Masters. 1 October, no year. The Harry Ransom Humanities Research Center, The University of Texas at Austin.

Sheppard, Richard. "The Crisis of Language." *Modernism.* Ed. Malcolm Bradbury and James McFarlane. New York: Penguin, 1976. 323–36.

Sherman, Joan R. *Invisible Poets: Afro-Americans of the Nineteenth Century.* 2nd ed. Urbana: U of Illinois P, 1989.

Simonson, Rick, and Scott Walker, eds. *Multi-Cultural Literacy.* St. Paul: Graywolf, 1988.

Sinclair, Upton. *The Jungle.* New York: Doubleday, Page, 1906.

Singh, Amritjit. "Black-White Symbiosis: Another Look at the Literary History of the 1920s." *The Harlem Renaissance Re-examined.* Ed. Victor A. Kramer. New York: AMS, 1987. 31–42.

Smith, Carl S. *Chicago and the American Literary Imagination, 1880–1920.* Chicago: U of Chicago P, 1984.

Sollors, Werner. *Beyond Ethnicity: Consent and Descent in American Culture.* New York: Oxford UP, 1986.

Sontag, Deborah. "English as a Precious Language." *New York Times* 29 Aug. 1993, late ed., sec. 1: 29+.

Sparks, Marion E. Letter. "Dialect, or English?" *Dial* 24 (1898): 39.

Spear, Allan. *Black Chicago: The Making of a Negro Ghetto, 1890–1920.* Chicago: U of Chicago P, 1967.

Spengemann, William C. *A Mirror for Americanists: Reflections on the Idea of American Literature.* Hanover: UP of New England, 1989.

Stanford, Barbara Dodds, ed. *I, Too, Sing America: Black Voices in American Literature.* New York: Hayden, 1971.

Starr, Ellen Gates. "Tenements, and a Name." *One Hundred Years at Hull-House.* Ed. Mary Lynn McCree Bryan and Allen F. Davis. Bloomington: Indiana UP, 1990. 19–20.

Stebner, Eleanor J. *The Women of Hull House: A Study in Spirituality, Vocation, and Friendship.* Albany: State U of New York P, 1997.

Stein, Gertrude. *Selected Writings of Gertrude Stein.* Ed. Carl Van Vechten. 1945. New York: Vintage Books, 1972.

———. *Three Lives.* 1909. London: John Rodker, 1927.

Steinem, Gloria. *Outrageous Acts and Everyday Rebellions.* New York: Holt, Rinehart and Winston, 1983.

Stuckey, Sterling. Introduction. *Southern Road.* By Sterling A. Brown. Boston: Beacon, 1974. xiii–xxxiv.

Szuberla, Guy. "Peattie's *Precipice* and the 'Settlement House' Novel." *MidAmerica: The Yearbook of the Society for the Study of Midwestern Literature* 20 (1993): 59–75.

———. "Reborn in Babel: Immigrant Characters and Types in Early Chicago Fiction." *MidAmerica: The Yearbook of the Society for the Study of Midwestern Literature* 13 (1986): 31–48.

Talbot, Margaret. "The Gender Trap: Are Women's Colleges Bad for Women?" *Washington Post* 20 Nov. 1994: Magazine 13–19, 30–35.

Tannen, Deborah. *You Just Don't Understand: Women and Men in Conversation.* New York: Morrow, 1990.

Terdiman, Richard. "Is There Class in This Class?" *The New Historicism.* Ed. H. Aram Veeser. New York: Routledge, 1989. 225–30.

Thompson, Mildred I. *Ida B. Wells-Barnett: An Exploratory Study of an American Black Woman, 1893–1930.* Brooklyn: Carlson, 1990.

"Three Centuries of American Literature." Editorial. *Dial* 29 (1900): 485–87.

Thurston, Henry W. Letter. "A Literary Phase of the Immigration Question." *Dial* 14 (1893): 41.

Tietjens, Eunice. *Body and Raiment.* New York: Knopf, 1919.

———. Letter to Alice Corbin Henderson. 17 July, no year. Alice Corbin Henderson Collection. The Harry Ransom Humanities Research Center, The University of Texas at Austin.

———. Letter to Alice Corbin Henderson. 16 August 1917. Alice Corbin Henderson Collection. The Harry Ransom Humanities Research Center, The University of Texas at Austin.

———. *The World at My Shoulder.* New York: Macmillan, 1938.

Tompkins, Jane. "Fighting Words: Unlearning to Write the Critical Essay." *The Georgia Review* 42 (1988): 585–90.

———. *Sensational Designs: The Cultural Work of American Fiction, 1790–1860.* New York: Oxford UP, 1986.

Trent, William P. "American Literature." *Dial* 28 (1900): 334–40.

Torgovnick, Marianna. *Gone Primitive: Savage Intellects, Modern Lives.* Chicago: U of Chicago P, 1990.

Untermeyer, Louis. *From Another World.* New York: Harcourt, Brace, 1939.

Van Wienen, Mark. "Taming the Socialist: Carl Sandburg's *Chicago Poems* and Its Critics." *American Literature* 63 (1991): 89–103.

Veblen, Thorstein. *The Theory of the Leisure Class.* 1899. New York: Random House, Modern Library, 1934.

Wade, Louise Carroll. "The Problem with Classroom Use of Upton Sinclair's *The Jungle.*" *American Studies* 32.2 (1991): 79–101.

Wallace, Kathleen R. "'Roots, Aren't They Supposed to Be Buried?': The Experience of Place in Midwestern Women's Autobiography." *Mapping American Culture.* Ed. Wayne Franklin and Michael Steiner. Iowa City: U of Iowa P, 1992. 168–87.

Washington, Booker T., N. B. Wood, and Fannie Barrier Williams. *A New Negro for a New Century.* 1900. New York: Arno and the New York Times, 1969.

Washington, Mary Helen. "'Taming All That Anger Down': Rage and Silence in

Gwendolyn Brooks' *Maud Martha*." *The Massachusetts Review* 24 (1983): 453–66.

Waterloo, Stanley. Letter. "Who Reads a Chicago Book?" *Dial* 13 (1892): 206–7.

Wells, Ida B. *Crusade for Justice*. Ed. Alfreda M. Duster. Chicago: U of Chicago P, 1970.

Wentworth, Michael. "'A Walk Through the Paradise Garden': Vachel Lindsay's Idea of Kansas in *Adventures While Preaching the Gospel of Beauty*." *MidAmerica* 20 (1993): 26–39.

West, James L. W., III. "Editorial Principles." *Sister Carrie*. By Theodore Dreiser. U of Pennsylvania P, 1981. 577–90.

"Who Reads a Chicago Book?" Letter signed J. K. *Dial* 13 (1892): 131.

Wiegman, Robyn. *American Anatomies: Theorizing Race and Gender*. Durham: Duke UP, 1995.

Wiget, Andrew. "Reading Against the Grain: Origin Stories and American Literary History." *American Literary History* 3 (1991): 209–31.

Williams, Ellen. *Harriet Monroe and the Poetry Renaissance, the First Ten Years of Poetry, 1912–22*. Urbana: U of Illinois P, 1977.

Williams, Fanny Barrier. "The Club Movement Among Colored Women of America." *A New Negro for a New Century*. By Booker T. Washington, N. B. Wood, and Fannie Barrier Williams. New York: Arno, 1969. 378–428.

Williams, Kenny J. "From Carl Pretzel to Slats Grobnik: A Study of Chicago Humor." *MidAmerica: The Yearbook of the Society for the Study of Midwestern Literature* 10 (1983): 152–76.

——. *In the City of Men: Another Story of Chicago*. Nashville: Townsend P, 1974.

——. "An Invisible Partnership and an Unlikely Relationship: William Stanley Braithwaite and Harriet Monroe." *Callaloo* 10 (1987): 516–50.

Wilson, Christopher P. "American Naturalism and the Problem of Sincerity." *American Literature* 54 (1982): 511–27.

Wolfe, Glenn Joseph. *Vachel Lindsay: The Poet as Film Theorist*. New York: Arno, 1973.

Wood, Clement. *Poets of America*. New York: Dutton, 1925.

Wordsworth, William. "Preface to the Second Edition of *Lyrical Ballads*." *Critical Theory Since Plato*. Ed. Hazard Adams. New York: Harcourt Brace Jovanovich, 1971. 433–43.

Wright, John S. "A Scintillating Send-off for Falling Stars: The Black Renaissance Reconsidered." *A Stronger Soul within a Finer Frame: Portraying African-Americans in the Black Renaissance*. Minneapolis: University Art Museum, 1990. 13–45.

Wyatt, Edith. "Modern Poetry." *Art and the Worthwhile*. Ed. Baker Brownell. New York: D. Van Nostrand, 1929. 113–49. Vol. 9 of *Man and His World*. 12 vols.

——. *True Love*. 1903. Urbana: U of Illinois P, 1993.

Yannella, Philip R. *The Other Carl Sandburg*. Jackson: UP of Mississippi, 1996.

Young, Iris Marion. "The Ideal of Community and the Politics of Difference." *Feminism/Postmodernism*. Ed. Linda J. Nicholson. New York: Routledge, 1990. 300–23.

INDEX